The Long Haul

Alex Hibbert

The Long Haul

Copyright © 2018 by Alex Hibbert

Photographs © their respective owners
Other images are public domain/expired copyright
Original illustrations by Vuk Žugić
Typeset in 11-point Baskerville

ISBN 9781912821112 (paperback)

First published 2010 by Tricorn Books
Second Edition (Limited Edition) published 2018 by
Tricorn Books, Aspex Gallery, 42 The Vulcan Building
Gunwharf Quays, Portsmouth, PO1 3BF
Updated 2019

Printed and bound in the United Kingdom

The Long Haul

10 Year Anniversary
Limited Edition

Dear Sam,

Good luck with
your adventures!

Alen H Uh

Contents

Maps of Routes

About the Author

Alex Hibbert was born in 1986 in Hampshire, England. He was educated at Canford School, then went on to study Biological Sciences at the University of Oxford, where his interests included large animal behaviour, language and evolutionary theory. His first major polar expedition, The Long Haul, still holds the world record for the longest unsupported Arctic journey in history. Hibbert is the author of four books prior to this edition, is a public speaker invited to address audiences in numerous countries, and his photographic collection has been published worldwide.

You can follow Alex Hibbert on Twitter and Instagram:
@alexhibbert

Website:
www.alexhibbert.com

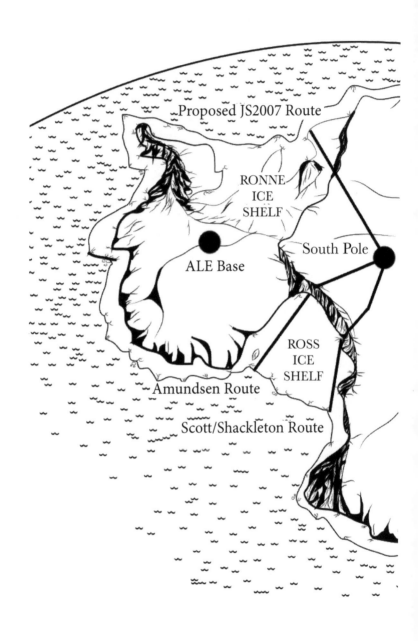

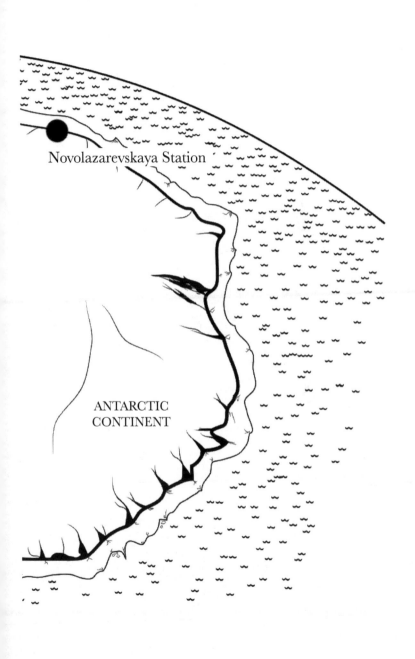

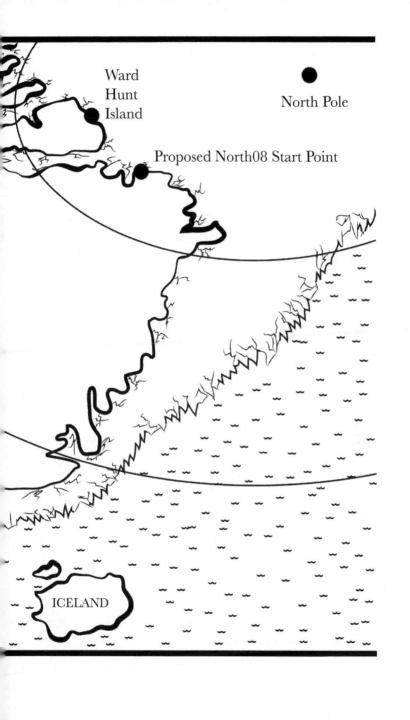

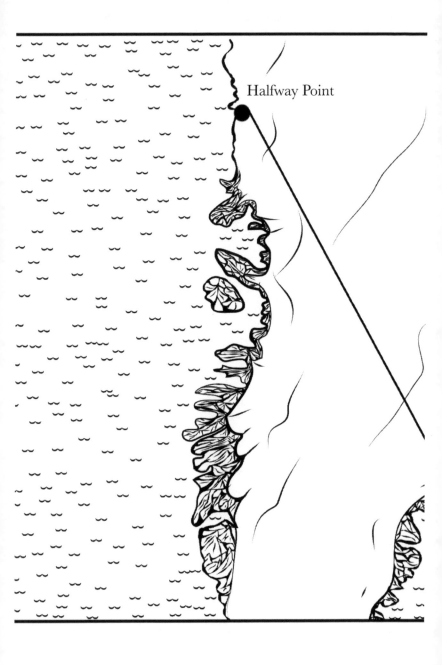

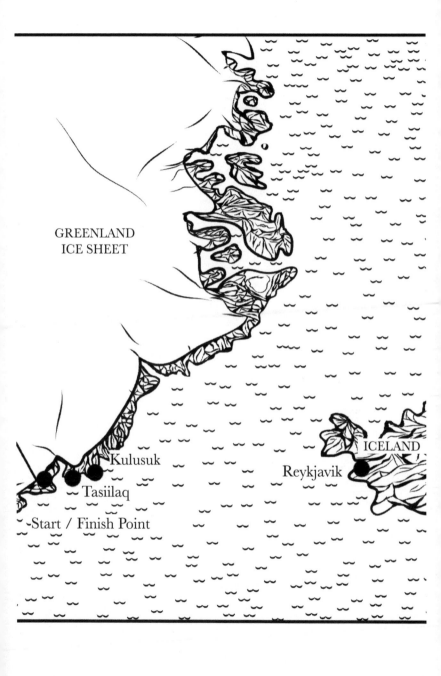

Foreword

It is a truth universally acknowledged that one saves time travelling only two hours from one point to another, instead of spending eight hours on the same journey. Or driving across Greenland with a skidoo rather than walking on skis, dragging all food, fuel and gear you need on a sled. While this holds up mathematically, my experience is the opposite: time passes more quickly when I increase the speed of travel. My speed and time accelerate in parallel. It is as if the duration of a single hour becomes less than a clock-hour. When I am in a rush, I hardly pay attention to anything at all.

When you are in a car driving towards a mountain, with small pools, slopes, rocks, moss and trees zooming past on all sides, life is curtailed; it gets shorter. You don't notice the wind, the smells, the weather, nor the shifting light. Your feet don't get sore. Everything becomes one big blur.

And it isn't only time that grows smaller as one's pace increases. Your sense of space does too. Suddenly you find yourself at the foot of the mountain. Even your sense of distance has been stunted. Having travelled far, you may be tempted to feel like you've experienced quite a bit. I doubt that's true.

If you were to walk along the same route, however – spending an entire day instead of a half-hour, breathing more easily, listening, feeling the ground beneath your feet, exerting yourself – the day becomes something else entirely. Little by little, the mountain looms up before you and your surroundings seem to grow larger. Becoming acquainted with these surroundings takes time. It's like building a friendship. The mountain up ahead, which slowly changes as you draw closer, feels like an intimate friend by the time you've arrived.

13

Your eyes, ears, nose, shoulders, stomach and legs speak to the mountain, and the mountain replies. Time stretches out, independent of minutes and hours.

And this is precisely the secret held by Alex and all those who go by foot: life is prolonged when you walk. Walking expands time rather than collapses it. After all, we were all born explorers.

Lev vel!
Erling Kagge

October 2018
Oslo, Norway

Aside from becoming the first, along with Børge Ousland, to reach the North Pole unsupported in 1990, and as the first person to reach the South Pole unsupported, Erling Kagge is a Norwegian philosopher, publisher and lawyer.

Anniversary Note

Irecently uncovered a photograph taken just hours after George and I were flown by helicopter to Tasiilaq at the finale of the Long Haul. For ten years it's sat unnoticed at the bottom of a 'rejects' folder on my computer. The poor lighting was such that, with the constraints of computer software of the day, I'd previously discounted it as the details were barely discernible.

I had been looking for new illustrations for this edition of *The Long Haul* and felt the photograph deserved some work. Surely enough, after some careful editing with ingenious software, the image emerged. I stopped and studied it for a time – a simple photo. It depicted me; starved, wild-haired, wind and cold-beaten, stood on a hill in front of snow-smattered mountains. I was holding a ski, named Rodney, that hadn't survived the journey.

I was smiling.

I'm not one for playing up to cameras with false smiles and poses – then as a twenty-two-year-old, or now. This smile though was a demonstration of an authentic crucible of emotions; ones impossible to fake in the state my mind was in. Relief. Disbelief. A slightly overwhelmed daze. Optimism. And true happiness.

This happiness was much more than the thrill of winning, or of the crest of the wave you ride after a moment of instant gratification. We had prevailed and completed our journey, not as an adversary of the ice sheet, and not as a friend, but just having accepted its indifference toward us. The deep-rooted contentment leading to my smile on that hillside was derived from my teamwork with George, the vindication of the journey itself, and the use of a sit-down loo for the first time in four months. But, also, due to what laid

15

ahead. A clear-headed ambition for what I was determined to create with my life. A decade on, I know the nuances of that ambition were naïve, yet not deluded.

Very few aspects of that decade have behaved as per the blueprint. It took a good portion of those years to fully shed the haunting spectre left by withdrawing from training to become a Commando Officer. This non-completion, made worse by the fact it was voluntary, left a hole. And, during that year I was in training, the financial crash belted the world squarely around its jaw. I emerged back into a civilian world that no longer had a penny to spare to ensure its own solvency, let alone the funding of polar journeys. It turned out that my time at school and university, the genesis of what would become The Long Haul, had been a boom-time for expedition sponsorship. The financial sector had, disproportionately, shovelled millions towards an assortment of ventures – some were innovative and purposeful, and others glorified adventure holidays. The media did little to differentiate the two.

Soon, much of it had evaporated. Logistics operators began selling their aircraft or ceased trading altogether. Some lamented they could no longer support polar expeditions and so focussed on other markets. Indicative perhaps of what had come to be, and then promptly collapsed, was the 'Polar Race' – a ski race in the Canadian Arctic to a place where in 1996 the Magnetic North Pole resided, many hundreds of miles south of the North Pole. Teams were invariably comprised of at least one banker who'd tapped into the office coffers. All returned home 'polar explorers'. The race ran from 2003 to 2011, the final year attracting just two teams. This rapid rise and decline represented much of what I now felt polar travel had become: disconnected, inauthentic, commercial, sanitised, the plaything of those who care very little for it. Those familiar with my writing and broadcasts will find my stubborn demands for authenticity and a maintenance of standards have woven through the boom, the bust, and now, if not through a recovery, into a new phase of polar travel.

For me, today, what brewed within me in that photograph in Tasiilaq in 2008 remains. I rallied and surged into the 2010s amidst a wounded industry. The playboys are long gone, as are some of the real deals, the latter simply no longer able to make it add up. Others, and newcomers, have gravitated toward 'appearing to be' on social media, rather than aspiring to really 'be'. The rewards they now reap are significant, albeit I suspect short-lived as the world wises up.

I have ventured out on the ice – to Greenland, to Iceland, to Svalbard – every year with companions, whether as a paid guide, self-funded on a shoestring, or with varying levels of business partnerships. I've worked with scoundrels, and with titans, and have learned from both. This frenetic pace has been central to me as I could not countenance the tedium of harking back to experiences increasingly far in the past. Funding is, even throughout the economic recovery the world has seen, not only still sparse, but the nature of how expeditions are funded is unrecognisable from what came before. Partnerships are a great deal more sophisticated and as a direct result, in my view no bad thing, far more dependent on having a tangible purpose. From the embers of the vanity and egos of the short-lived commercial era of faux-polar explorers, a warming fire can and will surely rise.

The demand for leadership and robustly peer-reviewed research and understanding in the cold regions of the world is growing at breakneck speed, not ebbing away in a pathetic nostalgia. And so, the need for innovative yet stubbornly-pursued polar journeys not only remains, but becomes imperative – on a technical and a human level.

The oversupply of half-baked expeditions that drowned public thirst for stories, and any corporate desire to supply cash, has simmered down over a number of years to reveal a concentrate of projects and individuals that deserve to exist. The scarcity of major journeys (there has been just one complete North Pole expedition in eight years, compared to one or more per year in the 2000s) is now not a gauge of poor health. It is an indication of difficulty in an era of changing ice conditions and harder-won funding. The public appetite for frank stories of hardship and endeavour across wildernesses hasn't dimmed but, depending on how you view it, has grown more cynical or more discerning.

My perspective regarding time-well-spent has undoubtedly broadened. This is perhaps best illustrated by the unplanned, and for me deeply poignant, time my team and I spent in Avanerriaq – detailed in *Polar Eskimo*. Skis made way for dog sleds, and wilderness for communities of warm, generous people unlike any I've found elsewhere.

George's and my world record, set on our 1374-mile Long Haul, stood for just three years until Aleksander Gamme of Norway pipped it by a dozen miles in the Antarctic. Our 'Polar' record became the 'Arctic' record, and that has stood to this day. No-one since Gamme, save for Saunders' 2013/14 attempt, has made a bid for an ultra-distance polar ski without resupply or power assistance – fully unsupported. I do not believe we have reached the ultimate maximum distance achievable by humans on skis, but the desire to commit to something so vast, and hard to distil into snappy Instagram posts, has waned. I truly hope that such a venture, perhaps mine, intertwined with a novel purpose aside from the distance record itself, will emerge.

Until then, my focus remains on my six-years-in-and-counting Dark Ice Project – to seek the North Pole unsupported in true winter conditions. The Antarctic must still wait. An expedition spends £10 there for every £1 spent in the Arctic. Distances, monopolies and a lack of coherent government in the South see to that.

In this significantly revised edition of *The Long Haul*, I have pointedly refused to excise the voice of that 22-year-old in the photograph – the image you'll find in the colour plates section. I make no apologies for that. *The Long Haul* written by a 32-year-old would be wholly pointless. It's the same man sat here now as who stood then on the ice – one with an unmoved core purpose a decade on. I most certainly look beyond ambitions of sledging through snowfields, but have anchors remaining buried deep within these curious things we have created from nowhere called expeditions – journeys we obsess over, commit thousands of hours to, and sometimes risk everything for.

This literary snapshot of emotions, fears, assertions, limited accrued life experience, flaws and perhaps qualities belongs solely to the man smiling in that photograph – and it has steered how I have treated the reworking of *The Long Haul*.

In memory of my grandmother, Mary Johnson

&

For my family; Richard, Suzanne and Oliver

--

In memory of

Frank Prendergast

Preface

I stared across the top of the wildly flapping tent and tried to make out George's shape as he struggled with the eyelets on his side. The drift and wind were so strong that even though we were only five feet apart, communication was impossible save a few desperate hand gestures. We had erected the tent, our home, dozens of times previously and had honed it down to a fine art. We had skied far too long into the storm; I knew this and cursed myself for putting mileage ahead of safety.

The process was usually so simple. For ease, we had never fully collapsed the tent each day, only releasing the pole tension and folding the fifteen foot tunnel into a neat sausage to be strapped to a sledge. We had previously managed it with minimal fuss and in only five minutes or so, despite the usual evening fatigue. Today was different, and we had been fighting the writhing mass of canvas and poles for over ten minutes. George and I were wearing our full inventory of gloves and mitts, making our hands about twice their normal size, with useless dexterity. Feeding the end of a pole into an eyelet is not a complicated task but, on what seemed to be our twentieth attempt, I started to turn my mind to our contingency plan. In the event of a lost, destroyed or unerectable tent the last resort was to retreat to the only other shelter we had: our sledges. The expedition was less than a third complete and the sledges were still extremely full. Squeezing in a freezing, shivering and scared occupant would be both a feat of determination and flexibility! Once the reinforced zip cover was closed over us, we would be out of the worst of the wind and drift and able to survive the storm.

My attention snapped back to reality as George yelled over from the other side that he had got a pole in. I could barely hear a word, but his body language suggested a renewed focus to get under shelter. I started to coordinate the remainder of the poles and the main structure of the tunnel was complete. As usual, even in calm conditions, the tent was already shackled to a sledge using a karabiner as an anchor against the wind. The wind caused the tent to act as a giant kite and it lifted straight up into the air, blowing hard into our faces. Since the tent had only one anchor at the windward end, our own efforts to tame the beast were futile. The powerful gusts were pushing underneath the ground sheet of the tunnel tent and lifting it up, making it impossible to use our skis as corner anchors or get snow onto the valance flaps along the sides.

It had been a quarter of an hour since we had stopped hauling and we were starting to get cold as we were not able to fetch our down jackets from the sledges. My fingers were like wood and George shouted into my ear that his were also deteriorating. In a final concerted effort, I grabbed a ski as George forced the tent down with his bodyweight and I managed to get a second anchor in. In what must have been only a few seconds, we forced the third and fourth skis into place and threw our tent bags into the inner compartment in an attempt to stop the wind flowing under it. The shovel was on my sledge, so I wrenched it from the top of the canvas and madly started to move ice and snow onto the valances to stabilise the tent. George dragged the remaining sledge into a windbreak position and then ran over to my obscured figure in the blizzard.

"Shall we get in?" George screamed with a hint of humour and then dived straight through the side opening of the tent into the outer area. I followed immediately after and we landed in a mangled heap.

We lay on the ground for a minute or so and began laughing in utter relief. The roar of the wind was still deafening and the tent was being thrown around horribly, but we were out of the wind and had not lost any equipment. It was time to pick ourselves up and move on.

Chapter I

'People, perhaps, still exist who believe that it is of no importance to explore the unknown regions… Man wants to know, and when he ceases to do so, he is no longer man.' Fridtjof Nansen

Travelling in the Polar Regions has no equal in terms of natural simplicity and demands placed on both body and mind. The very nature of polar travel and the expeditions venturing to the extreme latitudes of our planet have also changed beyond recognition in recent years. Even the environment itself is in a state of constant change, much of it apparently due to the actions of mankind itself. The task of writing an account of a journey in the Polar Regions in the twenty-first century certainly differs from the Heroic Age of the early twentieth century. Contentiously, public perception of expeditions and access to the Poles has transformed with the communication and commercial revolutions. The great early accounts of pioneering travel by men such as Fridtjof Nansen, Robert Scott, Knud Rasmussen and Apsley Cherry-Garrard are staggering acts to follow. The National Geographic voted Cherry-Garrard's *Worst Journey in the World* the greatest travel book ever written and it is clear that few endeavours grip the human imagination more than the efforts of explorers battling terrible conditions in remote locations.

The challenge in recalling my own journey across a region of the Arctic is not to regurgitate my frantically scribbled diary or to produce a polar travel guide. Rather, it is to attempt to let the reader into the world of travelling on ice, discuss and justify my views of polar exploration and, if possible, place the journey into context. Scan the travel and adventure sections of the few remaining bookshops and presented with a swathe of paperbacks by 'intrepid explorers'. In the process of my polar education, I naturally worked my way methodically through these mixed accounts. They further stirred my building desire to experience and test myself in these inhospitable places. Despite this, I found myself constantly turning back to the early books. Most were a breed apart to the modern adventure books in terms of measured humility. Once you had become accustomed to the Edwardian style of Scott's diaries or Shackleton's *South*, there was another dimension to the story that they were telling. Bruce Jackson commented rightly that 'few of the great writers about the Arctic seem capable of narrowness or parochialism.'

I wish to tackle the first obvious question straight away. It is the question I am often asked and does not come as a surprise. It is, of course, the question 'Why?' Those who have gone before have enlisted a whole host of responses including George Mallory's witty one liner: 'Because it's there.' Whilst certainly a cunning way to respond to such a tough question, I wonder whether it was used as an instrument to avoid any further inquisition. From my own point of view, I used to enjoy the fact that I just 'do' and did not feel the need to justify. Did Mallory really believe his own words, and was his much quoted response an understandable façade to deflect uncomfortable questions? There are a number of motivations behind polar expeditions. They range from the scientific to raising funds for good causes and sometimes, even the much vilified, raw ambition. Like Mallory, others voiced well-documented comments on this subject.

'To impress girls at parties,' explained Robert Swan. Sir Ranulph Fiennes claimed his polar endeavours were simply 'to pay the bills.' Wally Herbert, who made the first surface crossing of the Arctic, wrote elegantly, 'and what of those who ask? It is as well for them that there are others who feel the answer and never need to ask.' Having considered Herbert's response, I feel that most other attempts would somehow fall short of his. That is not to say that polar expeditioners should fall back on their laurels and smugly claim that 'mere mortals' would not understand – quite the opposite. It is the duty of every person to explain his or her motivations if they are to receive support, either financial or intangible.

The great polar leader, Ernest Shackleton, blusters that the lure of the Poles 'can hardly be understood by the people who have never got outside the pale of civilisation' but then immediately counters with a humble acceptance that he would be trying his 'fortune once again in the frozen south.' This surely cushions him from accusations of complacency and elitism by his being conscious of inevitable human inferiority in the face of such powerful environments.

These quotations still somehow fall short of explaining why someone would voluntarily choose to spend prolonged periods in extremely cold, windy, dangerous and lonely places. I found that one way of looking at it was to draw a parallel with the sporting world, with which polar travel has some tenuous links. My logic follows that no-one ever asks a sprinter or a cyclist why they run or cycle. It is assumed that they do so for challenge, enjoyment or to satisfy a competitive desire. There is the added benefit that the Arctic and Antarctic happen to be stunningly beautiful places, Roald Amundsen observing in the Antarctic that the 'land looks like a fairytale'. This privilege never wears thin, especially when you consider that you can often be the only person to have witnessed a location in decades, if ever.

There is also a darker side to the lure of the Poles. The South African Mike Horn, who attempted the North Pole in the winter of 2006 with Norway's Børge Ousland said, 'I love nature when it is at the peak of its violence and its splendour, because when it forces me to undergo the worst pains imaginable, it nonetheless allows me to be part of it, and that is a real privilege'. The point being made here echoes in my own thoughts. This point is that the violence and attraction are, in a way, one and the same. I have chosen to undertake expeditions for a number of reasons. Firstly, I want to travel

27

further, harder and more simply than anyone else over routes that have been untrodden: a desire to lead and not to follow, ambition and competition, pure and simple. Secondly, I want to use the inevitable publicity to generate funds and awareness for matters I feel are important. This curious combination of both selfish drive and empathy has a critic in Mike Horn.

He said, 'anyone who does what I do and says it's for science or for the blind or deaf, they're full of it. It's just an excuse. Really, you can't keep yourself alive out there for charity. You do it for yourself. You come back for family. But you go out for yourself'. I am the first to admit that I saw charity fund-raising as a fortuitous side-product of my plans, not the purpose itself.

The trend I wanted to distance myself from was the fashionable environmental bandwagon. I studied environmental biology at university and care deeply about the fate of the natural world. However, the token inclusion of 'to raise awareness of global warming' in expedition brochures in the hope of more funding for an adventure holiday is, to me, vacuous. The fact that, to gain credibility, every organisation needs to 'carbon offset' and have other badges of dubious value, is evidence that the 'green revolution' is running way off target. This is largely due to half truths which spread like wildfire amongst an audience that is not always fully aware of the intricacies of environmental science.

This, alongside other common media-hooks, includes invented 'world records' which become more and more pointless and along with wholly exaggerated low temperatures. I read a claim on a website that an Antarctic expedition would endure temperatures of minus eighty. This is close to the lowest winter temperature ever recorded on Earth at Vostok Base and would never be approached in the summer. Surely a return to honesty and simplicity is the right path.

It is sometimes suggested that polar travellers and mountaineers have a morbid desire to be close to danger and death. This could be by placing themselves on a thin skim of ice over a freezing ocean or on a weak snow bridge over a crevasse. I completely reject the suggestion and even insist the complete opposite is true. In my experience, living and working on icecaps and also in the mountains, you never feel more alive. After all, life is about experiences – packing as many in as possible can never be a bad thing. Another attraction of travel in remote regions or mountaineering is the simplicity and tangibility of success and failure. For those days, weeks or months, the focus on the task in hand exists to the exclusion of all else. The freshness of perspective is exciting beyond description.

Now the scene is set and the overall intentions laid out, it is necessary to travel back to the very infancy of my polar plans. What is perhaps most striking is the very different form they had compared to the reality of four years later. I was sitting at my desk in my small room at the end of the Victorian corridor in St Hugh's College, glancing through the copious notes and tutorial discussions which dominated my studies at university. I have always had a very deep passion for the natural world, one that began to develop at school. It had provided a great deal of motivation in terms of my academic eagerness. A few teachers at school had made a huge impact on my direction and I consider them almost entirely responsible for whatever successes followed. They had an energy for their subjects I have never seen paralleled and taught me that the key to avoiding mediocrity was to have a combination of enthusiasm and the resolve to translate it into results.

This passion, developed in my teenage years, is still as strong today, but what I realised at Oxford was that I am not a modern biologist. As my tutor dryly commented, I would have been more at home as an eighteenth century natural historian travelling the world and discovering new species in strange and distant lands. Sadly, the reality of modern-day biological science was dominated by mathematics and other processes which, for me, rather spoilt the magic of studying life on Earth. I wanted to 'get amongst' the natural world, not peer at it from a distance.

My attention shifted again from 'evolutionary systematics' to the wider world and I found myself thinking about a way of combining all the things important to me in a single event, the 'big project'. Of course, I loved the natural world but I was also fascinated by endurance and the art of pushing the human mind and body beyond their comfort zones. Even at the age of just fifteen, I had made moves into the worlds of ultra-distance kayaking, long-distance running and cycling. These would, over the years, develop into serious competition in both triathlon and rowing. Finally, there was another aspect to my personality that I simply could not ignore, no matter how conflicted the motivations behind it were. I craved the opportunity to do something different and utterly break the mould. I thought this exclusivity and possibility for creativity irresistible. This did not stop at simply wanting to join a group of people who did something different, or at least appeared to. It involved wanting to be at the forefront of even the smallest niche of people, pushing into the unknown in an age where adventures are seen to be ten-a-penny and available at the click of a button. This, of course, brings us back to the concept of raw ambition and the egotist. I believe that there has to be some portion of ego in every person who attempts to go that clichéd extra mile. History tells us that many of the most celebrated characters share this trait, regardless of their popularity.

This big project had to be physical, distant, unusual and have some form of long-term legacy. I could not contemplate the idea of having an achievement sink into obscurity after putting life and soul into capturing it. Like anyone who finds themselves captured by the Polar Regions, it was first by the stories of the pioneers, the real explorers. It was this classic starting point which turned my attention to the Poles, in particular the Antarctic. I was sure that the moment when I decided to pursue a certain goal would cement in my memory forever. It did not, however, seem to happen like that. There was no eureka moment, no point of realisation of what I must do. Instead, what followed was a gradual development with a growing sense of excitement and purpose, which did not dim once in the years which followed.

There were a few main components which I lacked. They were, to put it mildly, quite significant. I had no experience, no team, no route and critically, no funding. One thing I knew for sure was that I did not want to join someone else's project or to be led. I wanted very much to see my own dream and concept from start to finish. My father once told me that leaders can go one of two ways when choosing a team. They can, on the one hand, surround themselves with those of lesser skill, experience and strength of character. This makes the team very easy to dominate and steer but is the choice of the weak and insecure leader who craves power.

Instead, as he explained at this early stage, "choose a team of those who are better than you." This way I would have a team full of creativity, experience, skills and ultimately, one capable of success. This seemed undeniable logical, but putting the plan into action would prove very difficult indeed.

Aside from my own team-seeking tasks, there were others in the polar community to consider. The few years following the millennium are a difficult period to consider in terms of identifying the key players who set the standard. This is due to the rampant increase in accessibility and expeditions, and also the often inaccurate publicity that some employ to promote their activities. Glancing through the features pages of the broadsheets during the northern and southern polar seasons, a casual reader would be forgiven for thinking that every soul on Earth is making Pole attempts. Especially in the financially buoyant years preceding 2007, sponsorship was relatively straightforward to achieve and so the number of expeditions grew.

In reality, the majority transpire to be one-off 'Pole bagging' exercises undertaken by those with only a passing

31

interest in the Poles and the associated self-congratulation and perceived glory. Many, once reaching a Pole by the easiest possible method, will abandon polar travel and move onto another symbol of achievement, often Mount Everest. A common rule of thumb to assist in sifting the phoney from the real deal is whether a person champions themselves as an 'explorer'. Those who hold a long-term passion for the Arctic or Antarctic and have made significant contributions to polar travel are usually reluctant to be labelled 'Polar Explorer'. This is largely due to the reverence which they hold for the early pioneers and true explorers who serve as their inspiration.

This community is remarkable for its small size and has a core culture of idealism, machismo and competitiveness. Jon Krakauer, a mountaineer and journalist on Everest during the 1996 disaster which left a dozen climbers dead, observed the parallel climbing community. He wrote that, 'Getting to the top...was considered much less important than how one got there: prestige was earned by tackling the most unforgiving routes...in the boldest style imaginable.' And so it is in the polar world. Needless to say, this leads to a spectrum of viewpoints on many aspects of polar expeditions. A disproportionate number originate from a relatively small number of countries. This is usually due to a long history of ski travel on ice, in the case of Norway and Canada, or due to a reputation for global expansion and exploration, most notably Great Britain.

For context, the group still active at the time of my expedition and who are considered major personalities in polar expeditions includes the Canadian, Richard Weber. He skied to and returned unsupported from the North Pole in 1995, completing what many have called the greatest feat in polar history. Successful on his second attempt with Russian, Misha Malakhov, they travelled enormous distances over tortuous ice.

Inserted to the Canadian Ward Hunt Island as winter was loosening its hold, they did not return until June, when temperatures saw the ice floes melt under their feet. The book of their Herculean effort, *Polar Attack*, even welcomes others to attempt to repeat the expedition but in nearly fifteen years, none have stepped up to the plate.

Another is Norwegian Børge Ousland whose prolific polar record involves both Poles, as part of a team and also solo. He has utilised a number of styles, usually without resupply, and also pioneered the use of immersion suits in the Arctic Ocean and para-sails on icecaps.

The major British contenders to play on the global stage are Pen Hadow, Ben Saunders and Sir Ranulph Fiennes. Hadow, who became the first to reach the North Pole solo and unsupported from Canada in 2003, did so after a number of attempts. He attracted controversy after the aircraft operators he was dealing with claimed that he stayed out on the ice later than agreed. Hadow had to endure a further week on the ice having reached the Pole before being extracted by Twin Otter aircraft. The point at which it is safe to land an aircraft on the melting sea ice is sensitive due to concerns for pilot safety but other expeditions have since been extracted from the ice weeks later in the season.

Ben Saunders, who reached the North Pole in 2004 after seventy-four days alone, is driven by a strong expedition philosophy. Saunders has since had plans for expeditions both Arctic and Antarctic but funding issues have plagued him and his team-mates, these woes eventually subsiding to make way for a South Pole return journey with resupply in 2013/14.

Sir Ranulph Fiennes, more commonly called Ran and Britain's most well known living polar traveller, has a mixed but prolific track-record both in the Arctic and Antarctic, both with and without outside support. The Norwegian Rune Gjeldnes holds records for mammoth crossings of the Arctic Ocean and Antarctic, and the American Will Steger is the undisputed world leader in long distance dog-driven expeditions. In 1989-90, he led a dog team across the Antarctic, covering nearly 3,500 miles. In the years since, treaty laws stipulate that dogs are no longer permitted on the continent. These men were and are a fitting group of individuals to bear the torch handed over by those who went before. They have a dedication to professionalism, the Polar Regions as an environment and to preserving the a spirit of exploration.

In contrast, a large number compensate for a lack of experience by employing the services of highly experienced individuals as guides. These guides include formerly husband and wife team, Paul Landry and Matty McNair, and also Canadian, Devon McDiarmid. As has been reported on a number of occasions, guides will play little part in any publicity about the expedition, will often be required to break trail for every session during the day and even be asked to step out of photographs of triumph on completion. Other episodes included teams leaving sets of skis at home hours before departure to the Antarctic and another being bankrolled huge guiding fees by family, having been abandoned by a sponsor. Needless to say, this spirit of travelling was anathema to myself and many others. The concept of using a guide totally removed the challenge of self-reliance, simplicity and also equality of achievement within the team. Guiding is best suited to when those with ambitions in the Poles or mountains are in the early stages of learning their art. These polar 'apprenticeships' are often impatiently forgone in deference to chasing immediate results. My own apprenticeship in the mountains is ongoing and I did not have any delusions about undertaking a major polar expedition without training in a polar environment beforehand.

My initial challenge was to find some other people who were similarly motivated and mad enough to want to get involved in my project. Before I could start on the team, however, there was a more pressing problem. I was an eighteen-year-old student in full-time education, not a professional polar traveller. As a result, I had no reputation and no credibility in the tight-knit polar community. Quite understandably, even my own family met my enthusiastic plans with a healthy amount of scepticism as I had a track record of ambitious and borderline-outlandish dreams and schemes! As the months rolled on and the depth into which I was researching the expedition became apparent, the slow realisation that this was for real emerged. Despite having no experience or interest in the cold or Polar Regions, my family in particular were behind the project from day one, always adding that vital alternative perspective to solving problems.

I thought to myself, 'Where do you look for polar expedition team-mates?' There was no easy answer, being such an unusual niche. I just started to put the word out amongst the circles of people I thought might be interested. This ranged from the university Exploration Club and the department where I studied, to a number of contacts I had in the Armed Forces. I put out posters on noticeboards and tried to get the word out primarily by getting people talking. I was very keen to try and find companions for the journey the old fashioned way, not by getting people to apply on the internet. It became increasingly clear that finding a team for something as demanding and specialist as a polar expedition would require a lot of lateral thought. It was not like signing up for a package holiday, although some companies have recently attempted to market 'polar experiences' along those lines.

My plan was to make the process as individual as possible and with the aim of finding the right personality for the trip, not simply a strong CV on paper. Letters and emails of interest were starting to flood in, some from teenagers with a love for the outdoors and some from those with simply mind blowing amounts of experience. I was really starting to feel that I was gaining momentum but I needed to gather my team together so that we could discuss my ideas and solve the inevitable endless string of setbacks. My plan was to meet each interested party individually and in a totally informal atmosphere. I did not want any hint of the meeting being an interview. Predominantly, this journey was about a couple of things. One was to achieve something significant and new in the Polar Regions. The other was to have the most extraordinary experience possible and I felt that this really had to be shared with the right people – the right team. I had to find a group who would gel on the ice and would meet the challenges together as a united front. Above all, we had to get on at a personal level, not just work as colleagues.

My first bit of luck came almost immediately. As it happened, the secretary of the Oxford University Exploration Club was not just content with circulating my appeal for team-mates to the club. He wanted to get involved himself. I immediately arranged to meet Adam Griffiths for coffee in a small French café on one of the quaint little streets that criss-cross Oxford. This was to become the scene of all of my discussions with potential expeditioners. By the time that the letters of interest had started to dry up, the rather bemused waitress must have wondered why on Earth I was meeting a long list of men for coffee on a nearly daily basis. I sat down in the café and waited for Adam to arrive. His six foot five inch frame walked through the small door at exactly the time we had arranged and we made our introductions. I instantly warmed to Adam, a real gentle giant, and we spent the next couple of hours chatting about ideas, looking at maps and talking about our backgrounds. It was exactly as I had hoped, informal and with the ice broken immediately. The topic of polar travel had bridged two complete strangers. I knew Adam had to be involved and he was only the first contender I had met. Adam had already travelled to the High Arctic with the charity, the British Schools Exploring Society (BSES), now British Exploring, which organises global expeditions for youngsters from various backgrounds. Adam's climbing and Arctic experience was impressive and he had a skill set I was keen to bring into my team.

As the days and weeks passed, the applicants came and went. The range was incredible, from the delightful to the downright arrogant. One in particular proceeded to lecture me for about half an hour about how well qualified he was and then abruptly left. Astounded, I glanced down at my notepad and, with a slight grin, put a line through his name. Some, however, had a passion and an energy which came bursting out and I was excited about having so many to choose from. Ultimately, the success of the expedition would depend on a positive and resourceful personality from every team member. One of my final coffee sessions was with a thirty year old called Andrew Wilkinson. He was serving full-time as a Royal Marines Reservist Officer and had one of those CVs that simply jumped at you. His climbing and outdoor experience took up much of the form and had touches of humour and energy that were apparent even on paper. His final comment was that his interests included 'eating chocolate cake with friends'.

I was looking forward to meeting Wilki immensely. Over our two hour chat and a number of coffees, to which Wilki was particularly partial, we discussed the whole project and his hopes for it. What struck me was that, despite his obvious experience and skills, he had a humility about his past and he did not consider his place on the team a matter of course. Wilki had driven some distance from his home to meet me and this reinforced my view that he was the right sort of guy to have around. Something had been niggling in my mind throughout our meeting and just before we went our separate ways, I asked him, "were you on POC in late 2002?" POC, the Potential Officers Course, was the physical component of Royal Marines Officer selection. With a widening smile as it clicked in both our heads, "Yes!" he responded. Wilki and I had been through selection together over two years previously. It was all starting to fit into place; what a small world!

The problem of team size was one that weighed heavily on my mind throughout the search for a team. There seemed to be undeniable logic behind teams of all sizes. Polar expeditions have successfully travelled solo, in pairs or even in large military style 'sieges' with dozens of support staff. Looking to history certainly seemed to be the best place to start as different strategies have been tried and tested over the decades. I certainly did not want to travel solo, at this stage of my life at least. I had great admiration for those who did, such as Erling Kagge, Børge Ousland and Pen Hadow. It struck me as something that you move onto at a later stage in life and perhaps the attraction for me will grow with time. The real question was whether I wanted one, two or three companions on the trip. There are many things to consider; the possibility of an early drop out, injury on the ice, conversation, team dynamics and so on. I decided to aim for three as this left room for one to drop out due to illness or a change of heart, a variety of ideas and conversation, and also the ability to spread the considerable hauling load.

Ran Fiennes, who made a number of attempts on the North Pole and also a long expedition across the Antarctic, had a strong view on the matter of team selection. He believed that choosing the perfect team is 'nearly impossible. There is no foolproof selection process and the longer, the more ambitious the endeavour, the more time there is for each person's failings to rise to the surface.' I can see where he is coming from but, from experience, I now know that it is possible to survive expeditions without fall-outs with companions. Essentially, since expeditions are so unique in their demands, there is no real way to replicate these through a selection procedure. Fiennes does, however, mention that he hoped to find a 'true companion' on each journey, which he most certainly did in a team-mate, Dr. Mike Stroud. Both Adam and Wilki seemed like ideal expedition team-mates and so, after a weekend on Dartmoor hiking with some other potentials, I settled on the team. Almost as if a sign of the flexibility that would be required in the coming months and just as I was due to finalise the team, I received a call from Wilki.

"Morning Alex. I know you're keen to have a three man team, but there's this chap at work who you just have to meet. I mentioned the expedition to him and his eyes popped out his head with excitement!" he explained.

"Ok then," I replied. "Where does he live and when will he be available for a chat?"

"Well, he's called Rich Smith and lives near Edinburgh. Oh, and he's already trying to book a flight down South to meet you."

Stunned by the enthusiasm of someone who had only heard of me from Wilki's description, I waited to meet Rich. I really started to get the feeling for the first time that I was surrounding myself with the people my father had described. True to his word, Rich flew down a few days later and I went to meet him in the aforementioned French café. Once I had Rich up to speed with the project as it stood and chatted about how he knew Wilki, he explained his reasons for wanting to get involved. He had already reached the summit of Alaska's extremely challenging Mount Denali, and was also a keen long-distance kayaker, like myself. Rich was looking for that next challenge and was attracted by my specific intention to make the expedition novel and independent. It did not take long to see why Wilki had wanted me to meet Rich and I was delighted to welcome a fourth member. Both Wilki and Rich were in their thirties and had a great deal of practical experience. Indeed, only a couple of years later Wilki was to summit Everest and Cho Oyu on independent and non-commercial climbs. The team was complete as 2005 drew to a close and I felt a mixture of both excitement and also a responsibility to deliver results. After all, as the project leader, I would expect dedication and a significant amount of time from these three men who worked in full-time jobs.

Chapter II

'Adventure is just bad planning.' Roald Amundsen

One initial hurdle to overcome, before any meaningful work could be done, was that of our dispersed team. The newly formed 'Journey South 2007' team was spread around the far corners of the United Kingdom, almost literally. If I was to ensure we met our own deadline of hitting the Antarctic ice in the winter of 2007, then communication would have to be excellent from the offset.

We devised a neat system of conference calling when we could not meet personally. This supplemented the obvious email traffic, without which there would have been massive headaches for the team. These phone calls were invaluable as they allowed a quick four-way discussion of the main topics which were circulated by email previously. Rather surprisingly, the first time we actually met together as a team was in the winter of 2005 when we gathered for a weekend of planning, walks in the countryside and large meals at Wilki's family home. With less than two years until we planned to embark on our journey, we were at last able to discuss the fundamental goals of the expedition and develop a game plan for the coming months.

Immediately I noticed that the team communicated well and so the first, and most important, part of the jigsaw puzzle was in place. We gathered in a living room at one end of the house with a large, open fire and crowded round a plethora of draft proposals, maps and plans. Just as productive were the long strolls through the woods where the four of us were able to get to know one another. Up until this point we had been working at a distance and very much as colleagues, rather

41

than team-mates. Despite the significant age gap inherent in the team – Rich and I were separated by over fifteen years – we began to find that the team was, although made up of individuals, very compatible in a benign environment. How we would fare in highly pressured and genuinely life-threatening situations remained to be seen.

The question of whether it is best to travel with friends or professional colleagues is an important one. As has been much publicised in the media over the decades, there is a belief that expeditions, especially polar expeditions, invariably breed contempt within teams. As for the sizes of the teams themselves, there have been successful examples of different team dynamics throughout history. The expeditions led by the pioneers such as Franklin, Amundsen and Shackleton were organisationally formal with strict selection interviews and a strong hierarchy in terms of command. What is particularly interesting is that, despite this seemingly inflexible and impersonal approach, the men in many cases worked well in cramped and horribly arduous conditions. A good example is the exceptional spirit displayed by Shackleton's *Endurance* crew who overwintered in the Antarctic and spent months awaiting rescue underneath an upturned boat hull.

In a characteristically pragmatic and frank way, Ran Fiennes makes a point of considering friendship from an expedition to be a bonus rather than an expectation. His own relationships with his early teams and long-term expedition companion, Dr Mike Stroud, were called into question by the media. On more than one occasion, arguments and 'mutinies' were reported by the press with apparently little grounding in reality.

Our team was undeniably diverse. I was a teenage university student, Wilki a serving Royal Marines Officer, Adam an outdoor instructor and Rich a technology and IT professional and also a Royal Marines Reservist. Somehow it seemed to work well and I was not going to complain as long as it continued to do so. I was keen to iron out the issue of leadership from the word go. It was always my intention for the team to forgo the formalities of a strict command structure. This was to ensure that I was utilising one of team's greatest assets, the experience of each individual. The four of us had travelled up to the Birmingham NEC for the annual Outdoors Show, and on one of our 'working dinners', in the newly developed city centre, I suggested that we discuss the way that we wanted the team to be run. Encouragingly, everyone outwardly had a very similar vision: a very open forum for discussion but with myself in place to maintain the direction and coordination. I had noticed that Rich had been a little quiet about the matter and so approached him away from the group. "Are you okay with the team running as it is? We haven't really broached the subject of our ages since we met in Oxford," I asked.

"It's fine. I agree that it's best to avoid anything too formal in such a small team," he replied, still not sounding entirely certain.

I resolved to leave the matter and see how the next few weeks went. Even from the early days following the team's creation, I had wondered how a highly proficient and confident outdoorsman such as Rich would react to being on an expedition run by a relative youngster. The discussion we had seemed to have smoothed over the issue and it never resurfaced.

It was approaching the end of 2005 and the clock was starting to tick. The amount of preparation and fund-raising to complete was daunting and we needed some advice and input from the experts. Adam, through his involvement with BSES, had been familiar with the Royal Geographical Society (RGS) in Kensington Gore, London for some years. BSES rent a number of rooms in one of the far corners of the RGS building and the two societies have very close ties. The RGS is considered the home of exploration for the British at least, playing a part in almost every major expedition since its foundation in 1830. The society has its headquarters in an imposing brick building with statues of exploration heroes set into the walls. One of its most distinguished Presidents, Sir Clements Markham, was instrumental in assisting the Antarctic expeditions of Captain Robert Scott. Unfortunately for us, the Society no longer makes financial contributions to expeditions, as in years past. Instead, it provides a hub for dozens of the country's most knowledgeable expedition experts.

Annually, the RGS hosts a conference, *Explore*, which brings hundreds of delegates together with panels of experts. I had previously decided that the November 2005 conference would be ideal for us to start building a public profile. In an attempt to give our relatively unknown team an identity to make the best of the conference, I quickly fashioned a logo for the team and had four polo shirts made. It read on the back in large, white letters, 'Journey South 2007 – unsupported to the South Pole'. The implications of the word 'unsupported' will be discussed in depth later. Early on the first day of the two day event, we headed past the imposing black statue of Shackleton set into the walls of the Society and into the reception area. Adam had agreed to volunteer as a helper for the day and set to work as the remainder of us circulated the stands and began to talk to other delegates.

Networking is a necessary evil in the world of expedition planning. Expeditions are expensive and the only practical way of raising the necessary funds, short of having a fabulously wealthy donor, is to gain corporate sponsorship. This was something of a black art to me and was the next major challenge. Indeed, the challenge of funding would be a constant menace throughout. The only practical way to gain access to the people who control large quantities of money is by networking. It was not something that came naturally to me as I enjoyed meeting and speaking to new people but did not revel in the constant financial undercurrent.

The shirts certainly seemed to have done the trick as, within minutes of us walking into the rather impressive Map

Room, we were inundated with advice from all quarters. I was keen to ensure that we would not appear with our ambitious plans completely unknown and so had drummed up some online press beforehand. Explorers Web is a website founded by a Swedish husband and wife team, Tom and Tina Sjögren, who had reached both Poles unsupported and had reached the summit of Everest. Their online magazine is the most widely read for news of expeditions in the Polar Regions, on the oceans or in the Himalaya. In a short email to their press desk, I spelt out my aims and hopes for the expedition in an attempt to get an article to start the press ball rolling. The Sjögrens have a reputation in the adventure world for being opinionated regarding the motives of adventurers and their claims. As such, and knowing that they had routinely published critical reports of British expeditions, I was not expecting a positive response.

To my surprise, within the day, I received a pleasant reply and a few days later a short article followed in the polar section with an all important link to our fledgling and highly unimpressive website. Within hours, messages of good will and offers of assistance flooded in, many of which asked to meet us at the RGS Explore event.

This initial contact with Explorers Web (now under new management) and my subsequent first steps into the polar community introduced me to its controversial side. As can be expected of people who make large personal sacrifices and endure significant physical hardship, the topic of records, claims and definitions is very divisive. The debates that rage could easily fill a book on their own, but in the four years or so since I became involved in polar travel, some things have become increasingly clear to me. One is the matter of support. This simple word is responsible for a vast amount of the arguments and bad blood between expeditioners.

There are two main factors that constitute support, and it is these that cause most of the confusion. Expeditions can either receive resupplies or not on their journeys. These

45

resupplies can contain food, fuel, medicines and replacements of broken equipment – a regular occurrence in such extreme conditions. Whether a cache is dropped by aircraft or left at a predesignated point by a support crew, this represents a major form of support. This is largely due to the dramatically reduced weight that needs to be moved across the ice. The other implications of resupply are stark when compared to the few expeditions which set out without it. They include the ability to heat the tent using plentiful fuel and the opportunity to extract injured team members.

Secondly, and more debatable, there is power assistance. Clearly, using outside sources of power to move is a form of support to the expedition. These sources range from the dogs used by Roald Amundsen on his successful South Pole attempt to the Snowcats used on Sir Vivian Fuchs' Commonwealth Trans-Antarctic Expedition of 1955-8. Although sails and rudimentary kites have been used to pull sledges along for decades, the 1990s saw a revolution in the power and control of so-called para-sails or kites. Despite significant sledge loads, a skilled skier can travel over a hundred miles in a single day using a large sail and favourable winds. An analogy which I have often used is a nautical comparison. Equating a man-haul expedition to a sail-assisted expedition is like comparing a swimmer to a sailor. There is no comparison. It has been suggested that using a kite is no different from using other mechanical aids such as skis, stoves and radios. It is a totally different matter. These other items serve to make the journey safer, but only the kite actually powers the travel itself. To many, myself included, either a resupply or power assistance constitute support. I had long since decided that travelling without resupply or power assistance was the way for me; it was polar travel in its purest form.

The more important question is whether this, perhaps arbitrary measure of difficulty, really matters. The spirit and style in which an expedition is undertaken is undeniably vital and every traveller has a different goal in undertaking their

46

journey. Polar travel is not a sport. There is no governing body, no world championship and consequently no rules. Whether a person wishes to abide by a set of guidelines is therefore entirely their own choice. Extreme pressure from the media and the community itself has been blamed for injuries sustained by expeditions whilst attempting to conform to the perceived 'rules of polar travel'. In the spring of 2004, the soloist North Pole hopeful, Franco-Finnish Dominick Arduin, waited to be inserted to her Russian start point at Cape Arcticheskiy. The National Geographic's Gordon Wiltsie called this corner of Siberia, scene of countless Cold War nuclear tests, 'a hateful, haunting place'. Weather conditions meant that there was a large compression zone and tracts of open water around the Cape itself and so the route onto the Arctic Ocean ice skin was impassable. The other expeditions attempting the North Pole from Russia elected to be flown by helicopter across the gap and to begin where the icepack was more substantial. Arduin rejected this plan and returned to the Russian Cape to begin her bid alone. After a day attempting to push north towards the Pole, her support team lost contact and she was never found, presumed drowned. Her motivation was to travel from the recognised start point to the North Pole, which is any point of dry land. Notwithstanding her own uncompromising focus in demanding her highly dangerous route, the pressure placed upon her by armchair explorers and the press should not be underestimated.

It may seem that I am at odds with the concept of rules and regulations in comparing expeditions. On the contrary, there has to be a method of putting expeditions in context and to separate the tourist trip from a landmark expedition. A line must be drawn somewhere. It is inescapable that journeys will be compared, as those who undertake them will invariably be competitive by nature. This is no new trend as the pioneers themselves raced each other for national glory and placed a great premium on competing by 'gentlemen's rules'.

Traditionalists, of which I count myself one in as far as maintaining standards, are inescapably troubled by the commercialisation of polar travel. This can be seen to debase the foundations of pioneering expeditions and even the environments themselves. As in the mountains, some of those with the financial means but without experience can find themselves reaching places totally impossible were they to forgo a professional guide. Thankfully, the financial lawsuits commonplace in mountaineering are not as yet present in polar guiding. Having parted with substantial sums, many Western climbers have attempted to sue their guiding companies when the summit eluded them. Peter Athans, an Everest guide, commented rightly that 'some people don't understand that an Everest expedition can't be run like a Swiss train.'

These were issues that I had to consider carefully whilst my team and I were in the formative stages of expedition planning and deciding what we wanted to achieve. Originally, the intention was to attempt the recognised route from Hercules Inlet to the South Pole. This was chosen due to its proximity to Patriot Hills, a natural blue ice runway near the Ellsworth Mountains. The commercial Antarctic veterans ANI and its subsidiary Antarctic Expeditions and Logistics, ALE, operate solely from Patriot Hills (latterly moving to Union Glacier). Until recent years, it had no commercial competitor in providing logistics to private expeditions. Government scientific stations operated by the US, UK and other nations had long since rejected supporting private ventures after a number of high-cost rescue missions. I reflected on Hercules Inlet and decided a couple of things. The inlet, confusingly, is nowhere near open water, which is hundreds of miles to the north due to the presence of the permanent Ronne Ice Shelf. Miles deep under the ice is the continental coast of Antarctica and so defining Hercules Inlet as the coast is somewhat academic. This instantly voided Hercules as a start point as I could not contemplate achieving the Pole on a technicality. The pioneers, such as Mawson, Scott and Amundsen, did not have the luxury of being flown across ice shelves to avoid longer distances. To disregard permanent ice in a place such as the Antarctic, whether as an ice shelf or as the icecap over the continent itself, invites the entire endeavour to descend into disarray. It is fairly clear that the creation of the Patriot Hills camp and the nearby Hercules Inlet start point, whilst signalling a revival in Pole attempts both North and South, has kick-started an era of questionable claims and other corner-cutting exercises.

My second point was that of the purpose of the expedition. I wanted our endeavours to stand out amongst others and take their place amongst the great polar journeys. A very easy conclusion to reach was that the route should be new and untried. This constituted real exploration and the unknown in an age where anyone who enters the Polar Regions is hailed an 'explorer'. My attention centred on a region of the Antarctic on the Caird Coast, near the British scientific station at Halley Bay. It provided a balance of novelty and achievable distance from the South Geographic Pole itself, at around a thousand statute miles. Although slightly taken aback by my change in tack for the route, the others embraced the new plan and we enjoyed a newly united purpose.

Mapping of the Caird Coast, a coastal 'hinge region' as the ice shelf meets the icecap, ice streams and mountain ranges, was limited. The areas were sometimes overflown but not well known on foot at all. My challenge was to research the area and develop a route. Luckily, I was contacted by a British Antarctic Survey (BAS) scientist named Alex Gough who had previously studied at the same university college. At that time stationed at Halley Station itself, he offered to dig through the archives to find photographs, advice and possible routes. I appreciated the gesture particularly as I knew that BAS had a policy of not officially assisting independent expeditions in any way.

Our first appearance at *Explore 2005* was dominated by meeting some individuals who would be long-term supporters of my polar plans and became good friends. One such man was Steve Bull, who ran his own expeditions company and had guided a team over the 'last degree' to the South Pole a few years previously. Steve is one of those exceptional people who would gladly give up his own time and experience in order to aid others' success. His contacts in the logistics world and practical advice would be a constant help to me for years to come. In particular, Steve sat down with Rich and me for an Explore afternoon to study the preliminary costings for the expedition before the sponsor hunt began in earnest. When considering sums in the tens of thousands of pounds and budget totals in the hundreds of thousands, which themselves fluctuated with exchange rates and oil prices, it is easy to make costly errors. Having Steve as a sounding board and as someone who had managed to previously cut through the inevitable red tape was very useful.

In order to combat the limited polar experience of the team, we started to discuss training expeditions amongst ourselves, soliciting the advice of those who had gone before us, such as Geoff Somers and Steve Bull. The perceived wisdom was to train in Finse, Norway in the spring and Southeast Greenland in the summer. After writing off Finse due to clashes with work and exams, we contacted the two major Greenland logistics teams who were both present at *Explore*. Paul Walker is an Arctic veteran who had made the first land winter crossing of the High Arctic island of Spitsbergen. He was a slightly built and unassuming character who specialised in the use of Twin Otter aircraft to insert teams onto the east coast of Greenland from Iceland. This inevitably entailed a high cost and, despite Paul's sales pitch, we looked elsewhere. On the first evening of the conference, the team and I were heading out of the RGS and began musing on which restaurant to choose for our 'working dinner'. Barely after we had walked out the gates, a voice called from behind.

"Alex, I hear you're after some Greenland logistics?" yelled a bearded man with his business partner, we presumed, in tow.

"That's right. We most certainly are!" I replied.

Within five minutes the pair, Matt Spenceley and Jon Russill, had us sat in a trendy Kensington bar and set a few beers in front of us. Relative newcomers to the logistics business but with enormous personal experience, Matt began showing us various training expedition locations on his laptop with Google Earth. He had previously been an ice climber and kayaker at international level. Matt and Jon, like Paul, also operated in the southeast of Greenland, used local helicopters and had a base camp in Greenland itself, in the Inuit village of Kulusuk. This brought the cost of logistics down dramatically as scheduled, albeit unreliable and sparse, flights could be used to travel from England to Kulusuk via Iceland. What attracted me particularly to the way Matt and Jon worked was the integration with the local community. As was evident over the next few years, Matt would always seek to put money directly into Inuit hands, rather than via Danish or Icelandic companies. We agreed that in the summer of 2007, our four-man team would fly onto the huge Greenlandic icecap, second only to the Antarctic, and train for a month.

A quote of around £11,000 was issued, our first solid costing, and we went away with serious concerns about funding. I knew that compared to Antarctic logistics, PR and equipment, £11,000 was a drop in the ocean but it still seemed like a major challenge.

Explore 2005 marked, for my team, the start of a two year struggle to gain corporate sponsorship for the journey. The key to delivering value for money to sponsors is via media and publicity for their brand. For this, I had to dip my toes into the alien world of public relations. Everywhere I went in the RGS that weekend, I heard the name Tina. After asking around, I was introduced to Tina Fotherby, the expedition publicity guru and director of Yes Consultancy.

51

Brimming with enthusiasm, she immediately began to divulge fund-raising and publicity advice and helped shape my plan for the first part of 2006. Tina had worked with the apple brand 'Pink Lady' and linked them financially to both ocean rowers and adventure racers. Tina was widely considered amongst the best in this PR niche and I was extremely keen to have her on board. After considering the significant fees we would be parted with in the months surrounding the planned expedition, Tina agreed to work with us on risk in the months leading up to our planned departure date, October 2007. We were all grateful for her confidence in us as 'unknowns' and travelled back to our respective corners of the UK with renewed resolve.

Why are expeditions to the Poles so prohibitively expensive? The core reason from which everything else flows is the inaccessibility. Putting aside commercial 'off the shelf' expeditions, a small independent expedition one-way to the South Pole will cost around £250,000 and to the North Pole £125,000. The inaccessibility and large distances to travel lead to low competition or no competition at all between logistics firms. This monopoly allows for 'take it or leave it' offers for flights and logistics. The companies are also famously non-transparent about costings. The expense of transporting fuel is enormous and long flights count for most of a budget. Add to this expensive custom-made equipment, a sledge for example can cost £3,000, search and rescue insurance and publicity fees, and the total is eye-watering. In 2018, you can easily double these sums.

An unusual option for our insertion to Halley, which is a long distance from any ice runway, came up whilst speaking to some friends in the services. The Royal Navy's HMS *Endurance* polar patrol vessel did venture into the Weddell Sea, which Halley lies near, and had assisted private ventures in the past. I wrote to Admiral Sir Jonathon Band, the First Sea Lord of the Royal Navy and requested assistance from HMS *Endurance* if she was due to be in the region. He replied a few days later and explained that although in principle the plan would be enthusiastically supported, the ship would be thousands of miles away from the Weddell Sea in our narrow time window of late October. Other talks commenced with commercial shipping companies who operated in the Southern Seas but we drew blanks with all for financial and practical reasons. A traditional ship-borne insertion was not to be.

We had made our choice in terms of a logistics firm fairly early on in the timeline of the 'Journey South 2007' planning. ALCI was a Russian-run company that primarily resupplied government research stations but had recently allowed private charters to operate from Novo Base. Novo, long name Novolazarevskaya, is situated on a blue ice runway in Queen Maud Land. Flights to Novo set off from South Africa, unlike Patriot Hills which is reached from Chile. My contacts were Victor Serov, a Russian polar veteran and Patrick Woodhead, a Londoner married to a South African who had completed a number of guided expeditions and now runs a super-exclusive Antarctic tour company.

The team and I met Patrick in a wonderful little pub in Notting Hill, which had apparently hosted a number of polar brain storming sessions in times past. I instantly warmed to Patrick who was charismatic, with a hint of rebelliousness, and an unusual honesty when tackling difficult questions. We all crowded around an old table in one of the many cubby-holes in the cosy, dark pub. We scanned over maps and brochures and talked finance, coming away with a payment schedule and budget which suited both parties. A 230,000 Euro fee for their services would be payable before travel began. This was not before I had managed to destroy any credibility I had accrued by head-butting the wooden frame of an unnaturally small door which separated the rooms of the pub, a door more at home in a JRR Tolkein book. On the subject of books, Patrick gave us all a copy of *Misadventures in a White Desert*, which told the story of his South Pole expedition.

Despite my reservations about guided expeditions, the book was excellent: light-hearted and self-effacing.

Meanwhile, we had turned our attention to a vital branch of the wider expedition project, the charities. With so many thoroughly deserving organisations, many with a personal link to a member of our team, we considered with due care. Rich had successfully fought testicular cancer twice in the years leading up to joining the team and had decided to use his experiences to raise funds for charity and raise awareness. This was, as he explained seriously in our London hotel before a meeting, far more useful than being secretive and hiding it away. I admired his fortitude and honesty over something that many men find embarrassing and would rather not discuss. Rich was keen to nominate the charities for the expedition and they were finalised as Cancer Research UK and Maggie's Cancer Centres. To kick-start our fund-raising, Rich, Adam and I enjoyed a long day in the Scottish Munro mountain range pulling car tyres up Ben Nevis, the UK's tallest mountain, although miniscule by international standards. This classic polar training, crossed with mountaineering, was a hit and received a great deal of publicity when combined with Rich's cancer story.

On a cold February morning, we stepped out of our youth hostel at the base of Ben Nevis and began our hike up the mountain, whose summit is a little under a mile above sea level. The tyres constantly became caught on rocks on the uneven path. We were also collecting footage for a promotional DVD at the time and so were accompanied by a broadcast quality film camera in the capable hands of one of Rich's friends. As the rocky path turned to snow and ice we donned our crampons and the going became easier. The day, which would accumulate over £12,000 in charity donations, also served as a good team-building exercise. We had been conscious that too much of our time had been spent under office conditions trying to kick the dream into action. We passed a large number of bemused walkers and climbers on the route, each of whom had a witty joke regarding our choice of equipment dragging behind us. We developed a stock answer.

"The rest of the car is on the summit. We're just taking up the last bits now," we would explain seriously. They chuckled as if to humour us – we had clearly been declared insane. I am not sure I would entirely disagree.

Once we had reached the top and taken some photographs, we began our descent, which was a lot more fun. The slopes down to the main path were fairly steep and so Adam was the first to try sitting on his tyre and using it as a toboggan. There was no way of stopping or changing direction so most attempts ended in a spectacular crash but we moved back down the mountain at a rate of knots. The day was deemed a success – the only sadness being that Wilki was not available due to work commitments. As it turned out, the footage from the camera was of the shaky variety, but some was salvaged to create the DVD that would accompany sponsorship proposals.

Our tour of Scotland concluded with a fascinating visit to Edinburgh's Maggie's Cancer Centre, which helped Rich during his treatment. We were given a tour of the brightly coloured building, which is on the same site as the main city hospital. Andrew, our host, gave an interview for the DVD and explained how they help those undergoing treatment handle the non-clinical side of things. This sort of first-hand exposure to the charity itself reaffirmed my confidence that Rich had chosen well.

A few months later Rich, Adam and I would aim slightly higher in terms of mountaineering altitude and climbed Mont Blanc. At 15,781 feet, it is the tallest peak in the European Alps and, although a popular peak, responsible for a large number of fatalities. Not long before writing this book, a fellow expeditioner and also Everest summiteer, Rob Gauntlett, was killed on its slopes with his climbing partner, James Atkinson.

55

Our climb was not without incident however. Severe food poisoning and a healthy dose of altitude sickness gave the climb an educational twist. However, we reached the summit with incredible views to the Matterhorn and Eiger in the distance. The three of us worked together well on a fairly tricky climb, despite it not being technically highly rated. Mountaineering and polar expeditions tend to attract similar types of people and share a great number of common skills.

Chapter III

*'Nothing will ever be attempted if all possible objections must
first be overcome.'* Samuel Johnson

For over two years, almost without respite, sponsorship
proposals or 'props' as they came to be known, were a
daily feature. This included weekends, bank holidays, even
a large portion of Christmas, such was the hunger to gain
the all important funding. No money, no expedition – and
all our long hours of work would be for nothing. The rest
of the team took their share of the list of target companies
and had to produce them around their own significant work
commitments. As I coordinated this mammoth campaign, I
insisted that a master list was kept up to date, to the occasional
consternation of the hard-worked trio. We attacked each
sector of commerce in turn – first management consultancy,
then investment banks, then construction, and so on.

An important secret, which our advisors highlighted,
was to ensure personalisation of proposals. Marketing
Directors and CEOs receive many such requests from all sorts
of ventures every day of the week. A clearly mass-produced
'default' proposal would go straight in the bin without even
being considered. As a consequence, the process of scripting
a covering letter and brochure, which had new iterations
over the months, was a long and drawn out saga. I do not
believe that many casual observers of the expedition world
appreciate the hours needed to undertake the public side
of the venture – the journey or climb. There is no proven
formula to corporate fund-raising, a notoriously challenging
task, but this is the strategy we used. The cycle would involve
an initial phone call to a front desk to introduce myself and

ask which department would be suitable for a request for funding. Often the receptionist would misunderstand and direct me to the charity department but through perseverance I usually reached the right destination. I once even received a response to a written proposal from a major car manufacturer addressed to 'Alex Hibbert, Exhibition Leader'. We were lucky in this case, however, as about a third never received a reply at all. Once I had reached the Marketing or Corporate Social Responsibility Department, I did not attempt to make a pitch for funding there and then to a disinterested recipient on the other end. Instead, I asked for the name and address of the appropriate person and asked if they might be informed that a brochure would be arriving by post. Emails and phone calls are so easy to ignore and dismiss; a hard copy, I felt, was less forgettable.

Two or three days later, we sent a brochure first class to the Director or Manager and then followed up by phone a couple of days later. Lewis McNaught, a previous head of Gartmore, impressed on me that follow up calls were the absolute key to ending up on the top of the pile. I would often get into a long phone dialogue over months with personal assistants of CEOs, Directors and those who control spending and would often be able to speak to the bosses themselves. Invariably, the answer would be a regrettable 'no', a dead end, and the search would continue. Companies such as Microsoft, Badenoch and Clark and Aegon listened intently over long periods of time to the media and internal benefits of such an association but the trail went cold after their margins and targets had been considered. It was all about the right place at the right time – and this knife-edge could become infuriating.

The IT and database company that Rich worked for were in talks about a total and exclusive sponsorship deal for nearly a year. Having established that there was insufficient marketing funding in their UK sector and that there was real boardroom support for the idea, their European counterparts were brought in and our chances for success seemed boosted for quite some time. The majority of the negotiations were being made by Rich on the expedition's behalf as he was the one with the personal contacts. As a consequence, I had to work with reports of his progress as he carefully followed up leads and discussions.

Rich had a tricky balance to find as he attempted to keep the pressure on whilst not becoming a nuisance to his employers. As it became increasingly clear that the deal was losing momentum and we might end up with nothing after 'courting' the company for months, I pushed Rich for more details in one of our regular phone calls. This led to the sole disagreement between any members of the team in our entire time together as a four. Frustrated and irritated at what I perceived to be a lack of urgency, I ended the call, not wanting it to descend into a mud slinging match. Equally annoyed, Rich left a voice message a few minutes later and I decided that a response would not do much to calm the situation. Rich had been trying his best and I was getting exasperated at the hands-off approach which I had with the negotiations. He had personally invested a lot in the quest to secure the cash from his own employer and I later appreciated that its imminent failure would weigh more on him than Wilki, Adam or myself. Ultimately, despite an excellent proposal, strong business argument and good support from the UK sector, the prospect of receiving a quarter of a million pounds from European Headquarters was officially rejected only weeks before our schedule dictated we should be leaving the UK for South Africa and then Novo Base.

What was fast becoming obvious, as Tina and others had predicted, was that 'cold' proposals have an infinitesimally small chance of success. The reserves of funding allocated for external marketing and sponsorship was always outweighed by the demand for it. From the early days through to 2007, we had only two poor experiences with sponsors who had actually made a commitment to the team. One was with a small, now defunct design company based in Oxford, who produced utterly half-hearted brochure designs and reacted defensively when concerns were raised. Needless to say, the relationship ended acrimoniously. They were our first sponsor – I hoped it would not become a habit.

The second sponsorship disaster come in a very different guise and was more a result of misfortune than poor professionalism. Doniert Macfarlane, an ex-surgeon who was building a remote medical support company, had expressed great interest for months and had committed to becoming a leading partner of the 'Journey South 2007'. He even made an initial payment as a show of intent and we earmarked his input to fund the Greenland training expedition planned for July 2007. The main contribution was to come following the culmination of his own negotiations with major investors. Only weeks later a very apologetic and rather heartbroken-sounding Doniert called me and said they could not agree terms; the deal could not go forward. Our money was gone and Greenland had to take place using stinging personal contributions. Although the situation left the team in a very shaky position, Doniert's honesty was appreciated and, having spoken to him months later, I found his business had recovered. If only the timing had been better, the partnership could have been very beneficial to both his company and my team.

The financial situation that we found ourselves in was becoming perilous. Oddly necessary in the world of expedition fund-raising, it is critical to maintain a public air of positivity and to make it seem as if funding is flooding in. Referring to 'when' the expedition happens rather than 'if' when talking to potential backers, perpetuates the feeling of a successful project. Rarely is it actually the case and often funding comes from a last-minute offer, if at all.

Right from the outset, Adam had been designated the duty filmmaker in the team. He had used broadcast equipment in the High Arctic in Svalbard, a skill that comes only with experience. My own background in photographic stills was also useful in terms of technical understanding, but it was very much Adam's remit. As such, it was also his job to secure the pathway to perhaps the greatest benefit we could offer a corporate sponsor, a documentary. The fact that we planned to travel unsupported meant that we could not take a film crew on the ice for any part of the journey. This would therefore mean that we would self-film whilst under the stresses of an unprecedented expedition – not an easy task. The key was to find a talented and open-minded film production team that was willing to work on location and had the ability to secure a good slot for the documentary. As became very obvious when Adam began to contact the multitude of production companies, every single one promised a series of hour-long documentaries on prime time BBC1. Not one would be able to ground their claims with evidence but it is a competitive marketplace and quality content is at a premium. The only real way to differentiate a quality company with genuine prospects of marketing a documentary well, and those without, is by studying their recent work. After speaking to a shortlist, all of whom were extremely keen to get involved with a project that promised to be unique in the sheer number of selling points it held, we signed on with Eye Film and Television.

Eye was run by a team that oozed confidence, fresh ideas but also experience from the 'old days' of television film-making. It is not an industry that I had much experience in and so I was keen to get involved and learn the way the process worked. Our initial meetings with Charlie Gauvain, Frank Prendergast and Mike Coles showed that they were friendly and excited but professional and had a quiet confidence that only experience and success can generate. After only a few weeks pitching to broadcasters behind closed doors, they had secured an agreement with FIVE Television to produce a one-hour prime time feature. The fact it was prime time, terrestrial and a full hour in length was spectacular and we knew we had a strong publicity tool to take to companies interested in sponsoring the expedition. The moment I heard the news was the highlight of the four-year expedition campaign.

"Alex, I've got some reasonably good news," Charlie said slowly down the phone in his comically understated way. "Congratulations, you've got a prime time documentary confirmed! Not just pending – confirmed!"

I was in my room at home in the middle of another batch of sponsorship proposals when I received the call and was not able to control my joy. Whilst bouncing around the room in relief and excitement, I tried to conduct a serious business conversation with Charlie on the other end. He had clearly done his jumping around previously.

The next few months would involve hours of filming to record the build-up to the expedition. After all, an hour of television dedicated solely to four men skiing across a white landscape would, at best, be boring. Also, it would not do justice to the hundreds of hours of preparation and planning which is often more of a roller-coaster than the journey itself. The team and our film-crew travelled the length and breadth of the country, filming aspects that would create a complete story of our journey.

It had struck me that since the conception of my polar journey some years previously, the intensity of the preparations had been frenetic. Not only was this the case for myself, for whom it had become an obsession, but also for family and friends who had become unwittingly embroiled in the inevitable ups and downs. Aside from the fact that I also wanted an opportunity to stir up some more interest from those who may have assisted with funding or contacts, I wanted to host an evening for them. Oxford would be the venue. Having been an undergraduate there would aid enormously in attaining special deals for room hire. It was a busy time for the team as we had set the date for our Greenlandic training and filming expedition shortly afterwards. This, combined with the increasing seriousness of the financial viability of the project, weighed on my mind. We managed to secure partial funding for the evening from a local catering firm and special rates from the Bodleian Library hire team. We chose the Divinity Schools, an imposing gothic hall and part of the larger Bodleian complex frequented by thousands of tourists every year. The hall had been used as the 'sickbay' for the Harry Potter films, amongst many of the university's colleges that had also been used.

As I am now aware, the organisation of an evening of drinks, a seated meal and charity auction is no mean feat. In fact, the launch party took significant amounts of time away from the main effort of the team. Regardless, I was determined that the event would be a success.

One major setback did occur a fortnight before the black-tie dinner was planned to take place in June. Adam and I decided to return to Mont Blanc with two friends of his and attempt the peak from another side. In an accident which I still cannot fully explain, I received second and third degree burns to the majority of my face below the eyes and round to below my ears. It must have had something to do with a cooking fuel leak and a strong sun at 13,000 foot altitude. I can only imagine that fuel on my hands came into contact with my skin and stripped off the sunblock that I had religiously applied. Two days of climbing in direct sunlight must have burned the skin so violently that it blistered badly and constantly oozed a thick pus. I was unable to move my mouth as my face become a hard, leathery mask, which I proceeded to hide behind a black balaclava. This was as much to protect me from the stares of those back in Chamonix as to stop further burning from the sun. Andy, one of the two friends that Adam and I were climbing with, was a newly-qualified doctor and was able to vouch for my condition with my insurance company. I then made my way home to hospital via Geneva – a long and uncomfortable journey. Andy even tried to explain to a French pharmacist which ointment I needed to soothe the excruciatingly painful burns and succeeded only after she had recoiled in shock, having seen the burns. Back home in

England, I was picked up from the airport by my father who drove me straight to a hospital near Chichester in West Sussex. In a foul mood due to the six-hour flight delay, the sheer pain and the indignity of having to shield my face from view, I was an awful passenger. Having received copious painkillers and paraffin ointments from the young doctor, we returned home and I started on a diet of smoothies: the only food I could eat through a straw. I saw a close family friend the next day, an experienced surgeon, who assessed the burns and gave me realistic expectations of scarring. He also sympathetically took photographs to show to poor medical students. At least my situation would be of some use!

In a two-week recovery that shocked both the experts and myself, the burns hardened further and then started to fall away. This left healthy skin beneath, not scar tissue which I had feared most. Sensation also returned to all areas of my face which was remarkable given the depth of the burning. A few days before the party and a Summer Ball at New College, Oxford, my face had returned to normal save some blotchy pigments that settled over the following weeks. I was free to rejoin the final preparations for the evening, including sourcing wine and a jazz band, looking slightly more like me.

My temporary injury and discomfort, unpleasant though it was, reminded me of the ordeal which those with permanent disfigurement have to endure. It was humbling to consider the tolerance which they must summon to cope with people staring, asking questions and treating them as fundamentally 'different'. For me, however, the story was over within the month and for that I was extraordinarily grateful.

The reception and dinner ran without a hitch. The four of us on the ice team along with our Patron, Admiral Sir Nigel Essenhigh, made brief speeches and then moved into a charity auction. Sir Nigel had served alongside my father in the Royal Navy and had agreed from the early days to become our high profile figurehead and advisor. He had flown from

Scandinavia that day to make the launch and had provided the expedition over the previous months with assistance and credibility amongst high-level business people. His suggestions ranged from safety and evacuation procedures to the best way in which to approach individuals when in pursuit of funding. We had representatives from both Cancer Research UK and Maggie's Cancer Centres present, and an auctioneer friend, Mark Hewitt, hosted the sale. Various shops and retailers in the South had donated items from teddy bears to silver necklaces and the auction proved a resounding success. Whilst Mark plied his trade with remarkable skill, seemingly capable of extending bidding with a few choice words, the four of us acted as display stands for the lots. As the evening came to a close, many of our guests, from family and friends to our logistics manager, Patrick Woodhead and his wife Robyn, retired to a bar on Oxford High Street until the early hours. The support of those present and the efforts made to attend meant a great deal to us; the polar saga was in its third year by this point.

Chapter IV

'Luck favours the mind that is prepared.' Louis Pasteur

Soon after the fun and excitement of the Oxford launch was over, it was straight back to business again. We had only days until we planned to fly to Eastern Greenland with our film crew in tow for a few weeks of documentary work and training. We had a team get-together and discussed the things we wanted to achieve whilst on the ice. It would be an expensive trip due to the sponsorship meltdown and so it was necessary to be efficient with time. Rich volunteered to make a running list of routines and systems which we would develop on the ice along with various tips to make life more bearable.

It is unusual for those who spend a great deal of time in the outdoors not to become somewhat interested in outdoor gear. We were no exception, but our undeniable kit expert was Adam. He loved every minute of UK-based kit testing and selection and was given responsibility for the team's inventory. There is a long history of those heading to the Polar Regions modifying their clothing and equipment beyond recognition. This originated from when clothing, especially, was entirely inappropriate for extreme cold weather. Often smocks and masks would have to be bought from high street outdoor retailers and then redesigned to be fit for their purpose. In recent years we have become more fortunate with the advent of advanced fabrics such as Pertex and Gore-tex. There are also companies which now manufacture top quality items ideal for use with little alteration needed. Examples include Brenig for clothing and Snowsled and Acapulka for sledges. There was a time when Richard Weber and Misha Malakhov, not wanting to haul large wooden sledges known as komatiks, would resort to children's plastic toboggans.

Some polar purists, especially from the old school and often necessarily from the 'unsupported community', are brutal with their equipment modifications. The purpose is to reduce the weight hauled on the ice. Small things add up to leave you with a sledge too heavy to allow an expedition to succeed. Stories circulate the chattering polar circles of people sanding the paint off ski poles to save weight and cutting the covers off books. In my mind, this obsessiveness is unnecessary considering the superfluous equipment many expeditions carry with them, technology for instance. I resolved that our equipment would be fit to do its job, that we would take nothing unnecessary, but not to go to extreme lengths. Spartan living is in the nature of unsupported polar expeditions but a forecast eighty to ninety days on the ice made a few luxuries vital to stay sane. It is only supported expeditions that can afford to be less exacting with their choices, having the comfort of light sledges, food, fuel, medicine and breakage replacements flown out.

Through all the fast-paced preparations and the proposal writing which, as ever, had to run alongside other vital work, I had almost forgotten to be excited. Greenland would be my first experience of the real Arctic. For so long I had run the expedition like a business; it had to be that way. Again, I was at last able to pour over the photographs of the Polar Regions with the buzz and magic that hooked me in the first place. Greenland is lesser known than the Polar Regions around the North and South Poles but is a formidable polar environment, sharing its altitude, katabatic winds and desolation with the Antarctic. The icecap, second only to the Antarctic, which covers the vast majority is, in places, over two miles thick and contains nearly two million square miles of ice.

As had been agreed weeks before, Matt Spenceley would provide logistics and equipment hire for the expedition as our South Pole equipment was either unsuitable for the

Greenlandic summer, was yet to arrive or was too precious to use in training. He had arranged for our flights from England to Reykjavik, Iceland and then a small, propeller-driven aircraft to Kulusuk, a small village but the only 'international' hub in Eastern Greenland. From there, we would cross the fjord by boat to Tasiilaq and fly in a helicopter piloted by a Dane to the edge of the dauntingly large icecap. After a week of filming orientated work around the crevassed coast, the film crew would be flown out and we'd spend a short time mountaineering and then undertake a short hauling journey inland.

As it was July, Matt would not be in Kulusuk himself, but we were to be met by Georg Utuaq, a local inuk, who Matt wisely described as 'the main man in Kulusuk'. Over the following years, Georg would become a regular player in my expeditions and we built a good rapport, despite never speaking in the same language. He was certainly the 'King of Kulusuk', very much the local businessman who ran a sweet shop called the 'Kiosk Mugu'. *Mugu* means 'little man' – also the name of one of his sons. His ten foot square shop remains the only store besides the village shop itself. The village shop was remarkable, with the most eclectic mix of stores imaginable; rifles and shotguns were placed next to confectionary. Kulusuk was also home to Johan, an Icelandic anthropologist, who had lived in the remote village with his wife for years.

After a spectacular flight towards the iceberg-strewn Greenlandic coast, we arrived at the small building which served as the terminal at Kulusuk. The first signs that we were about to reach the island were small bergs in the bright blue sea. They began to increase in frequency and soon the sea was filled with ice from tiny blocks to bergs the size of buildings. The coast of Greenland is jaggedly mountainous and in the summer, most are only partially snow-covered, leaving the brown rock exposed.

The terminal had been built fairly recently and was remarkably Western in design. It was an indication that the Greenlandic people were keen to develop their industries in line with the rest of the world, despite their reliance on traditional hunting as a way of life. Kulusuk itself means 'the chest of a black guillemot' and is a small hunting and fishing village of only three hundred Inuit. The villagers lived in small wooden cabins, all painted in bright colours; blue, red and yellow being the most popular. It was a photographer's paradise. We stayed in a cabin owned by Matt's company, Tunu, and then having collected food, fuel and a weapon, travelled across the fjord to Tasiilaq. Throughout the year, Greenland's coast hosts a population of polar bears and the shotgun was a final defence against an unlikely attack. In summer, the fjords are navigable by boat although heavily filled with floating ice. Georg's son was our helm and he expertly steered through the ice at speed. By this point, we had been joined by Frank and Mike from Eye Film and they were thrust into filming amazing sequences of the boat journey. As Matt was quick to point out, as with any polar region, Greenland is a frontier territory where life does not work as in Europe. Things do not go to plan and timings are totally flexible. Once you embrace and actually enjoy this way of life, it is thoroughly refreshing. Frank and Mike were well travelled but still clearly took a time to feel at home.

Once in Tasiilaq, meaning 'like a lake', a larger settlement of nearly two thousand, we moved our equipment and sledges to the helicopter landing site. This included the three cumbersome high definition film cameras to be used by Mike and, in time, ourselves. We were to be taught how to film as we would have to bring back footage from the expedition ourselves. The unsupported nature of the journey meant a film crew was impossible. We managed to persuade a local man to help us move our kit in his old pickup truck the half mile from the shoreline to the pad. I confirmed the location we were aiming for with the pilot, the top of the seldom travelled and remote Hahn Glacier, and we were airborne within an hour of arriving. Inuit did not, as a rule, travel onto the inland ice. This was due partly to superstition over icecap-bound spirits, but more the fact that there was nothing of interest or value to be found there!

The views from the Huey helicopter were spectacular, although the flight only took twenty minutes as we flew low over the mountains, fjords and glaciers. Adam filmed out of one window and I shot stills out of another, mesmerised by the landscape and determined not to miss a second of it. The environment looked so welcoming, so serene. We had arrived on a still day with blue skies and a warm sun. I knew from history that this place, along with the Antarctic, can turn on the unwary in a heartbeat.

The pilot spotted a safe landing spot above the bergschrund of the Hahn Glacier. A bergschrund is the uppermost crevasse of a glacier and separates it from more static ice, in this case the giant icecap. They sometimes extend all the way down to the bedrock below and are usually among the largest of the intimidating cracks in the ice. This one was about ten feet wide, enough to swallow a family-sized car. Anyone intending to travel on the great icecaps, especially the Greenlandic or the Antarctic, must, at some point, face these monsters. We would encounter them close up over the coming days.

We flew lower and I looked out of the helicopter in both directions. To the east was the sea and the mountains. To the west lay an indescribable flat whiteness: the icecap. The contrast was extraordinary. As we touched down on the ice, the downdraft threw up clouds of snow which totally obscured any view out of the aircraft. The pilot shut down the engine and we opened the slide doors to welcome a chilly wind into the cabin. After ten minutes or so of shuffling the four sledges and camera equipment out, we lay on our equipment to avoid losing it as the helicopter departed.

The first job was to set up a base camp. We planned to stay put for the first week in order to film as the crew were due to leave us afterwards. Due to our proximity to the coast, prime hunting ground for the polar bear, we took great care to ensure our weapon and flare deterrents were always at hand. Bears rarely wander inland due to the total lack of food there, but can be curious animals. Besides avoiding the wildlife, we could also make some attempts on mountains yet to be climbed whilst in the vicinity. After all, we had auctioned the name of a Greenlandic mountain for charity at the Oxford launch. Now we had to deliver and summit a new mountain – a tall order certainly but very exciting. The team had good experience in the mountains. Adam and I had climbed in the Alps whilst Rich had been on teams working in some of the most challenging ranges in the world. Only months previously, Wilki had taken some time out from work and the team for his successful attempt on Mount Everest – he has since ascended the Eiger's North Face and dozens more routes. We were confident that between us, we could make some first ascents.

Our base camp was very comfortable and the temperatures were mild due to the high sun of mid-summer. Daytime temperatures were warm and only at night did the really cold air descend. We dug a latrine twenty feet or so from the line of four tents. Two dome tents were pitched on flat ice for Mike and Frank. One was for them to sleep in, and one was to protect their large quantities of equipment. Mike's tripod alone needed a packhorse to manoeuvre it. As for the team, we were testing two designs of tent, as kit testing was one of the main aims of this expensive expedition. One was a dome mountain tent and the other a Hilleberg 'tunnel' tent which was longer with a partitioned inside. However, it had to be pitched facing into the wind, otherwise the occupant would have an uncomfortable night. The views from the camp were ideal. We were on a dome and so could see the routes onto the icecap and also good approaches down the glacier towards the coastal mountains. The crevasses began in earnest only about five minutes from the camp and so they were accessible for the film crew, who were not on skis.

The next few days included crevasse rescue demonstrations where I, the lucky volunteer, walked out onto a weak snow-bridge over the bergschrund and hopped up and down until it gave way. I fell ten or twelve feet before the rope attached to my harness pulled taut, jerking me to a halt. As the other three worked away on a pulley system to haul me out and as Mike filmed, I had one of the film cameras passed down to me so I could film from inside the crevasse. It was a fairly large 'slot' with an unstable snow ledge about twenty feet below the lip. I doubted that it would hold my weight. Instead, it would most likely collapse down into the guts of the crevasse which could have been two hundred feet deep. To either side of me was blackness but the ice itself was a beautiful azure blue, glistening in the shafts of sunlight. The walls were smooth as glass and I knew that climbing out unaided would be near impossible. I was quickly pulled out of the crevasse and we then practised our rescue drills until we worked quickly and efficiently. In reality, the victim of a fall could be unconscious and would need to be out of immediate danger as fast as possible.

We gave a number of interviews and sledging demonstrations for the documentary and had an all important business meeting on the ice – surely the best venue and views for such a meeting anywhere in the world? The first week passed quickly and we sadly had to help Mike and Frank, with whom we were developing a great rapport, to pack up their gear and await the helicopter pick up. The helicopter had been confirmed for 1400hrs but, during a solo ski I was enjoying a few hundred yards from camp at midday, I heard rotor blades. From all our respective locations, we stared in disbelief at the approaching red helicopter and I skied at double speed back to camp. Our equipment was not yet strapped down safely against the down blast of the rotors but we leapt on them in time. We returned the pilot's enthusiastic wave as he landed twenty feet from our tents. I decided that he must have one of the best jobs in the world – flying across the remote regions of the Arctic and getting paid for it.

The following days were spent as a four, the first time we had really spent valuable time alone together on an expedition. We began to gel and I was confident that we had a fighting chance of staying a cohesive unit on the ice in November through to February. We began some climbs from the base of the glacier, often having to ski downhill at speed across a myriad of smaller crevasses or slots, which served to desensitise ourselves to their presence. Wilki was by far the best downhill skier and despite all of us being confident, there were some impressive falling displays from the remaining three of us. In our defence, the ice had precious little snow cover and so ski control was tough.

We all had different motivations in attaining a new ascent, beside the thrill of climbing on rock and ice that had never been previously trodden. These included the charity mountain ascent and dedications of peaks to members of our families, and to friends who had died in mountains elsewhere in the world. Between us, we reached the summits of five new peaks and laid cairns on top to indicate precedence. We had occasionally split into two pairs in order to get more climbing done and so we could explore more of the coast.

On our final return up the glacier, much less fun than the descent, we suffered our only slight mishap. We were not roped together as the terrain seemed amiable. One minute we were skiing along in a line, Rich second in the line and myself third, the next Rich seemed to fall awkwardly. I quickly realised that he had put an entire ski down a hidden crevasse. The closest to him, I grabbed Rich's rucksack straps and helped him extricate himself. Rich sat on the ground for a moment, a little wide eyed, and merely said, "I guess we'd better rope up then." We did so and had an uneventful return ski to our tents.

The climbing portion of the trip completed, we proceeded to pack up camp and prepared to head fifty miles or so inland onto the icecap. This was to familiarise ourselves with the sledging routine that would become our whole lives on the ice for months. About thirty minutes into our very first session of sledging, I heard Rich's characteristic northern accent over my shoulder.

"Guys, are you bored?" he asked, with perfect comic timing. He got his reward and the three of us were bent double with laughter. Luckily, we managed to gain what we wanted from the sledging journey in terms of learning little tricks and gaining experience. My ski binding came a little loose after a while and began depositing small spots of grease on the white snow, but it lasted until the end.

The dynamic between Rich and Wilki, the closest to each other in terms of age, was fascinating. We were setting up camp on a particularly cold evening after the sun had set – using our wide skis to stamp down the soft snow in order to get a good sleeping surface and much care was taken to ensure a good night's sleep. As Rich was completing the surface under the tent he and I planned to share, Wilki accidentally walked over some of the carefully flattened snow. Mischievously, Rich decided retaliation was in order and proceeded to stomp across Wilki's own pitch. It was the closest I had ever seen Wilki to losing his cool. Our verdict on the tent choice after swapping between them a number of times was unanimous. The tunnel design Hilleberg was the winner in terms of size, wind stability and ease of use. We accepted that the North Face dome tent was the clear choice for high altitude mountaineering, but for polar work, the Swedish Hilleberg was the king.

With some regret, we had to return to our previous base camp position to await the helicopter for our own pick up. Needless to say, we arrived with time to spare, the night before in fact, to avoid missing our transport. That last night on the ice had a final twist. In an area we considered to be slow-moving and stable ice, we pitched camp for the final time. The Arctic treated us to a spectacular final night with a sunset of so many colours you did not know where to look next. The mountains and sea glowed warm in the sun's beams.

As we all slept deeply after a few days hard work, Adam ventured outside to answer the call of nature. I wearily woke to muffled calls of, "guys, a hand would be good." Adam had clearly intended a lightning visit to the latrine and was not fully clothed. Now he was stuck, slightly embarrassed, with one leg halfway down a hidden crevasse. His boot had become jammed in the tight slot and needed to be extracted. The crevasse ran straight through our camp and we concluded that many similar ones surrounded us. It was exactly where the helicopter was due to land. The solution was simply to ensure that the helicopter landed perpendicular to the direction of the slots, alleviating the chance of a skid going down a crack. We set up the landing site with black bags accordingly. The helicopter did arrive on time on this occasion and our journey back to civilisation was interesting – I wondered how I would feel. Encouragingly, I found myself missing the environment and knew this boded well for our plans in the winter.

A final reminder of the risks emerged on the boat trip back across the fjord to Kulusuk Island. The water was still thick with ice, much of it hidden insidiously below the waterline. Georg's son was driving the boat at about twenty knots and was busy weaving it through the channels of clear water. Adam and Wilki were sitting on the bow of the boat, enjoying the view. Suddenly, with a deafening bang, the boat's bow rose out of the water and we were flung to the stern. Adam and Wilki managed to hang onto the rails at the front. As the boat settled, we looked around at each other in silence and then peered over the side. There was a submerged metal container from a cargo ship in the water and we had collided at speed.

We assessed the side of the boat and thought it safe to continue as before, with all those onboard holding on that bit tighter. On reflection, if the hull had been damaged and the boat had sunk, we were miles from help and our satellite phones were in our sledges. The only refuge would have been the floating ice. In addition, we were a long way from the world of Health and Safety and as such had no buoyancy aids. This scenario provided us all with food for thought on the journey home to the UK. In the weeks that followed, our minds were a million miles from a valuable and unforgettable expedition in Greenland. Funding and publicity were the focus as we neared the all-important payment deadline for logistics.

Chapter V

'Every pro was once an amateur.' Robin Sharma

Early on the morning of the press launch, August 21st 2007, I travelled into central London from Upminster where I had stayed with a good friend from university and his family. I made contact with Rich, Wilki and Adam, Tina and her PR team and the various guests for the launch – organisation for the day running from the start without a single hitch. I was met by Nick Leevers from the RGS and he introduced me to the various staff who were working on the mechanics of the event. Signs advertising the launch had been displayed on the outside of the building and, at the planned time, members of the press began to file through reception and into the conference room. Press attendance at events such as ours is unpredictable at best. Despite messages of intent from many of the media, a major news story in Parliament or a natural disaster will ensure that all resources are moved to where they are most required. Tina and her team were, as ever, ahead of the game with respect to this and had planned the conference to occur on a Tuesday in August, maximising our chances of a large press attendance. This forethought paid dividends and by nine o'clock, the presentation room was awash with film crews, journalists and radio interviewers. Referring to their hectic schedule for interviews, Tina, Carrie and Giselle rushed the four of us from camera to camera, giving us any important advice we might require.

It was a completely new experience for me but before the conference had even begun, we had already completed around half a dozen interviews. The main focus for the press seemed to be myself due to my youth and also Rich due to his fight with cancer.

My first ever interview on live television could not have been worse. In order to add some interest for the assembled media we had all, in the height of summer, donned down clothing used on a previous South Pole expedition. Since there were only three down jackets and one full length down 'Michelin Man' suit, it was a case of pulling the short straw. I conceded defeat and spent the rest of the morning roasting like a chicken whilst trying to respond to interviewers' questions. I had been brought over from a newspaper journalist by Tina to prepare for a live 'on location' interview for Sky News. These are, I subsequently discovered, the hardest interviews to do and so my baptism was one of fire. It is necessary to attempt to respond to the presenter through a camera lens and seem natural despite the questions being fed to you through an impossibly quiet earpiece. I was given the thirty second countdown and the technician checked the microphone levels. As the interviewer began to ask his first question, I realised to my horror that I could not hear him properly.

"I'm sorry, could you say again?" I had to say into the camera. It was not a good start and I was furious. It turned out he had simply asked for my age.

The remainder of the interview went well enough and I was able to mention most of the critical points I wanted to get across, most notably the need for funding. The rest of the team was otherwise engaged whilst I was live and so did not hear the initial hiccup. By this time, I had started to sweat horribly in my totally inappropriate garments and was worried that I would come across on television with sweat dripping down my face. By some miracle, on later inspection, it was not noticeable in any of the broadcasts. I put it down to clever work by the lighting man.

Even as the event progressed, Carrie was constantly on the phone to various television stations who still had not committed to covering our story. It was the nature of the business but the news fed to me by Tina was increasingly positive. All of the major networks who had expressed interest had made an appearance, plus others were joining the growing crowd. I could not help but be impressed by the hive of activity and the recognition that the media was paying attention.

After Sky News came Channel Four/ITN, The Press Association, LBC and a number of major newspapers. As we entered the main scheduled event of the day, the conference and photo-call, the room was full of photographers editing their images on laptops and wiring them directly back to their agencies. We had already set up the presentation and made sure that Frank, Mike and the rest of Eye Film had a good position from which to film the event. I had asked Dr. Dan Martin from CASE, who had reached Everest's summit just months before with the Caudwell Extreme Everest Expedition, to outline what our team would contribute in terms of scientific data. CASE was University College, London's extreme environment scientific research team and Dan was a key personality within the group. The sustained nature of our expedition and the gradual starvation our bodies would suffer was of interest to doctors researching critical care. I opened the conference with a short, five minute speech which served to introduce the various personalities and provide some background context for what would follow. We were on a tight schedule, as the press would quickly lose interest if events began to drag on, and so Wilki, Rich, Adam and Dan made their contributions in quick succession. The key facts and unique selling points had been emphasised and so Tina nodded to me that I should signal the start of questions from the floor.

Most of the questions were predictable but luckily none were designed to pick holes in our plans or motives. The often caustic expedition press had decided not to make an appearance, which was a great relief. Some months later I would attend a similar launch, in the same room, for Pen Hadow's multi-million pound Arctic Survey. He and his team

81

had to tackle a number of questions from some journalists who were unconvinced by the stated motivations behind the expedition. The expedition was, in my view, notable by its absence of egocentric ambition.

The photo-call was an eye-opener. We were placed outside the Society in the gardens with our tent, down clothing and some skis. About half a dozen photographers then spent the next twenty minutes or so trying to get our attention so that we would look into their lens. The competitiveness between them was amusing as they fought for the attention of the team. For a group of professionals under such time pressure, they were exceptionally cordial.

I found Tina as the various film crews and journalists began to leave the RGS and asked her if we were drawing to a close. "Absolutely not!" she exclaimed with an excited grin on her face. "The BBC News channel wants to interview you in their studio. We're just booking a taxi to take you and Rich there now."

I had never seen the iconic BBC Television Centre before and we received our guest passes as we were hurried through reception. Only minutes after we had sat down outside the BBC News 24 studio itself, we were placed next to the newsreaders and had our make-up applied, which Rich found hilarious. What surprised me most was the state of the studio. It was placed directly in the middle of what could only be described as the chaos of the newsroom. The famous red and white news studios of the BBC were not as pristine as they appeared on the television. The white desk was chipped, the floor covered with paper; clearly a by-product of the ferocious pace at which the team had to work.

Within thirty seconds of our press release being printed directly behind the newsreaders, they had highlighted the main points and were ready to interview Rich and myself. I am sure that few casual observers of the BBC News fully appreciate the professionalism and speed of thought demanded all the way down the process.

Having concluded our seemingly epic seven-minute interview, during which we had covered iPods, cancer and science, we were ushered out. Carrie had been seated just outside and had been watching the broadcast live on a flat screen on the wall – delighted at how we came across.

The key in the few days following the press launch was to capitalise on the publicity with regards to fund-raising. We hoped to strike whilst the story was fresh in people's heads and I was keen to contact Sue Newton of Barbour from the press launch. Very politely, she thanked me for her invitation to the launch and expressed her admiration for the endeavour but said that financial input was beyond their budget for the year. It was a real disappointment, especially as we had all taken attendance in London as a good sign. It transpired the next day that we had earned a large photo article in the Metro, the London Underground newspaper, which was widely read by exactly the people we were after: London businesspeople. However, as the days passed and we began to run out of corporate figures to contact, it become increasingly clear that funding was again at crisis point.

Ever patient, both Victor Serov and Patrick Woodhead had continued to work on our logistics plan for insertion to Halley and extraction from the Geographic South Pole. Victor had sent me the deposit request form and contract with ALCI, the logistics firm, for me to complete. The deposit was for around £20,000 and had strictly been due a month previously. I contacted Victor to explain the situation and then received a call from Patrick the next day.

"Alex, I understand the realities of polar expedition fund-raising and that in the past money has come through for expeditions in the final week. Obviously, we need to know whether we can sell your cargo space to government scientists and so really need a no messing-about assessment of your chances," he reasoned. I explained to him that although we had a couple of reasonable leads, the time it would take to clear large sums of sponsorship in order to pay him would not be feasible. Patrick was a super guy and the two of us had always maintained a policy of total transparency throughout the time we worked together. I said that I could provide no certainty of payment. He thanked me and sincerely expressed how gutted he was for our team. After the call I placed the phone down and stood still for a minute. I knew deep down that the end for the project was coming but the moment it hit was still devastating. Not only was it the end of three years of total dedication and hundreds of hours of work, it had knock-on effects for so many other people. Many of these people had become friends and I felt a personal responsibility for letting them down. I proceeded to telephone the team and tell them that despite the loss, I would develop a new expedition along the same concept of the 'Journey South 2007'. I then called Tina Fotherby and broke the news that after her hours of work 'on risk' for us, we could no longer employ her for the expedition itself.

The hardest phone call was to Frank at Eye Film. They had put their necks on the block for the project and invested serious cash in the equipment and time for the initial filming. I had spent hours with Frank and Charlie in meetings, on filming location and on the icecap – I had come to trust them as friends. FIVE had released initial funding on the understanding that the main bulk of the filming costs would be met by a small portion of the sponsorship. The lack of funding also had a knock on effect for Mike and Dan at CASE, who would no longer be able to contribute to the scientific side of the endeavour.

After a day of feeling thoroughly miserable I went to see some good friends from university. They were always the right people to help regain perspective and after a small reunion across a swathe of Oxford's best pubs, I returned home with renewed drive. If Plan A was not going to happen, why not Plan B?

Chapter VI

'Difficulties are just things to overcome, after all.'
Sir Ernest Shackleton

It was now a few days into October and so the chances of an Antarctic journey were gone for the 2007/2008 season at least. I had made some last chance calls via Steve Bull and Mike Sharp of ALE to try and secure some flights to Patriot Hills but the costs were beyond personal funding.

In a refreshing contrast to the team's financial problems, there was some fantastic news. Rich and his long-term girlfriend, Hils, had been successful with IVF treatment on what was their last chance. I knew that the preceding months had been very hard for the couple. In particular Rich, who had been worried for her health, also had to juggle the stresses of work and a failing expedition. Also with the knowledge that the team would struggle to secure time off from work outside the months established for the' Journey South 2007', I forged on ahead with the new expedition knowing I would have to remain flexible.

In the final months of our Antarctic planning, I had considered the worst case scenario and what I would do if funding did fall through. Despite the significant technical differences with the type of ice travel, I turned my attention to the North. In a change of direction which mirrored that of Roald Amundsen in 1911, we would now attempt the Geographic North Pole. Amundsen had publicly announced his plans to achieve the first undisputed crossing to the North Pole but turned his ship, Fram, south instead. This was much to the surprise of Robert Scott and led to the legendary South

Pole race, on which Scott and his team would ultimately perish.

I hoped that if the expedition could be launched in the spring of 2008, only five months after the 'Journey South 2007' was due to begin, much of the media interest and partnerships, including the documentary, could be saved. In the same way that the Antarctic journey was set to be novel and ground breaking in its approach, the 'North08' should achieve a genuine, non-contrived first. Speed records struck me as somewhat arbitrary, since the expeditions were not races, and so were certainly off the menu.

Whilst leaning over a large chart of the Arctic Ocean, the answer came to me suddenly. There had always been a limit to the number of directions from which expeditions could approach the Geographic North Pole. Firstly, this was due to there being a limited number of landmasses with realistic proximity to the Pole: Alaska, Canada, Greenland, Svalbard and Russia. Secondly, more critically, was the ice current that dominates the ocean. The strongest forces are the cyclic Beaufort Gyre and the linear Transpolar Drift towards the Atlantic Ocean. Unlike the great icecaps of Greenland and the Antarctic, the Arctic Ocean is totally at the mercy of these currents. This is due to the surface being constructed from a mammoth jigsaw puzzle of frozen seawater and snow, often only a few feet thick. The 'pans' of ice crack, collide, spin and drift their way across the ocean, creating a nightmare for travel. Since the currents are very persistent, the ice tends to move in a constant direction when viewed over a long period of time. Ice moves from Russia towards the Pole and down towards Svalbard and the Atlantic. It drifts across the Pole and towards the North American continent, where it either deviates, collides with the ice shelves or travels through the narrow 'Nares Strait' bottleneck between Ellesmere Island and Greenland into Baffin Bay. The result of these events is that ice on the Russian side is often flatter, faster and divided up by perilous black 'leads' of water. On the Canadian side,

86

particularly close to the mainland, the ice is mashed up into rubble as it compresses and pressure ridges appear, often up to twenty feet in height.

The early attempts on the Pole by Cook, Peary, Plaisted and Herbert began from the extreme tips of Canada and Alaska. The first successful expedition to the North Pole is still unknown, as both Cook and Peary are widely believed to have fabricated navigational accounts. Ralph Plaisted, an American, was the first to reach the North Pole overland and without doubt in 1968. Another epic surface expedition which certainly reached the Pole was the Trans Arctic expedition of the British leader, Wally Herbert. His achievement in 1969 was overshadowed by Neil Armstrong landing on the moon and Herbert was only recognised with a knighthood in 2000. Herbert died in 2007 and I was lucky enough to meet him at the RGS shortly beforehand. Subsequently, the Russian Islands at Cape Arcticheskiy began to be used as a start point following the fall of Communism and the resultant access for Westerners into Russia.

Despite its close proximity to the Pole and relative accessibility, Svalbard has never been used as a start for an over-ice North Pole attempt due to the fierce Transpolar Drift flowing in the opposite direction. Anyone brave enough to attempt such a journey would be pushed out into the frozen North Atlantic very rapidly. For me, the answer then was obvious – Greenland. Not only was Greenland the nearest land to the North Pole on Earth, it had a broad northern coast that provided a multitude of insertion options. I used NASA satellite photographs and sea ice reports to attempt to ascertain why no team had used Greenland previously. The first reason was the strong current pulling the ice south-east but the effect was, the satellite animations showed me, most active on the eastern edges of Greenland. On Peary Land, nearer to the traditional Canadian start point of Ward Hunt Island, the ice drift was not too pronounced. The second reason, I deduced, was that there was no pilot able to fly a team to the north

87

of Greenland. Without logistics, no expeditions could take place.

I made detailed enquiries with Steve Penikett of the Canadian Kenn Borek Air and Victor Boyarsky of the Russian VICAAR agency. They were, for their respective areas of operation, the sole polar operators available in the Arctic and the costs reflected this. Kenn Borek Air supplies the Twin Otter aircraft used by ALE in the Antarctic season from November to January. In what would become an enormously complicated puzzle of dates, deadlines, quotes and counter-quotes, I developed a plan. In order to avoid the $100,000 fee for a Twin Otter pick up from the Pole by Kenn Borek, I elected to accept a 30th April deadline for a far less costly Russian extraction by helicopter. Kenn Borek explained that they could not provide a flight to Northwest Greenland for political reasons. So, for the time being, we had no means of reaching our start point.

Expecting a negative reply, I was ecstatic when Peter Lyberth of the Air Greenland charter division agreed to send their only Twin Otter to the north of Greenland for our flight. I felt that I had achieved something significant in persuading a new aircraft operator to fly a polar expedition in the High Arctic. He stressed, however, that his pilots would not fly over the ocean as they were not trained to land on sea ice. I believed that I had solved the two main issues with a Greenlandic North Pole bid.

Despite only intending to set foot on Greenland itself for a matter of hours before setting out onto the Arctic Ocean, we would require a permit from the Danish Polar Centre, which governed Greenlandic access to areas not within the boundaries of villages. They had a strict safety rule of no expeditions before the 1st April, now unwisely shifted to the 15th. This would leave us with only thirty days to reach the Pole, far faster than even the supported speed record. I spent weeks negotiating with Kirsten, the very helpful DPC representative, until she and the Chief Constable of

Greenland granted us a permit valid from 20th February. It was critical that we set off that early, a time in the spring when the sun had not made an appearance and temperatures were at their most brutal.

Unlike the £250,000 budget for the 'Journey South 2007', the 'North08' had a smaller but equally daunting £110,000 shortfall. The world's economy was starting to show signs of major fragility and I knew that I had to act fast in order to obtain the necessary funding. Aside from the traditional fund-raising techniques that had failed the 'Journey South' expedition, I enlisted a couple located near to me in Hampshire. Gail Baird and Dan Bernard were a photography, design and PR double act who ran 131 Design from home. I came across their advertisement in a local magazine and met them both the next day. That meeting was the beginning of a great friendship and both Gail and Dan's enthusiasm and 'can do' attitude were infectious. Whilst the remainder of the team, all still reeling from the Antarctic failure, were working full-time jobs and continuing to send proposals, Gail, Dan and I worked as a trio. They had agreed to work on risk with the end result of a commission from the sponsorship input – a not abnormal PR arrangement.

In the short weeks that followed, and as I continued to organise all of the practical aspects of the new Arctic trip, we tried everything. In our long brain-storming sessions in 131's basement office, lateral thought was very much the order of the day. We even used an eBay auction as a media hook to drum up added interest. As the days passed by with frightening pace, Charlie and Frank from Eye were becoming worried and it was clear that we were fighting a losing battle. The climate just was not conducive to securing large sums of cash. I had been contacted some months back by a hedge fund manager for ABN AMRO called Charlie Newington-Bridges, who wanted to join the team. Charlie had strong endurance credentials and seemed very easy to get on with. Ultimately, despite being willing to make significant personal contributions to the expedition, he was unable to persuade his employer to supplement this.

Adam and I had made plans a long time in advance to visit the North Wales workshops of Graham Ogle and his company Brenig. He was a specialist clothing manufacturer who started from scratch in the business, gradually becoming the brand of choice for many expeditions. Adam and I were keen to test a number of garments, including smocks, all-in-one suits and the all important immersion suits – vital for sea ice travel. The only comparable immersion suit competitor was Helly Hansen and they charged an enormous custom fee direct from their factory, the suits not being a common choice for those checking out their local Millets or Blacks store! We decided to get stuck in and go for a float in the winter sea off the Welsh coast.

After a fascinating tour round the workshops, complete with expertly skilled ladies on manual sewing machines, Graham found a suit. It was the only one and was too small for Adam's six-foot-five frame so I was the lucky volunteer to try it out. I only had the clothes I was standing in so hoped that the immersion suit would perform. We drove to a concrete jetty and I clambered awkwardly into the yellow rubber suit.

We tightened the cords around my face and I ambled into the water. It worked perfectly and after ten minutes or so happily floating about, I was reluctant to come out. Adam was spending half his time laughing and the other taking photographic evidence of how ridiculous I looked. The trip was a success but after the drive back down South, it was back to business.

In the first few days of 2008, I was again receiving phone calls from concerned logistics operators asking after their deposits. I was again forced to tell them the grim situation and on the 6th January, I officially pulled the plug on 'North08'. It was a simple fact, although not a particularly comforting one, that the vast majority of independent expeditions would not gain full funding. This was a total disaster, especially for Eye

Film and TV. They had invested large sums of money and hundreds of hours in the project and faced the prospect of a displeased FIVE and worse. I felt hopelessly sorry for Charlie and Frank and felt entirely responsible for their plight. Frank reassured me that they entered into the whirlwind of a project with their eyes open and that they had very much enjoyed our months together, especially on location in Greenland.

The time around Christmas and New Year had been punctuated with a number of phone calls between Charlie and both myself and Gail at 131. The situation had become so desperate that it transcended professional business and became deeply personal. The failure of the second plan sent me into a very black few days. Rich had recently announced his removal from the team due to the need to be with his girlfriend during her twin pregnancy and Wilki soon followed due to work commitments. Adam and I remained but he soon had to pull out of any future plans due to a string of important job interviews in the spring of 2008. I found myself alone in my team, having spent three years working unremittingly on the journeys. I had no funding and time was running out. I would start work as a Royal Marines Young Officer in the autumn of 2008.

One glimmer of hope remained. Tiso, the Scottish-based outdoors company, had been a long-term supporter of Craig Mathieson, a friend of Rich. They had also agreed to supply the expeditions with clothing and equipment. I wondered whether Tiso would be prepared to increase their involvement in a new, low cost expedition. I could not contemplate the concept of not undertaking a polar journey that season but the standards and goals could not drop. After speaking to Louise Ramsay, Tiso's marketing director, she agreed over the telephone to become Title Partner of a new expedition. Plan C, as I originally coined it, would need to be developed and be ready to launch in a matter of weeks. This was in alarming contrast to the years which had been used to plan 'Journey South 2007' and 'North08'.

91

Greenland was logistically more accessible than the Antarctic or Arctic Ocean but shared the same fearsome reputation. I resolved to match the technicality of the 'North08' and new route of the 'Journey South 2007' with sheer distance. What would become the 'Tiso Trans Greenland Expedition' would attempt to be the longest polar expedition ever undertaken without any support whatsoever. I looked at the competition. Roger Mear's 1985 South Pole journey covered 883 miles and the various attempts from Berkner Island to the Pole were over 800 miles. In the Arctic, two fabulously difficult unsupported expeditions stood out. Weber and Malakhov's 1995 return journey to the North Pole at 960 miles, still unrepeated, and Larsen and Gjeldnes' 1,070 mile Arctic crossing in 2000. Doctors reported of the latter two Norwegians that, on completion of their crossing in Canada, they were forty-eight hours from death.

I proposed, although still without a team-mate, to ski 1,400 miles. I knew that Ben Saunders had long been planning a 1,800 mile unsupported South Pole return and I wanted to bridge the mighty distance gap. Ben, ever since his seventy-four day solo expedition to the North Pole in 2004, had been trying to secure the large sums of cash necessary to support his two-man journey. This drought only ended nearly a decade later, but an emergency resupply on his Scott Expedition stymied his unsupported status. In the interests of making the expedition fundable, I decided again to use Kulusuk as a base camp. We would then start and finish the journey on the east coast, near to Kulusuk, with a half-way turnaround on the West Coast.

The season for Greenland expeditions is, as for any polar region, very specific. The winter provides very little opportunity due to the lack of light and the difficulty of getting a Danish permit to travel. The late summer causes problems as the accumulated sun causes the ice and snow to deteriorate. The window is between spring and early summer and it was vital to be clear of the ice before this 'melt'. I proposed, since this expedition was of a duration previously unheard of, to set off in early spring and hope to complete the journey of over a hundred days by the time the ice went out of condition. I aimed for mid-March as I did not believe that I could complete the numerous preparations before that time. A permit that early would also cause potential headaches as would the length of time we proposed to be on the ice. Despite the hours taken to secure a special early permit for the 'North08' access to northern Greenland, I was informed that a fresh application must be made to access the inland ice before April. This was, with no small measure of luck, again secured by Kirsten at the DPC with great efficiency. Due to the one hundred and ten day projected duration, we would need to secure a visa to remain in Danish territory. This paperwork was fast-tracked and confirmation arrived with only days to spare.

We planned to be flown by helicopter to a glacier near Kulusuk which spilled out into the sea. This ensured we could begin right on the edge of the icecap. From there, we would travel up the glacier and reach the icecap itself. The route then took us north across the icecap and over the dome-shaped icecap, reaching 8,600 feet before descending to the West Coast. We would lay our own supply depots as we crossed, in order to release weight from the sledges. There was no purpose in hauling our supplies for the return leg all the way across the icecap. The region on the West Coast was chosen for its distance from Kulusuk, 700 miles, as it fitted my 1,400 mile total target. There were a number of glaciers which, having assessed satellite images and charts, were potential access points to the sea. I settled on a region known as Ussing Braer, an extremely remote tidal outlet glacier that was part of an area where the icecap is separated from the sea by only a narrow rim of headlands. Having negotiated the technically difficult West Coast, which had perhaps never been assessed on foot, we would retrace our steps back across the dome to our start point on the east and be flown out again. No-one had previously achieved an unsupported man-haul return journey across the icecap. If I did not attempt the journey then someone else would inevitably do so.

The concept of a return rekindled an art from the Heroic Age of polar exploration: depots. They would serve to reduce the sledge weights and psychologically break up the expedition into phases. In the interests of continuity and due to his excellent performance the previous year, I once again employed Matt Spenceley as our logistics manager along with his team.

In terms of equipment and nutrition, I was able to use the majority of the planning from the 'Journey South 2007' as the principles were almost identical. The only changes were forced due to a more restrictive budget and so, for example, sledges (otherwise known as 'pulks') would be made by Roger Daynes of Snowsled out of glass-fibre, not Kevlar. What I was most notably missing was a team. Having noticed the success of two-man teams in ultra long-distance polar expeditions, I was open to the idea of a single companion for the journey. I found myself in a strange situation. Only five weeks from the proposed start date for the expedition, I had funding and equipment but no team. I began to put the word out in a similar manner to three years previously and met with similar success. The interest was significant, especially from the ranks of BSES, the Royal Marines and OUEC. One particular individual stood out in terms of enthusiasm and mental approach to the task. George Bullard, who I had arranged to meet at the RGS, was an experienced open water swimmer and had recently travelled to South Georgia with BSES. He was seeking something more substantial and challenging, outside of the guided expedition arena.

George was introduced to me by Lucy Bruzzone of the RGS and we hit it off immediately. George was tall, thin and confident and before long I had decided that he was the strongest candidate. There was a certain quality to his enthusiasm, tempered with humility, which I became convinced would be a recipe for success. Most importantly, apart from his athletic ability and proven mental resolve, I felt that we would get on well together as a team. I also had the opportunity to speak to his companions from previous travels and his family that served to reinforce my thoughts. I would not have the luxury of spending months working on preparations and training with George and needed to get him up to speed with the complex project. My gut instinct was that I would find no better companion, even if I had been given many more months to search. Importantly, George had the opportunity to commit to the four months away from work, a stumbling block that meant that most interested parties were unable to become involved. My parting words to him, after we had agreed to meet at my home to familiarise him with equipment, was to put on weight as a matter of urgency. Despite the 5,500 calories we were planning to consume daily, the strain and length of the expedition would still cause significant weight loss. It has been suggested that on some sledging days in the Antarctic in 1992, Mike Stroud and Ran Fiennes used around 11,000 calories per day. Stroud, a doctor specialising in nutrition, would carry out extensive tests on both himself and Fiennes. They even resolved to retain scientific instruments when choosing items to discard in order to jettison weight.

George was naturally athletic but, as he explained to me, found it hard to 'keep the fat on'. Not an ideal situation, especially this close to D-Day. So, with George sent off to consume cheese, full-fat milk and lots of red meat, I made the final arrangements with Tiso and our food sponsors, Be-Well. Brian Welsby, who worked with Kees de Kijs at Be-Well, supplied Fiennes with his rations on previous polar journeys. They had improved the compositions over the years and learned from the horrific starvation suffered on the early journeys. The importance of nutrition and our expedition food would reoccur throughout the journey. Since the expedition was, by all intents and purposes, organised prior to George's arrival, I gave him the choice and responsibility

95

for charity fund-raising. Fittingly, he chose another cancer charity, this time Breast Cancer Haven. Both of our families had experience of the disease and so it was a popular decision.

As was predictable, given the very tight schedules involved, deliveries were rushed and often needed correcting but the efforts on the part of both sponsors was remarkable. For example, when the wrong skis were sent from Scotland, I received the correct Fischer endurance cross-country skis the next day. In terms of a skiing system, there were many schools of thought and every person has their own opinion. I opted for a rope-hauled single sledge with a full body harness. This would be easy to control, would avoid broken hauling poles and distributed the load across the hips and shoulders. The skis were two metres, metal-edged and non-waxed to allow easy use of skins. Skins are mohair-nylon strips that allow glide in one direction and grip in the other, aiding the hauling process on slopes. We screwed them into the skis to secure them for the miles of abuse ahead. One critically important issue was that of boots and ski bindings.

Bindings were notorious for failing and many travellers had suffered blisters and expedition-threatening infections from rigid-style boots. My original plan to defeat the well known fragility of Berwyns, the most popular flexible bindings, was to take spares and rely on redundancy. This was, of course, an unsatisfactory solution to solve a problem which could be a show-stopper. Hannah McKeand, with substantial Antarctic experience, pointed me towards another flexible binding. I opted for a soft and highly insulated mukluk boot system from Baffin, as the famous Sorel boots were unavailable, and 'Flexi' flexible bindings. The bindings were manufactured in a day by Eric Philips of Icetrek in Australia and arrived in England with a day to spare, his efforts saving the expedition before it even began. They were manufactured from an expensive plastic plate which was able to resist the extreme cold and repeated bending almost indefinitely.

Eric, a veteran of the Arctic, had strong views on the unsupported debate which were largely at odds with my own. Like myself, he attributed some responsibility for Arduin's death in the Arctic Ocean in 2004 to community pressure. However, he believed in a 'best effort' approach to start points. This means that when ice conditions on the Arctic Ocean do not allow expeditions to step off land directly onto sea ice to begin their journey, being flown out to meet the safer ice further north is considered the same. This translates into expeditions to the North Pole potentially varying in length by hundreds of miles yet being compared as equals. Instead, I believe that if the climate causes ice to retreat away from land in March, then you must find a way to begin your expedition in February or even earlier when the cold aids ice coverage all the way to land.

Due to the time pressures on us, George and I met in London to discuss various expedition issues, exchange paperwork and familiarise ourselves with the new equipment. Armed with our expedition tent and our crevasse rescue kit, we headed into one of the capital's royal parks. After ensuring that we could erect and collapse the tent together without any fuss, our attention turned to the ropes. We practised the crevasse rescue pulley systems that neither of us had performed in a few months. It was reassuring to go over these life-saving skills that had become rusty. Our afternoon in the parks came to an end when a police car slowly drew up beside us and the police officer stepped out, looking somewhat bemused. After looking over our bright red tent and ropes, he explained that there was no camping allowed in the royal parks and that he had been alerted by a local resident. I explained that we were simply testing and intended to leave after an hour or so. Very reasonably, he allowed us to stay, but we had covered everything we had planned and so began to pack up. George and I joked about the local residents who were clearly peering round their curtains at our 'clandestine' scheme to camp in the middle of the park with a red beacon of a tent.

As an important part of our final weeks in the country before heading north, I made a visit to the Tiso Headquarters in Edinburgh. Its showpiece store and centre represented the size and breadth of the outdoor pursuits it promoted. Despite months of communication, negotiation and short-notice equipment orders from around globe, I had never met my sponsors in person.

After the long train journey up the spectacular English East Coast, I made my way to the Tiso offices and met Louise Ramsay, the Marketing Director, and her team. We spent time going over the intricacies of my demanding equipment requests. Many of the items were not from the simple accounts that Tiso had with major outdoor manufacturers such as Rab and Mountain Equipment. Some, such as the boots and sledges, were made either abroad or by craftsmen in backyard workshops. The common thread was that, understandably, lead times were long and orders bespoke in nature. The Baffin boots were ordered from Canada after I had confirmed that getting hold of Sorel's was impossible. This boot choice would have a varied outcome for each of us.

Scott Shaw, the man in charge of bulk orders for Tiso, went through my requirements and we had to compromise in a few areas due to availability. Scott had been personally recommended for his efficiency by Craig Mathieson, and he did not disappoint. The vast load of his work had been done previously and we were simply tying up loose ends and making sure that, for example, the critical choice of base layers was optimum. Base layers are one of the most important aspects of expedition clothing and we opted for expensive but excellent merino wool garments. Avoiding the garish bright colours that are often chosen for expedition suits, we opted for black smocks and trousers. This would, most importantly, be the best for heat retention but also easy to spot against a white blizzard.

Louise and I also finalised the publicity details that would ensure that the expedition 'delivered value' to the company in return for its support of the team. This included the logo branding for the clothing and sledges, the website, and also our PR arrangements to generate television and press. The moment as I placed the logos of sponsors onto our equipment and especially our sledges was, if mundane, significant for me. This could not be done before collecting the seven-foot sledges, the largest available, from Roger Daynes' workshop in the Cotswolds. From my very earliest days reading about the expeditions preceding mine, the signal of potential was the beacon of a sponsor logo on a sledge. It represented success in the notorious sponsorship game and meant that the talking could be left in England. The walking could now get underway on the ice. I had always read the books of Fiennes and Weber with jealous glances at the photographs – the funding is always considered the barrier to being released into the cold. My team and I had been through a rough ride with funding and I had to remind myself that the 'business' side of things was over and the expedition was real. An unexpected final touch came from our long-term supporter, Steve Bull, who had first been in contact in 2005 in the fledgling months of my polar endeavours. He sent me a personal letter commenting on the perseverance to push through two losses of funding to being ready to deploy on the ice. His efforts and advice played a significant role in that success. He also stressed that 'every expedition should have a flag' and provided a donation to cover the purchase, as well as a farewell beer.

George arrived to pack the sledges in my garage at home, as Be-Well's food arrived on an enormous pallet. The size was terrifying and my mother stared wide-eyed as we manhandled it into the garage. I wondered whether the supplies would physically fit in the sledges. The art of packing a sledge was not to be underestimated. The weight distribution was important in order to make sure that the sledge ran evenly over the ice. Also, we needed to position various items in order of priority by how often we would need to use them. For example, the GPS handset would need to be more accessible than the backup solar charger. Some past teams had decided that due to ease of freighting, they would transport sledges empty and the contents in blue barrels. Due to the mammoth size of our sledges we were being charged by volume, not weight, and so resolved to pack them fully for the ice.

The perceived wisdom was to place the rations into a number of dry bags, each large enough for a week. Also, fuel had traditionally been carried in individual litre fuel bottles. It is all too easy to follow the crowd in terms of equipment or techniques in polar expeditions. The undeniable fact is, however, that many of the systems championed by veterans of the past have been superseded. On the flip side, many, such as Amundsen-style boots, still hold strong after being used on the ice for decades. There are relatively few who are true innovators of polar equipment and systems.

Having assessed the weight of the dry bags and metal fuel containers, which would be required for my estimated one hundred and ten days, it was clear a new direction was needed. Extra weight is justified if the item serves a purpose but these seemed unnecessary to me. We replaced the choice of small metal bottles with five-litre cold-rated plastic containers. This saved us an entire 5kg, not just a few grams. Similarly, I abandoned dry bags and chose instead to group the various items in a daily set of rations and shrink wrap them together so they were easily accessible in a potentially difficult situation. The added benefit was that the packs of food were easy to pack tightly in the sledge and we could see the contents through the plastic wrap. Additionally, there was no need to keep the rations watertight as the packets were themselves resistant to damp. Although surprising, damp can still occur in extreme sub-zero temperatures if wind is excluded and sunlight is constant.

As a lucky coincidence the tubs of high-calorie ghee butter, key to high energy and low weight, fitted perfectly into the grooves running down the belly of the sledges. We each took 22kg of the unpalatable fat that contained 8,800 kcal per kilogram. George and I then placed a tower of flapjack, our staple food during the skiing day, down the centre of the two 'torpedoes' of ghee tubs. We took 44kg of flapjack apiece and, for variety, had three flavours: raisin, chocolate chip and banana. The fuel containers fitted into the rear of the sledge, partitioned from the food, as contamination would cause a premature end to our plans. Equipment, clothing and technology were placed strategically around other areas of the sledges.

George, who was still very thin, and I were not able to complete the packing until the last few days due to a constant stream of deliveries frantically arriving from all corners of the globe. Finally complete, we sealed the sledges onto protective wooden boards. They were then shrink wrapped in polythene. The sledges were to be couriered to London via our freight agent and then flown ahead. As the van driver arrived to collect the sledges from our garage, it dawned on me that they had never been shifted, let alone been lifted. They had been loaded static on the floor across a pair of sturdy metal cases. They would be approaching 200kg in weight per piece, far in excess of our early estimates of 160kg. There was also 30kg of white gas fuel to add when we arrived in the Arctic. White gas, or naphtha, is a very clean burning stove fuel and would be used in our stoves to melt ice and heat our food. Four people each located at a corner of a sledge could just lift it and shuffle slowly to the van flat-bed. Our life-lines were soon on their way to London. The next time we would see them would be offloading them from the aircraft in Kulusuk. The thought of whether we could haul these monsters was left at the back of my mind – it seemed better that way.

My mother provided endless calorie-filled home cooking in our final days in England before heading on our quest. The concept of actually beginning the journey of which I had dreamt for years was a strange one indeed. In mid-March with only rucksacks, as our sledges had long since flown, we drove to London Stansted airport with our families in order

101

to fly our first leg to Iceland. My parents were quite clearly happy, relieved and excited that the expedition was underway but also with the understandable undercurrent of concern. I reassured them, feebly, that it was just like a long-term at university and we waved goodbye after a 'before' photograph.

Up until that moment, the big expedition had been but something in my imagination; now it was within my grasp. For the journey to Greenland I kept a note in my pocket that my ever-reliable godfather, Chris, had given to me shortly before departure. It read 'Keep your head when all about you are losing theirs and blaming it on you!'

I had visited Iceland the previous year for another brief stopover with the 'Journey South 2007' team. However, this time it was March, not summer and my next stop was not a dress rehearsal. It was the real thing. In the interests of cost effectiveness in the city of Reykjavik, pre-financial crash, I had arranged with Matt for us to stay the night in the conveniently placed Salvation Army Hostel. All we required, after all, was a warm place to sleep after our 'last supper' in town. In our down jackets and huge expedition boots, we clambered into the city centre, very quiet at that time of year, and set about finding a restaurant selling large portions. Successful, I quickly made my way through an enormous burger and a couple of Viking beers – the last I would taste for many months.

Iceland is not a normal country. Its economy is based largely on tourism, fishing and banking and it appeared that the entire population smoked heavily. As the pubs and bars had smoking bans, everyone seemed to spend their evenings on the pavements outside. The people of Iceland, we found, were either delightful or very brash with nothing much in between. Halfway through my excellent burger stuffed with guacamole and bacon, we were interrupted by a woman in her twenties who we initially believed to be paralytically drunk. It transpired, once the barman had ejected her from the restaurant, that she was a local drug addict and would work her way from restaurant to bar to restaurant all evening. He explained that it was not an unusual thing to see in Reykjavik. In the years since, I've visited Iceland and Reykjavik nearly a dozen times, and now find it hard to reconcile this first impression of the place. I see Iceland and its people as amongst the most welcoming, and least-troubled, I have visited anywhere in the northern nations. The growing popularity of the city as a mid-Atlantic stopover destination, a key strategy of their tourism industry, is critical for the country's economy but has led to the small capital losing some of its unique charm.

We returned soon after to the hostel in order to sleep well before our aircraft flew the next day to take us to Greenland. The flights to such a small frontier village were very infrequent and unpredictable but this was the nature of travel in the Arctic. For some reason, I was worried about us sleeping a little too well and missing our flight and so we made an ingenious alarm amplifier using an mp3 player and two plastic cups. The next morning it was a simple case of loading ourselves into a prearranged taxi. The driver saw little reason in looking at the road ahead but managed to deliver us to the tiny airport from where charters operated.

Once our twin-propeller aeroplane was airborne, we cleared the Icelandic coast and before long began to spy sea ice far below. Only about half an hour into our flight, the pilot informed us cheerily that the electronics on board had failed and that we would have to turn back. Luckily, little time was wasted back in Reykjavik and we were soon on our way once more. Following our rapidly devoured in-flight meal George, clearly trying to pass the time, had constructed a rose out of a paper napkin. In a botched attempt to present it proudly to the typically attractive attendant, George dropped the white rose and had to make do with her bemused smile. With vivid memories of the landscape from the previous year, I left my seat and peered out of a window on the right-hand side of the aircraft, hoping to catch my first glimpse of our new home for the next few months. I was rewarded immediately. We had

103

begun to near Greenland itself; the increase in sea ice was the giveaway. We then spied the mountains on the horizon and slowly the mainland came into view. I had not previously seen the coast in early spring and the vista was stunningly pristine. The sea gradually developed from being ice free, to being dotted with large ice floes and became a patchwork of interconnected ice pans. This skin of ice on the open ocean merged seamlessly with the endless fjords and upwards into the dramatic snow covered coastal peaks. I remained in situ for the remainder of the flight, staring transfixed at the panorama. The aircraft flew over the coast itself and spent some time lining itself up through the dozens of tricky peaks and valleys. We finally saw the airstrip as the pilot brought the plane into a dive. It was totally unrecognisable from the previous year, when it had consisted of a strip of dusty rock and earth. Now it was completely snow-covered, as was the entire landscape. The snowdrifts were clearly so deep that the staff had needed to carve a mammoth slit in the snow that became a runway. The scale of this labyrinth of channels was extraordinary, as they clearly included routes for the aircraft to taxi through as well. The local helicopter was stationary on the ground near the terminal and the walls of snow towered above it; it was a massive feat of snow moving.

Our pilot expertly brought us into the landing strip and touched down with a minimum of bumps. To the left and right of the aircraft was a wall of snow, hurtling past the window. We taxied round to the left and came to a halt fifty yards from the strangely modern-looking terminal building. Local Inuit were employed by the terminal and they were helping to offload equipment and cargo from the plane. These infrequent flights are the rare opportunity that locals have for supplies during the cold months when ships cannot dock.

I had spied the large white barges, the two sledges, soon after we got off the aircraft. The sun was bright and in our goosedown jackets, we were comfortably warm. We approached our sledges having had our passports checked.

Customs and security procedure is more of a token effort in Kulusuk, largely due to the fact that crime is more or less totally absent. The sledges themselves were intact and safe but the wooden boards they had been strapped to were cracked, torn and splintered. I dreaded to think how roughly they had been handled from Heathrow, via Iceland and onto our aircraft. If those boards had not been used, I imagined that the fragile runners would now be hanging off our sledges in pieces, ending the journey before it began.

George and I started to drag the monsters round to the front of the building in order to meet Georg, who was to help us move them into the village itself. In the thick snow, our efforts were futile and a kind local offered to move them round on the back of the airstrip's mini-tractor. Having thanked the Inuit man, who was characteristically friendly and helpful, Georg appeared on his all-terrain-vehicle at breakneck speed. I smiled as it turned out he had not changed a bit, even down to the same blue boiler suit he always wore, summer or winter. With some difficulty, we hauled the dead weight of the two sledges onto his trailer and then leapt on also. I had learned from the previous year to hold on tight as the ride is fast and bumpy between the airstrip and the village.

"Hold on!" I called back to George and he responded with a slightly nervous smile.

We sped down the hill towards the fjord and the small hotel used for the small number of day trippers who visit briefly in the height of the summer. We headed straight out onto the sea ice, which was a much quicker and flatter route than going via the hills overland. The sea ice was punctuated with large blocks of ice which, apparently, sat on top of rocks underneath the waterline in the harbour. As the tides come in and out, the sea ice rises and falls but the ice on top of these rocks stays put, unable to drop down. They resulted in amazing ten-foot-high columns of ice.

I caught sight of the village beneath the flawless blue skies and it was again a different place from the Kulusuk of the previous summer. Like on the airstrip, routes through the slope from the harbour to the village had been cut into deep snow and Georg weaved through the roofless tunnels of snow. We halted outside his house and were shown a free spot to strike camp near the school.

In what could have been considered a controversial decision, and one that I am not sure George was convinced about, we were to spend the few days in Kulusuk under canvas, not in a cabin. The last few days before the expedition would therefore not be spent with chairs, showers and a boiler. Matt had made it clear there was a cabin free should we need it. My reasoning was to ensure that we were conditioned to the tent routine in a relatively benign environment, not thrown in at the deep end at the base of the glacier. Skills such as tent pitching and collapsing were practised, as were crevasse rescue skills. The knowledge that we were not rusty was important and I believe would pay off in the long run.

We were waiting in Kulusuk for the green light from Georg to take our equipment from the village to Tasiilaq, where the helicopter was based. We planned to cover the short distance over the fjord using dogs. I was keen to use the traditional Inuit way, instead of airlifting the sledges to Tasiilaq using another helicopter charter. The state of the sea ice was critical and Georg would regularly head up to the brow of the hill to look at the sea. During the frustrating wait, a storm brewed in the region and the winds grew, ensuring that any good ice that had developed would be rendered useless. George and I had taken the opportunity to rest, send a few updates to England and meet the mischievous children of Kulusuk. They were fascinated by this strange pair of Westerners in their bright red tent. We also went for a brief test of the skis and bindings on the sea ice, where the local children were playing football. There were also lots of villagers making their way around using dog sledges, a perfectly suited mode of transport. The dogs were kept outside and were fed meat scraps, even raising their pups out in the cold and wind. They were hardy, working animals unlike their domesticated cousins at home.

On one evening return trip from Matt's storage hut on the hill overlooking Kulusuk village, where we had been collecting the weapon and ammunition, I spied a green glow in the now clear sky. We stood, mesmerised, for a quarter of an hour as the glow developed into a magnificent display of aurora borealis – the northern lights. They flowed, brightened and dimmed very slowly and calmly, unlike their time-lapsed counterparts often seen on television. I realised how lucky we were to see such a show, mostly thanks to our being in the Arctic in the cold early spring season before expeditions usually begin. Back in our temporary home, the peace was broken by Matt's voice from outside the tent and the bad news that the ice was looking like it would be fractured for the foreseeable future. We would therefore have to load the sledges onto the helicopter and fly to Tasiilaq, allow it to refuel and then fly to our insertion point a few hours later. Though disappointed that we could not use Georg's dogs, George and I made our final preparations and planned to fly early the next day. With the schedule now fixed, we decided to have a final meal in the small bar area of the guest-house near the airstrip. The meal was, as we were warned, expensive and pretty awful but the experience of eating hot food at a table with a plate was something we would soon miss.

After our meal and before our final early night in Kulusuk, I spoke business with Matt to confirm various procedures regarding logistics and Search and Rescue. The only job we had in Tasiilaq was to collect the thirty litres of white gas fuel from his contact there. More important was the policy about rescue. Our safety equipment comprised two satellite phones with spare batteries always kept in separate sledges and a 406Mhz Personal Locator Beacon (PLB). A press of the big, red button would send out a homing beacon for around a day and would, with luck, initiate a rescue in an emergency. For much of the expedition, we would be hundreds of miles from the nearest settlement and even further from those with access to aircraft. There were only two Twin Otter aircraft in Greenland capable of landing on ice. These were the realities and we understood them; serious polar expeditions, even in the twenty-first century, still carry significant risk.

The predicament was over communication loss. If we were, as was highly likely, to lose satellite phone contact for a few days then it could be due to two reasons. Either there was a technical issue which could be resolved in time or we were injured and could not operate them. However, sending a rescue aircraft hundreds of miles onto the icecap only to be sent back by a bemused George and myself would be disaster. Not only would it be a waste of the pilot's time but it would cost the expedition around £15,000 and would not be covered by insurance. The decision was a serious one and could only be taken by George and me. We resolved the best system was not to initiate Search and Rescue on loss of communications and only to do so if the PLB was activated. We knew the facts and knew that if we were in trouble and were unable to activate the PLB, no help would come.

The next morning we rose after having had plenty of sleep, both feeling more tense about the challenges ahead. I had written in my journal:

Day 0   25th March
'Pre-match nerves abound – plus a sense of responsibility...'

We moved the sledges back to the terminal where, predictably, the helicopter flight was heavily delayed. In an example of typical Inuit hospitality, the manager who spoke unusually good English invited us into his office for coffee. We went over the freight costs and haggled the costs based on sledges which had, according to their scales, increased in weight by 40kg each on the journey from the UK. As the rescheduled arrival of the helicopter loomed, George jokingly referred me to the sign on the wall which listed items prohibited from flying. We decided that we had most of the items in our sledges, including razor sharp ice axes, knives, a shotgun, live ammunition and lighters. No-one seemed in the slightest bit worried however; in this place Health and Safety makes way for common sense.

George and I moved the sledges, along with our new paperwork, out to the front of the terminal and awaited the helicopter whose distinctive engine we could now hear. In an impossibly dramatic manoeuvre, the bright red Twin Huey appeared round the corner of one of the ice walls in a tight turn, churning up clouds of loose snow which glistened in the Arctic sun. With our gear stowed onboard, we made the stunning but short flight across the coast to Tasiilaq, where we loaded the waiting fuel and awaited the pilot to let us know he was ready. After roughly an hour, and a welcome and somewhat symbolic final use of a real loo, we were beckoned through to the pad once more. We climbed onboard and tried to relax.

Chapter VII

'When your feet are cold, cover your head.' Inuit saying

As the rotors began to rotate and violently shake the fuselage of the helicopter, I tried to look forward out of the windshield. Obstructing my view were the two monstrously large sledges that we and three Inuit had struggled to lift onto the cargo section and strap down. It was March 25th and after the wait in Kulusuk, George and I had become impatient. I now felt slight regret as I contemplated that this village and helicopter landing site were the last features of civilisation we would see for months. We momentarily glanced at each other, as if to say, 'Well this is it then,' and then looked in wonder out of the filthy side windows of the helicopter. I love every moment of flying over the Arctic, especially in the cold spring when the sea and countless inlets are frozen solid in an endless plain of glinting white. As we flew higher and away from Tasiilaq, the buildings, boats and people grew smaller and I noticed the oddly modern church perched on the prominent high ground next to the sea.

Inuit people of Eastern Greenland, Tunumiit, moved to Protestant Christianity (more precisely, Evangelical Lutheran faith) some time ago and largely due to the increasing influence of Danish colonial settlers. Today, an overwhelming proportion are practising Christians and the church plays a conspicuous part in their lives. It would be wrong to criticise the modernisation of the Inuit way of life and see past days of more traditional lifestyles as superior and more authentic. It is true that in many Inuit settlements the inhabitants will be more likely to be wearing clothing from the West and boots from Canada, as well as riding quad bikes and using the

111

internet. In fact, the capital on the West Coast, Nuuk, has a network of roads, traffic lights and a business infrastructure. You would be unlikely to encounter an inuk who is against this progress; they are not interested in being frozen in time as curiosities. Nevertheless many traditional pursuits, such as dog-sledding and seal hunting, exist as they are the best way of living in such a remote location. The Inuit language is highly complicated and is a mean feat for any linguist to master. The eastern dialect varies from the official language of Greenland, Kalaallisut, and since the 1700s has been based on a reduced Latin alphabet, not atypical amongst Inuit languages. Thus far, we had survived quite well on enthusiastic hand gestures and drawing shapes in the snow.

Tasiilaq disappeared into the distance as our pilot took us west along the coast and briefly out to sea before heading towards the profusion of tongue-like glaciers flowing into the sea. We flew low and fast, often below the level of the prominent mountains and nunataks. We had been flying for about twenty minutes and so, being close to our Nagtivit Glacier insertion point, I scanned the coast for landmarks. The co-pilot passed me back a headset with microphone and the pilot asked me to point out where we would like to land. In his characteristically laid back way, the only previous discussion we had prior to the flight was for me to point roughly to the glacier on a chart. I described the area where I wanted to be set down at the base of the glacier and as close to sea level as was safe. Despite the evidently very heavy snow layer on the coast that year, there were still enormous open crevasse fields scarring the Nagtivit and the ice to its east and west. I could now see the problem troubling Georg over the previous three days, as the sea ice was heavily fractured and resembled an endless white jigsaw puzzle.

The pilot quickly brought us to a couple of hundred feet over the ice and glanced outside the cockpit for a relatively solid area on which to land. As we made contact with the ice in an extremely smooth touchdown, snow and ice were being picked up by the downdraft and churned around outside the helicopter. Once the pilot had switched the engine off and released our side hatch door, George and I stepped onto the white surface that would become our home for four long months. We had not really spoken to our pilot a great deal but as we struggled to slide the sledges off the helicopter, he and his co-pilot began to enquire further into our plans. He could not fathom why we would be out on the icecap so long. His parting words, along with a warm handshake and a grin was, "Most people try to get away from the cold of Greenland!"

George and I dragged the sledges, one by one, away from the body of the helicopter and lay down on top of them, anticipating the awesome gusts produced by a helicopter take-off only feet away. In a final enthusiastic request, George asked the pilot to 'buzz' us at low altitude as they departed. They duly responded, waving at us and flying only fifteen or so feet over our heads as they returned to civilisation. I will never be able to forget the feeling of loneliness, dread and anticipation as the familiar 'whoop, whoop, whoop' of the Huey's rotors faded into the distance. More than three years of endless toil, disappointment and borderline obsession had resulted in standing on the edge of this unimaginably massive icecap. The time for talking and persuasion was over and now the hard work began. In that instant, a massive weight dropped from my shoulders and I was able to concentrate on the actual purpose of the expedition. I relished the simplicity of the journey ahead of us.

There was no momentous speech made by either party as we stood alone on the ice. We simply got down to work immediately. I was aged only twenty-one and George was over a year my junior. I still had significant reservations about the initial climb with our monstrous weights and whether it was physically possible. George had very little experience on glaciers and crevassed terrain, so I had agreed to lead all of the sledging sessions until we reached the less chaotic and unstable icecap itself. We pointed our sledges and fastened

113

our full-body harnesses for the first time. After taking a GPS reading and setting our initial direction on my compass, I leant forward on my rope traces that connected me to my sledge. To my deep relief, the 195kg sledge creaked slowly into motion. I turned round to check on George who had also got his moving. He had a delighted grin on his face. We began to haul up the steep slope which was, as always in March, shrouded in deep snow. Although the dominating crevasse zones were obvious, the glacier would be littered with other hidden cracks. These varied from a six inch slot to a chasm able to swallow a car. The difference between a safe crossing of a crevasse and a fatal fall can be a few inches of snow and ice wedged in the opening.

The realities of crevasse rescue when in a pair or with sledges are frightening. My previous experience had included a crevasse fall in the Italian Alps and moving on crevassed ground in a trio, but here, travelling in pairs with sledges is considered the most risky. A sledge of the weight we were hauling could easily break through and pull its owner backwards into the abyss, or follow a falling skier downwards and crush his body on an ice ledge. Additionally, the chance of the second skier on a rope being able to arrest the fall of the first is negligible. Many pairs in fact choose not to rope up at all but I had decided in favour, fuelled partly by optimism and also the psychological support of being roped up.

In order for the helicopter to land safely, our drop-off point was slightly above sea level on the lower slopes of the glacier. To begin the expedition from a definite start point, I aimed at an angle towards a suitable position lower down before moving north up the glacier. Matt Spenceley had given me some way-points which were found to be safe from the previous year and this became my rough guide for picking a route. The glacier is a dynamic, flowing system and as such the structure changes from year to year. Despite this, it was invaluable to be able to identify likely trouble spots before we reached them. The snow came up to our ankles and the sledges creaked and groaned as they were hauled through the powder. Contrary to common assumption, only light sledges on a hard surface will glide freely and our 195kg monsters were resisting our efforts with every step.

I wanted to clear the majority of the disturbed ice by the end of first day and so we skied long and hard sessions to take advantage of the good visibility. We climbed higher and higher and, with each rest-stop, were rewarded with an ever better view of the coast. There was a distinct dip set into the glacier and so, to avoid the steeper and more dangerous zone, I chose a route around the edge of this. There was no sense in dropping down into a low area and then having to haul up an unnecessary slope.

As we reached the transition zone where the glacier met the icecap, the gradient of the slope became more pronounced and both George and I struggled to haul our loads. After a brief rest and acceptance that we were not hauling effectively, we made the decision to relay. As was discussed whilst in England, we began to set up a rope and prusik system that allowed us both to haul a single sledge and then speed down the glacier to retrieve the second. This laborious and demoralising relay was repeated around a dozen times until we had reached a flatter surface and were able to sledge alone. I cheerfully reassured George that the speed and ease of moving without a sledge would be more like the latter parts of the expedition. Although not totally believing my own words, I had noticed George's manner become more sombre and I thought it important to keep spirits up at this fragile stage of the journey. Perhaps the true scale of our undertaking was starting to sink in. It was no longer a theoretical journey on paper and would demand our blood, sweat and tears. It was undeniable that we were moving at a snail's pace. It was expected that our early mileages would be around four to five miles per day but this did not make the reality any less daunting. We needed to average around fourteen miles per day in order to complete the expedition without running out of food and fuel. Regardless of the slow pace and temperatures of around minus thirty, I felt George was pushing the pace too hard and not obeying the age-old 'polar plod'. I noted in my journal that George '...pulls a little fast and sweats a lot'.

Our first night on the icecap was uneventful thanks to the three days that we had spent in the tent in Kulusuk as a 'dry run'. Our drills were slick and before long we were rewarming our extremities in our down bags with snow being melted above the roaring stove. The first few weeks of the expedition, being in the grip of the polar spring, would be the most extreme in terms of temperature due to the sun being below the horizon for nearly half the day. Before long, it would not set at all − staying in the sky for the bulk of the remainder of our time on the ice.

Especially during the twenty-four hour sunlight of the polar summer, the effect of the sun on a pitched tent is enormous. Once the doors were closed and wind thereby excluded, it acted like a greenhouse, the temperature difference inside to outside often being up to fifty degrees. However, in March we would not have that comfort for many days to come. For the majority of our tent-time in those early days, we worked by torchlight and dreaded the moment when we would need to crawl out of our bags and brave the bitter cold. Even without wind, minus thirty or minus forty degrees hits you like a sledgehammer.

Day 4   29th March
Approx. 20 miles covered '...dread the morning rain of ice but love the evenings. Will depot early at 50 miles.'

These conditions of 'polar night' are experienced by a very small handful of expeditions, besides those who 'overwinter' in Antarctic science stations and of course northern native people. In the Antarctic, no expeditions can take place outside a four-month summer window, during which the sun never sets. Similarly, many Greenlandic expeditions takes place in the milder summer months from July to September. On the Arctic Ocean, the polar night is inescapable for travellers as it is necessary to begin in March or even earlier, to ensure ice conditions remain safe until they reach the North Pole in April or May. At the same time as George and I were making our first ski tracks in the Arctic early-spring, Ben Saunders reported minus forty-eight degrees in his tent on Ward Hunt Island, Canada. Ben, attempting a lightweight North Pole speed record, would have to be evacuated days later due to a broken ski binding.

As part of my agreement with the Danish authorities, and due to the fact that we were travelling on the ice long before the recognised weather window of mid-April to September, I made a satellite call to Greenland Home Rule. They were based on the West Coast of Greenland in Nuuk and I simply quoted our reference number and informed the friendly assistant that our expedition had just reached the icecap and was heading northwest.

The most important thing to success on a polar expedition, especially on such a large scale, is routine. A reliable sequence of systems which could be done without confusion or hesitation would make our progress across the ice more energy efficient and less likely to run into an accident. Our average day began at 4.30am in the early days but this altered as the sun's position in the sky changed. In any case, the time of day which we chose to adopt did not actually matter in the slightest – the only people it was relevant to was us. In fact, it is not unknown for expeditions to invent their own day lengths to improve mileage. One example is of Weber and Malakhov on their 1995 North Pole return, with days reaching 30 hours long. This can allow longer sledging periods whilst not shortening sleeping allowances. Biologically, the circadian rhythm of a human is a little more than twenty-four hours, around eleven minutes more, and so lengthening a day can have relatively little effect. We chose to stick to twenty-four hour days for the bulk of the journey, only changing if the situation necessitated.

As our alarm, which was built into our wind-meter and thermometer, chimed away, we would both awake from our often disturbed sleep. Many times I woke expecting to be in my bed at home, only to be somewhat disappointed by the reality. Due to the physical nature of every day's work on the icecap, what George termed 'our day in the office', we would wake with stiff, aching muscles. The first job was to persuade each limb in turn to start communicating with the rest of the body and slowly bring ourselves back to life. All of this had to be done with the minimum of shuffling around as even the smallest shake of the inner sheet brought down another storm of freezing hoarfrost onto our faces. My hands could then wiggle their way up from my sides to the hood of my sleeping bag which had been pulled tight around my mouth with a draw-cord. This meant that my breath was able to escape from the sleeping bag cocoon and not ice up the inside of the hood with frozen condensation. In these early days my eyelashes froze my eyes shut overnight and so I slowly rubbed the ice away before attempting to open them. A flood of light then overwhelmed my eyes as the light poured through the tent skin.

What would usually follow was a slow greeting with George and an enquiry about how he slept. He then let me know how our breakfast was coming along. One of the jobs that George had ended up with was the stove duties in the morning. Most jobs in the tent only required one person at a time and the cramped conditions of even our sizeable three-man tent supported this approach. Depending on how many layers I had slept in, I could then apply my outer garments and feel around on the outside of my vapour barrier for my socks. Socks were a tricky item to oversee in the Arctic. They were the only item which would routinely end up damp at the end of the day and therefore could not be left to freeze solid overnight. It was vital to remove socks each night for reasons of foot hygiene and to inspect for frost damage before putting on our downfilled tent boots. The vapour barrier was an impermeable bag which lined the down sleeping bags in order to stop water vapour entering the down compartments. Damp down feathers lose their loft and insulating properties fast. Placing the socks outside the barrier but inside the bag itself allowed my body heat to dry the socks and allowed the minimum moisture content to escape into the bag. As with anything on polar expeditions, it was a compromise that worked.

George's routine began by priming and lighting the stove – I ensured the night before that the fuel bottle had sufficient fuel for the morning. Priming involves releasing the valve until a little fuel drips into the stove cone and then screwing it shut quickly. That fuel is lit with a lighter or a flint and allowed to burn. This action draws vapour from the pumped fuel bottle to work its way along the fuel hose into the stove. As the hissing of the vapour was heard, George released the valve and allow a flow of fuel to power the stove. Often, along with the enormous morale lift provided with the jet engine-like roar of the blue flame, large balls of flame shot upwards towards the roof of the tent. We would jokingly look at the hopeful safety notice in the tent that strongly warned against cooking in the tent. However, the fire risk was very real and so we ensured that fuel was carefully segregated and cooking done in the 'outside' area of the inside of the tent. A burnt tent would leave us with no shelter and unless rescue was quickly summoned, we would be unlikely to survive. A recent death in Greenland was due to an incident just like this.

Breakfast, usually a wheat and oat-based porridge with added ghee butter, could follow once a pan of water had boiled. This powered us for the early hours of our day and contributed to our huge daily calorie intake. Unlike many expeditions, we decided never to have anything in the pans but water. This avoided the pans descending into a filthy state and meant that portion sizes were identical. The water was simply added to the bags of dried food and left to stand in order for the butter to melt.

Solid ghee butter is one of the most disgusting things anyone could have the misfortune to taste. George would later develop a taste for it; something I never achieved. After carefully licking every last morsel off our spoons, we set about packing away the tent gear into rucksacks. I then booted up and sat in the entrance, packing up the stove equipment whilst George dealt with the sleeping gear and mats. Whilst George was finishing off and getting dressed, I unzipped the tent door. It was always a nervous moment as, regardless of how the tent felt, you could never fully predict the weather outside, the wind, temperature, visibility or surface. After peering out the door, I turned my head to report back to George, who would always sit expectantly hoping for good news. I used to try and dress up my description so as to raise his spirits and to persuade myself it was alright. As the designated porter, I then moved the few items of equipment from the tent door to each respective sledge, trying to remember George's latest layout for his equipment. This was done whilst allowing the minimum of drift into the sledges. Once George had also left, the tent collapsing had to be done quickly. Until fully untensioned and rolled into a sausage, it was kept attached to a sledge using a climbing karabiner for security against wind.

Having been out of the tent in the cold, spring air and wind without having generated much body-heat, George and I were always at our coldest before the daily sledging began. My own way to combat the extreme cold was to undertake what became known as the 'cold dance'. Prior to attaching to the sledge, I hopped and ran around like a dervish, circling my hands over my head like windmills. This was the most effective solution I found to the problem and served to push warm blood to my extremities, where cold damage will tend to originate. It looked undeniably barmy and George, on one occasion, drew his camera without me noticing and recorded my performance for posterity. I reasoned that there are few places on Earth where you can behave like a madman and be almost certain of avoiding an audience.

The only jobs that remained were to set the direction of travel using a compass and clipping into our harnesses. The process of clipping on was always torture due to the fiddly karabiners and our large mitts and gloves we used in the cold mornings. We would end up clipping each other on as we could see better what we were doing. The whole saga left our hands cold and they took a while to recover once 'on the road'. It was just one of the series of small daily rituals that defined our teamwork on the ice.

In this way, our journey across the icecap itself began in one of the toughest times of the year. It was surreal to be finally out on the ice doing the job that I had pined after for so long. The daily mileage was indeed dismal, but not unreasonable and we were hauling strongly. We slid into a good daily regimen and the mileage began to creep up. The milestones of ten and fifty miles were important psychologically. In order to make sense of the appalling distances involved on the trip and to visualise the depots, we drew a timeline on the roof on the tent and we annotated it every night. Using a black marker, we agreed that I would complete the entries on my side of the tent until the West Coast, and George would take over for the return. At first the crosses, which indicated a day's progress, would be very close together but we hoped that as time went on and the weight lessened, they might spread apart. Aside from our diaries, we also wanted a pictorial record of the conditions we faced and so for entertainment, more than anything else, we drew symbols to represent weather. Some days would show white-out, others sun. More often than not, the wind symbol was a feature.

As another psychological aid, we named the depots and phases of the expedition. This was to attempt to rationalise the distances involved in our heads with something familiar. Given that the distance of the outward leg was some seven hundred miles, roughly the 'height' of the United Kingdom,

121

we used well-known towns. First came my home on the south coast, via London and Oxford and culminating in Aberdeen. The completion of this giant timeline was a constant source of amusement and much thought was given to daily entries. The most exciting target was always the depot; it was an opportunity to lose some weight from the sledge and also a confirmation that we were making headway. Our first foray into depot laying was after fifty miles. It involved burying a container of fuel, a few measured days of food and our rubbish, all to be collected on the return. In total this reduced our sledge weights by around 5kg. It felt like a great victory in the face of pitiful daily gains and we had an enormous distance to go. 54 miles covered.

Day 8   2nd April
'Tough couple of days with strong winds, a cairn to lay (inside the tent) and shoulder pains...hope the cairn lasts!'

The timeline entry we dreaded most of all and totally dominated the opening hundred or so miles of the expedition, was sastrugi. It occurred at the worst time, when the sledges were heaviest. Sastrugi are snow formations created and sculpted by the relentless polar winds and resemble blades or waves. They are a major obstacle on both the great icecaps of Greenland and Antarctica. From a distance, sastrugi are quite beautiful as they flow in a single direction and often grow into an overhang. Despite being made from the accumulation of drift against a small lump on the surface, they become hard as rock and it was possible to ski over an overhanging blade of snow without breaking it.

It became a sport of ours, futile as the attempts were, to break the sastrugi as we skied past them. It was our way of fighting back against the inanimate objects that made our lives a living hell. There was no escaping them, no route that would avoid them. Sastrugi would stretch for miles, as far as the eye could see, and there was no indication that they would end. Some were no more than three or four inches in height but for the most part, they were significant barriers, some up to five feet high. As the days passed, seemingly endless and featureless, the only stimulation, and it appeared topic of conversation, was sastrugi.

An illustration of the extent of our exhaustion is the lack of photography. Also, partly due to the technical and practical difficulties we had getting our cameras to work initially, there is precious little evidence of those first days. Photography is one of my greatest passions and I was determined that I would document the expedition no matter what the conditions. This entailed hauling heavy professional equipment onto the ice; it was my one extravagance but I felt it was worth the extra weight. The complicated battery and charging arrangements for the camera pushed it to the bottom of the solar charging priority list and for days on end, I could not get it to power up at all. We used George's smaller camera, which could also capture video, as a replacement for these periods. This was an era long before the advent of the GoPro action camera.

Much of the time, it was impossible to drag our 190kg dead weights over the sastrugi. Time and again, whoever was following would have to push on the back of the leader's sledge with a ski-pole. The result was that, after the supreme effort of getting the sledge to the crest of a given sastruga, it then shot down the other side, often twisting as it picked up speed and eventually slammed into the ankles of its hauler. So it continued for mile after mile with an effort that caused us to sweat and our shoulders to ache, followed by a desperate attempt to move out of the way of a 190kg blunt object, hell-bent on throwing us off our feet.

The sweating was a larger threat to our well-being than it may have seemed at first. Although our clothing was woven from the newest materials, including smart merino wool base layers and Pertex soft-shell outers, sweat did accumulate after strenuous hauling and it became a major enemy. The key aim when travelling in the Polar Regions is to balance body

123

heat – not being too hot when skiing and not too cold when resting. It is a difficult juggling act to achieve and the usual solution was to haul in only two light layers, despite bitter temperatures and then don a down jacket for the brief ten minute rests.

Meanwhile a problem was developing with our ski skins. The repeatedly uneven surface had caused the front corners of the skins to lift and act as a snowplough as the snow became wedged. This clearly had a major effect on the efficiency of the skis on the ice surface. Despite the special ski glue and screws that had been used to secure them, the skins needed an added adhesive to hold them onto the ski. Having scraped out the caught snow and dried out the entire area, I retrieved the super strength contact adhesive from my sledge and set about trying to apply it to both surfaces. Having a narrow nozzle and with the temperatures being low enough to freeze most gels, the glue was not forthcoming. Learning a valuable lesson of the Arctic the hard way, I proceeded to squeeze, hoping to unclog the obstruction. The crimped other end of the tube suddenly popped and glue came oozing out, covering my contact glove with the impossibly sticky substance. I could see immediately why the glue was marketed as being able to adhere 'anything to anything'. Having finally managed to stick the skin securely back to the ski, I set about trying to remove the excess from my clothing with partial success. I resolved to have more patience in the future, heating glues or other liquids and gels using body warmth until ready for use.

Day 9   3rd April
60 miles covered 'Started off like any other! Heavy sastrugi and horrible gradient. After lunch the surfaces improved a little... so enjoyable evening with long dinner! Little concerned over progress but upbeat.'

As we continued our way on a magnetic bearing, which coincidentally turned out to be exactly magnetic north, the sastrugi did not subside and I began to worry after making the usual mental calculations as I skied. We expected low initial mileages, to be countered by rapid ones in the coming weeks but we were still not even breaking one mile per hour. We were falling behind and, despite knowing that sastrugi were due to recent weather and that they could arrive and disappear in a few days, I called Matt for the first time. Although the only feasible satellite communications option in the Arctic, the Iridium system was not very reliable and a call often took a few attempts. It also had a curious habit of requiring a call to be made before receiving incoming messages. However, once connected, the clarity was remarkable given how isolated we were from the civilised world.

"Matt," I asked in a serious tone, "do you have any weather reports, forecasts or any other information that might signal an end to the bad surface? Our mileages are dismal and the sastrugi never-ending."

"Alex, I'm sorry but the current weather pattern is forecast to stay for the time being. You're just going to have to do what you can now and make the time up later," he replied, echoing my gut feeling.

We had two satellite phones and they resembled a mobile phone from the early 1990s: large grey bricks with a long extendable antenna. As our only two-way form of communication, batteries had to be conserved as a matter of survival and they were never kept in the same place at once. Using the handset's SMS function, we were able to send daily updates in a pre-iPhone age to our website, detailing the day's mileage, minimum temperature, maximum wind speed and a short message. This was a much-coveted privilege and we would take turns to make the nightly broadcast. As a further safety procedure, we would also transmit the GPS coordinates of our depot locations back to our home team via this system. What we really needed to clear the sastrugi and to allow us to ski on an even surface, was snowfall with low winds and some cold temperatures. This would bury the sastrugi without

125

wind to create new formations, then cold temperatures would harden the snow into a surface ideal for sledging. Our hopes would not come true for some weeks yet. In the meantime, the conditions would further deteriorate with the arrival of whiteout, and the climb continued.

'We had discovered an accursed country. We had found the Home of the Blizzard.' Sir Douglas Mawson

Whiteout, when it is impossible to distinguish between the snow and sky, is where there is zero contrast. It is far worse than simple low visibility. By July, with the early weeks being the worst, we had spent nearly six weeks in this disorientating nightmare, especially so when accompanied by high winds. At times, it was difficult to see the end of your ski just three feet in front of you. It became extremely difficult to see George to my front or rear and we had to ski very close together in order to avoid getting separated. Doing so would certainly condemn one of us to a cold and lonely death as we had only one tent and no means of finding each other in the whiteness. This only resulted in the annoying habit of skiing into the lead skier's sledge when he came to an abrupt halt to check his compass bearing. I wrote in my journal that 'the ruts and sastrugi jar my back. Hard to drift off in sessions due to need to concentrate.'

An added hazard of the whiteout was an inability to see crevasses. Having not travelled over such hostile ground previously, this was something that was clearly starting to prey on George's mind. He often spoke of them in the evenings as we worked in the tent. All I could do was to reiterate the procedure of probing the surface with a pole if unsure and to say that crevasse fields were increasingly infrequent as we climbed the icecap, away from the coast.

Another drawback of the conditions we found ourselves struggling through – sastrugi and whiteout combined – was that we could not see the sastrugi. As whiteout removes all

126

visibility, it also destroys any shadows, the telltale signs of white sastrugi against white ice. As a consequence, it was sometimes possible for the rear man to use the shadow of the lead skier to identify where the larger ridges and waves were. Unfortunately, the one of us breaking trail at the time had no such luxury and skied forward using pure guesswork. The sastrugi continued to be huge in size with sheer drops off the edges of many. I was the first to fall foul on April 6th – Day Twelve. As I led my session, I felt the ground disappear under my left ski and, with no warning, I tumbled awkwardly to my left down a slope and landed in a heap at the bottom. My trusty sledge followed directly after me and slid into my back. Lying there, skis stuck in the snow and face down, I struggled to extract myself alone. George followed down soon after, and to my indignation, had first to stop himself laughing uncontrollably before being able to assist. Once standing again and after confirming that neither I nor my sledge was damaged, I also saw the funny side and the absurdity of our predicament. George would follow suit only minutes later and balance was restored.

I managed to inflict the first damage to my equipment that night as I left my insulated mug, used for hot chocolate, too close to the windshield of the stove. Before I had time to realise, it had blistered the outer skin of the mug and formed a curious bubble that I reasoned gave the mug character. This was not to be the only mishap with the stoves. Our stove-board, the heat-proofed and waterproofed plywood which provided a solid platform for the fuel bottle and stove had quite a polar pedigree. We had forgone a new model in deference to one which had visited both North and South Poles with various expeditions. Of all the pieces of equipment which had been loaned to us for the duration, it was the one I wanted to bring back in one piece. Although we had only been on the ice for ten days or so, the heat-isolating rubber seals on the stove bottoms had perished, most likely due to the cold, and allowed the stove base to heat up. After an hour or so of use one evening,

George noticed a burning smell and we investigated the stove. The board now had a black circle of burnt wood in the centre, although its function was unhindered. I did feel a pang of guilt over the board which had a sentimental attachment to others, although it was now just part of its story.

Chapter VIII

*'Who is the third who walks always beside you? When I count, there
are only you and I together.'* T.S. Eliot

Navigation in a whiteout is a very tricky exercise indeed.
Our usual system was to make minimal use of the power-
hungry GPS units and rely on magnetic compasses.

The Magnetic North Pole, located north of Canada,
was far enough away at this point to use a fixed-plate Silva
compass and nautical 'floating' compass. The latter was more
effective in motion as the needle does not need to settle in
order to take a bearing. If required, we could use a light, wire
frame to mount the compass on our front in a sort of 'hands
free' configuration. The normal procedure in good visibility
is to take a bearing, spy a prominent sastruga on the horizon
on that bearing and ski to it, repeating this cycle endlessly.
Clearly this would be impossible in whiteout or in heavy snow
and so we employed two main solutions. If the sun had made
an appearance, we also used ourselves as a sundial and could
maintain a bearing using the position of our own shadow. The
first method was to watch the nautical compass mounted on
one's front constantly and ensure that you stayed on course.
It was a great relief to swap positions at the end of a sixty-
five minute session as this could be quite draining mentally.
The second technique was to use the elements to our own
advantage. As there was consistently a wind, usually of quite
some strength, we would watch over our gunmetal grey skis as
the drift and snow was blown over it. Providing the direction
of the wind was maintained for a few hours at a time and
that we made regular checks, we were able to ski in a straight
line but making sure the drift stayed at the same angle. In this

way, we skied for days on end into the blank landscape. The psychological aspect of the expedition, perhaps as significant as the physical toil, was becoming obvious even in these early weeks.

Most apparent in these hard, early days and in the whiteout especially, was hallucination and the extraordinary tricks your mind plays on you. The first, which has been written about on polar expeditions since the dawn of the twentieth century, is the phantom third skier. Noted by both Shackleton and Roger Mear in the Antarctic, no matter what the size of the sledging party, there will always be that presence of another. This phantom is not menacing but instead provides moral support, especially since our own team was so small. I found this extra companion so real that I would often look over my shoulder, even if skiing second to George, to check how he or she was getting on.

Even more bizarre than the phantom skier was an hallucination apparently unique to my own mind. No doubt as a result of the total visual deprivation that we suffered when hauling in these conditions, I saw man-made objects in the ground to the side of me. Most commonly this was a railway platform, just the sort I would sit on whilst waiting for a train to another sponsor meeting in the months past. What was most curious was that it was always just out of sight, no matter how much I turned my head to look at it, and always to the right of me, never to the left. Despite this perturbing onset of mild insanity, I found that I was becoming accustomed to life in the white wilderness.

Day 14   8th April
75 miles covered 'I chose not to sledge due to very high winds. Very frustrating and a hard call. Right call? I think so. Vital not to let ourselves slip back however. Must make 250 miles by 25th April. Woke with a full blown piteraq. Strictly on 8 hour days hereafter.'

The first storm hit early on for us in the expedition. The *'piteraq'* katabatic storms in both the Arctic and Antarctic are notorious and it arrived without warning as they so often do. My journal entry highlights the first signs of conflict in my own mind regarding progress and safety. It is so easy to be a wimp and ride out high winds but you end up using up supplies and travel nowhere.

Although relieved to be out of the melee, on the few occasions when we rode out a storm under shelter, guilt and a feeling of laziness can overcome you. George and I tried to sleep through the storm and the hunger induced by reduced rations. If we were not travelling, we could not justify full rations. When it was too loud to sleep, we played chess with George's miniature wooden set. So the next day proceeded to the endless soundtrack of howling wind and creaking tent poles.

'But I have never heard or felt or seen a wind like this. I wondered why it did not carry away the Earth.' Cherry Apsley-Garrard

After what must have been only an hour's sleep, George and I woke to totally different surroundings. The tent was no longer being thrown around and the quiet was almost eerie. The *piteraq* had subsided as fast as it had arrived. I decided to venture outside the tent to assess the icecap and check our equipment for any damage. Despite the large snowwall constructed the previous day, snow had piled up all around the tent, weighing down on the roof and blocking both side doors. It took a few minutes with the shovel to dig through the drift and see bright sunlight burst through the gap. The icecap was at peace once more, ready to be travelled again. George and I, both having been on next to no rations, felt weak and dizzy. We shared a single breakfast of hot cereal, tidied away the chess set and ventured outside. The tent took some time to dig out and the sledges themselves were totally submerged under three feet of drift. Amazingly, the effect of the ferocious winds and the air currents around our tent, the sole feature on the ice, had produced a strange effect. I had expected to see the surrounding ice covered in drift as well but once a few feet from the tent, the surface was devoid of any drift or powder. This was a welcome surprise and I was optimistic for our day's skiing and attempts to make up the lost miles.

It was at this point that I realised all was not well. The weakness had not diminished despite taking on water and food and I felt debilitated whilst collapsing the tent. Suddenly, despite the temperatures hovering in the mid minus-twenties, I felt uncomfortably hot and had an overwhelming desire to remove my down jacket. Soon after came an extreme nausea, head rushes and my legs could no longer support me. I slumped onto the front of my sledge and George came rushing over. I tried, in between deep breaths, to explain what the problem was and we shifted the sledge so that the wind was on my back. I sipped water and began to feel improved, although I was puzzled as to the cause of such an extreme reaction. I was reasonably well-fed and hydrated. I took a single stomach tablet, the only medication either of us would use in the whole four months.

"Well, we'd better head off then," I said. George nodded and we both slowly stood up and attached our harnesses. As usual, I was to lead the first session of the day and I thought this sensible to maintain. If I were to have another bad turn, I could collapse and George may not notice for some time if he were ahead. As if my morning could not become much worse, a persistent problem re-emerged almost immediately as we began to haul.

My goggles, which in tandem with my 'Gorilla' face mask provided protection against the worst headwinds, had iced up. They could go from totally clear to opaque within only a few moments. Now blind and with poor visibility due to conditions, I could not navigate in anything resembling a straight line. Still feeling appalling, I became increasingly frustrated and stopped, throwing my poles to the ground in irritation. It was approaching the end of the first hour and George offered to take over until my goggles cleared. He forged ahead with me in tow, becoming less agitated as time passed. I was able to follow him only by peering out of the corner of one side of the goggles where I could make out his blurred shape in the whiteness.

Removing goggles in anything but darkness or dusk is very unsafe due to snow-blindness. The intense sunlight and reflections off the white ice will quickly overcome naked human eyes. The burning sensation and feeling of 'sand' in the eye is agonising in minor cases and totally crippling in severe attacks. On the early expeditions where modern lenses were not available, card lenses with slits cut in were used to reduce the amount of light reaching the eye. Scott's 1911 expedition administered cocaine to those affected in order to reduce the pain. After a couple of hours progressing in this manner, my goggles had returned to normal and I felt a lot stronger. I resumed my position at the front, navigating and we pressed on with a long day in the harness.

Despite an unusually mild evening, I spent too long answering the call of nature whilst exposed to the wind. I returned to the tent wincing in pain as two of my fingers were solid as wood, not able to move in the slightest. They were totally white and did not respond to touch. I was enormously relieved as the pain intensified and colour slowly returned to the flesh. It was a close call with frostbite and a reminder to tighten up on my skills. The day was so mixed that my journal read: 'Worrying night. Every bump was a guy line snapping!... Nausea, shivers and the urge to 'void'. Lovely evening – cold – got nip on two fingers whilst on WC.'

Soon after, we received news of Ben Saunders' abandonment of his North Pole bid but also of the healthy birth of twins to Rich and Hils. I felt gutted for Ben, especially since he had failed due to equipment failure but I was ecstatic for Rich. It was the first I had heard from my previous 'Journey South 2007' team mates whilst in the Arctic.

As the main method for personal expression at the time, written journals were the portals into the ordeals and challenges the pioneering expeditions faced. Only the awe inspiring photographic plates of early photographers, such as Herbert Ponting, can provide extra insight into the realities of Edwardian polar exploration. Regardless of what conclusion you reach over his competence and judgement, Captain Robert Scott's diaries are exceptional in their detail and stretch over many months of Antarctic travel, much of it unsupported. It was these journals and accounts which first stirred a polar interest for me and I put a great deal of thought into what I wanted to achieve regarding my own record of the journey. Excerpts from my entries are included throughout this book.

My journal, small with a black cover and elastic strap, was to become my best friend and worst enemy almost from one moment to the next. On reflection, this seemingly mundane task of journal writing was where I showed some of the psychological strains of this epic walk. These were increasingly apparent as we entered the third month on the ice. In stark comparison to concocting the daily satellite dispatch for the public, which was often a motivation in itself towards the end of a long day sledging, the journal was, at times, a pest. Despite our relatively low tech approach to dispatches, which involved short, daily messages to our web site, we could not have hoped for better support. As we would later learn, hundreds of people were following our progress on a daily basis and many used the satellite service to send messages of support directly to us. I decided to conduct all of my administration in the period around 'dinner time' in the tent. Having laid out the interior of the tent, George's jobs were largely over for the evening and he would settle down in his sleeping bag and spend often over half an hour neatly penning his daily entry. I never have found out what he wrote, especially on the hardest days but I will always wonder about it, the most private of documents. Particularly, I wonder whether he found the same things the most draining and how he really viewed our rare differences of opinion. In the meantime, I would cook dinner, muddle through the inevitable electronic tinkering with batteries and chargers that seemed to never end, and complete my own single page journal entry.

My handwriting is atrocious even in the comfort of my own home and with numb fingers and awkward contact gloves, the situation was even more dire. I am certain I am the only person to be able to decipher the scribblings, and often even I struggle, but perhaps it was a subconscious attempt at privacy! Some days, usually those where whiteout, excessive wind and sastrugi were absent, I enjoyed the process of unloading my thoughts onto the page. More often, I saw the long term benefits of a permanent record of my thoughts and our progress but I was too exhausted to care. Even in the early days of the expedition, George and I fell into the tent after around twelve hours on the move and just craved food and sleep. We rarely received a disturbance-free night due to the wind and cold and the food, although barely sufficient in calories, was just not bulky enough to satisfy. As a consequence, my journal entries were often a hastily scribbled note of the day's events and rarely contained the thoughts and insight which they deserved. They also contained the recordings of maximum wind speed, minimum temperature and mileage achieved that day.

I was certain that a trip of such epic length and day to day similarity would merge into a single memory once home. Luckily, this has not been the case and I still recall the sequence of journey and intricate details of our time on the ice. The disappointment of a fairly basic journal has been balanced by this bank of memories and has served as inspiration and reference for telling the story in the subsequent months.

Our journey began to settle down into sixty-five minute sessions with short food breaks in between. We developed a strong routine even down to the way we would, in synchrony, stop after a session, push our poles into the snow, turn to the side and answer the call. Regular as clockwork.

As one hundred miles came and went after eighteen days, I noted in my journal 'some slightly erratic navigation [from George] which needs changing. Direction is too rigid which means too much clambering!' It was only a minor point but one that I wanted to nip in the bud. Instead of skiing 'head down' and assaulting each bump head-on, we needed to steer a path with intelligent deviations to minimise our energy expenditure. After listening to my concerns, George quickly altered his technique, although he still somehow managed to scrape off many of his sponsor logos from the sides of his sledge. I can only suppose that he chose a path that brushed against tall sastrugi and ridges.

We both had a chuckle in the evening as a message came through by satellite from my brother, Oliver. I wrote: 'Msg from Ol. 100 miles awesome work. Ditching joke as the punchline sucked. Tracking you on Google Earth. Looks white for the foreseeable future. Keep pulling. Ol.' It was just what we both needed. We knew the opening weeks would be amongst the most testing. We were drained already, only a fourteenth of the distance in.

As my birthday approached on the 19th April, Day 25 of the expedition, we had some hard days sledging. Comments in my entries included 'spirit beginning to be affected by the never ending toil' and 'finger tips still gone'. These were buoyed by endless support from the UK. Sean Chapple, an expedition leader previously in the Royal Marines, sent a characteristically buoyant cheer of, 'All others aborted, you're the only heroes left out there.' Whilst certainly not heroes, we were the only team on the ice on a major expedition following the unfortunate injury of Hannah McKeand whilst making a solo attempt on the North Pole.

The navigation was still causing problems as skiing on a direction dictated by just the windblown 'grain' of the sastrugi fell down when two or more different 'grains' appeared. Grain was created by the wind carving longitudinal shapes into the surface. The sastrugi also seemed to be set perpendicular to

Amundsen's 1911 South Pole expedition

Alex and Adam on Mont Blanc's summit ridge, 2007

Douglas Mawson and companion in an Antarctic blizzard, 1912

The JS2007 team and crew from Eye Film, SE Greenland, 2007

The JS2007 team in Greenland and at the Oxford Launch, 2007

JOURNEY
SOUTH
2007

Alex and Adam at the RGS Press Call

The extreme topography of the Greenland ice sheet

Alex on BBC News 24

SOUTH POLE EXPEDITION
1,000-mile trek to geographic South Pole
BBC NEWS 24 14:54 :IN ARE FACING TRIAL FOR ALLEGEDLY SUPP

Flapjacks being pre-packed

Practice camp in Kulusuk

The start - dropped off by helicopter on the glacier

A menacing cloud system

Early cold days

Sastrugi, our nemesis for hundreds of bumpy miles

Filling the pan with snow to melt - a daily ritual

Follow the leader

George building a depot cairn

Supplies to be depoted

Home

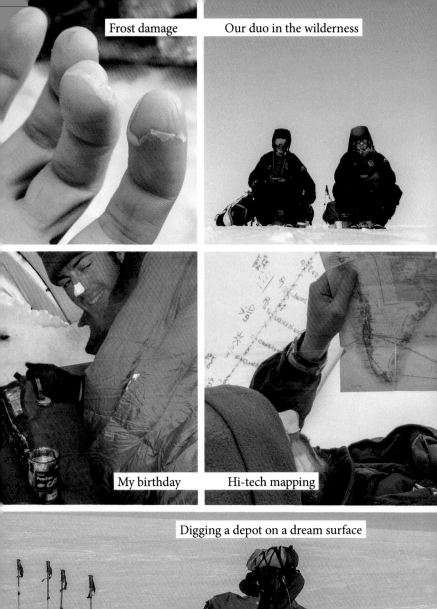

Frost damage

Our duo in the wilderness

My birthday

Hi-tech mapping

Digging a depot on a dream surface

George ventures onto a refrozen melt pool

The West Coast - crevasses and slopes

The sticky summer snow surface

Finding a depot cairn

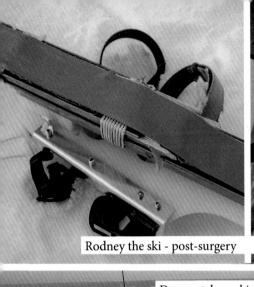

Rodney the ski - post-surgery

A view from the tent door

Desperately probing for the penultimate depot

The summer high pressure system

Starvation

The dizzy final push

Completion - calling in a pickup

After 113 days, our pickup - elation beyond words

Happiness

Georg Utuaq

London homecoming

our direction of travel – perfectly positioned to block our path toward the West Coast. Good news followed on Day 21 as snow started to fill in the gaps between ridges and a smoother surface resulted. We were approaching days of ten miles as we climbed further towards our icecap 'summit' at over 8,000 feet. Visibility also started to return after so many days' absence.

The icecap looked just like an angry sea, frozen in time. The ice was grey in the overcast light with the sastrugi resembling 'white horses' at sea. It was quite beautiful and totally static. My birthday held an enormous surprise, besides the satellite messages from home. Predicting the craving for fresh fruit on the expedition, George had secretly stashed a tin of peaches in his sledge. He had even wrapped it. We shared the present and savoured every last taste. Not only that, but we had broken the ten-mile barrier for a single day of sledging. Things were looking good for us at last.

Food became the obsession. When thoughts of house-building, expedition mental arithmetic and home had become stale, I fell back on food. Sometimes it was dreams of great feasts to come when the hell of the long marches had ended and sometimes simply anticipation of the freeze-dried curry and ghee butter to come. Although we spent much time keeping ourselves occupied with culinary inventions, such as the chef, Gordon Ramsay-inspired 'F-Word' pudding fashioned from flapjack and ghee, volume was the key. Our stomachs were never filled or satisfied with the extraordinarily calorie-dense food, as weight was the controlling factor on such things. With experimentation and patience, we decided that we could increase the perceived volume of our main meals and cereal breakfasts. By adding far more boiling water than suggested by the manufacturers, we left our food pouches on the warm water saucepan and let the contents swell with the water. Water was, after all, the only resource we had plenty of, fuel allowing. The result was, especially with my favourite cottage pie and rice-based meals, a puffy and 'larger feeling'

137

meal. I always felt, even from the early days of the expedition, that my greatest failing in preparing nutrition was to exclude a small supplement of dehydrated potato to swell and satisfy our hollow stomachs. Aside from a general lack of luxuries, I desired this more and more as time progressed.

It was decided that George should consume a larger proportion of the energy rich ghee butter than myself for two reasons. Firstly, I was still concerned about his lean physique and the impact on his survival later and on the return leg. The extra calories were vital to his retaining bodyweight. Secondly, I could not face the sheer quantity of ghee that George could consume. Our appetites could simply accept different amounts. I certainly suffered from 'ghee poisoning', the extreme nausea following a ghee butter 'overdose', more often than he. One such incident amused George so much that it found its way into our precious daily satellite update to the wider world.

As Day 26 gave way to Day 27, a miraculous change came over the icecap surface. We had christened the icecap Myrtle, as we named most inanimate objects in sight. It was most likely an attempt to create human character when the place was almost entirely devoid of it. Myrtle, we reasoned, just sounded like the name of someone, or something, with mixed moods. The icecap was certainly that. My comments one day stated that I was 'fed up of whiteout. Nothing to navigate off...dread it. No feeling in toe or finger tips.' The next, it enthused that it was 'the best day yet. Flattened off with great surface. Will it continue? Optimistic about the future at this rate.'

Despite the weeks of previous poor conditions our progress had actually been consistent, if slow, and we had accumulated distance. We were only falling a little behind schedule. We were also working together well and I had not begun to experience the negative feelings towards George that most predict on journeys of that length, not even when he accidentally stabbed my thin, inflatable mattress through both sides with a large knife. He had slipped whilst cutting the freezing cold ghee butter. He looked up at me sheepishly, knowing that our air-beds were one of the few items of comfort we had.

I was annoyed – really annoyed. Cutting something hard a few inches away from something full of air was asking for trouble. What would be gained by flying off the handle? Nothing, apart from a day of tension over something which was a simple mistake. I would make plenty, such as skiing half a mile past my outer mitt which had come unattached from my smock cuff. I skied back like a man possessed to find it but knew that it was a chink in my armour I could not afford. Back in the tent, I went to the bottom of my small box known as the 'Oh Shit Box' which contained emergency spares and repair kits and retrieved the puncture-repair kit. I handed it to George and said nothing. We shared a smirk and he set to heat up the glue between his legs before it could be used to patch up the hole. The resulting repairs lasted the remainder of the expedition as if new. Meanwhile, on the ice, the improvements in our performance continued.

Day 28   22 April
193 miles covered 'Twangs of home but still motivated 100%.
Seems really very possible. Looking forward to warmth, though. Surface
more crusty.'

A sign that things were on the up was that we were starting to think about fine tuning our skiing system rather than just hanging on for dear life. I found, for example, our rucksacks were giving us stiff and aching lower backs. The combination of rucksack and harness straps meant that there were a multitude of configurations and we experimented to get them comfortable. I finally managed to minimise the inevitable pain of hauling over 160kg by moving a lot of the weight to my waist and resting my shoulders. Another problem was that neither of our sledges were running straight along our ski tracks. Both tracked to the right and this was most noticeable in thick snow when the runners carved deep ruts into the soft surface. We were wasting energy as the second man skied along the leader's path. His sledge forged a new path and had to shovel new snow out of the way. We spent a few days fiddling with our bungee-softened hauling traces to get them running straight, eventually succeeding.

Throughout the bitterness of March and April, which was compounded by our altitude and the wind, warmth was my light at the end of the tunnel. The icecap is shaped similarly to the Antarctic, with steep gradients around the coasts and a central dome which gently rises to a summit. I kept on telling us that 'May would be warmer – the coming of summer'. The cold made just the basics of living in the Arctic so hard. The wind was also extraordinary. I recall vividly that on one beautifully clear and still day, one second it was still and the next the wind blew. Not gusty but just a constant stream of air. I had never before experienced weather that reacted as if to an 'on/off' switch.

We were, just as momentum was building, starting to experience problems with power. Our source was a flexible solar panel which was draped over a sledge canvas throughout the working day. It was designed to operate in even overcast conditions but had started to charge the vital satellite phones only intermittently. I had long since abandoned the idea of charging my 12v battery packs to power my brick of a professional SLR camera and investigated other solutions involving packs of smaller batteries.

The technical issues did not stop there. We also had communication issues via the satellite back to Matt and Dagmar, his weather forecast expert. As such, we did not receive regular forecasts and those we did receive were very approximate. They almost always underestimated the wind-speed, which became a source of slight amusement for George and me. This was through no fault of Dagmar's though, as forecasting in the Arctic is a tricky art with little useful data to work from.

George's use of the satellite phone became a source of slight irritation to me. The satellite phones and their limited supply of lithium batteries were, as I saw them, a major safety item. They were predominately for emergency and logistics conversations between myself and Matt Spenceley and for daily text dispatches. The proven unreliable nature of solar charging and the limited battery lives of the telephones supported my feeling that their use should be heavily rationed. Of course, I understood the effect of family contact on morale but I felt there was a line of professionalism and practicality that should not be overstepped. Especially around the days surrounding major landmarks on the icecap, George made long calls to those whom I considered relations far outside close family. I would have been thrilled to have spoken to friends and those apart from my parents and brother but I did not feel it justified. However, there was a great strength from these conversations, catching up on the latest from home but perhaps it could also cause us to miss home even more. At the time, I did raise my concerns but did not pursue – perhaps it was a passing irritation. I did not wish to risk an argument over something like phone calls. On one of the couple of times I spoke to my brother, Oliver, an engineer in Bristol, I managed to call him whilst out at dinner with a friend. Rather apologetically, I offered to call back later but he, sensing the absurdity of a phone call from the High Arctic, excused himself and we spoke for a few minutes.

Day 31   25th April
228 miles covered 'Found another bloody bowl today. Hope [it] is not a habit. Without weather forecast.'

An unexpected hurdle to overcome on our outward journey was that of bowls. Although the inland icecap is largely crevasse-free, it is not flat as a pancake as most would

141

imagine. The landscape gradually undulated in dips and rises, some miles wide. The implication for us was that even the slightest incline caused the heavy sledges to resist our attempts to haul and we gained precious little extra pace from the declines. Given the extraordinary appearance of the icecap, it causes a myriad of optical illusions unique to the place. For example, with no landmarks there was nothing to give a feeling of scale and so distances were impossible to guess. A dip or a large sastruga on the horizon could be one hundred yards or five miles away.

We soon experienced a dump of snow which, along with cold temperatures, improved the sledging surface by evening out the bumps. This was followed by another of the Arctic's spectacular shows – ice crystal showers. Quite unlike the horrible rain of hoarfrost inside the tent, these light speckles of frozen moisture fill the sky like glitter. The treat which the two of us received that day did not end with snow and ice. Despite being at one of the furthest distances from the coast we would ever be, we had a visitor. With a quiet chirp, a black and white bird appeared from our front quarter and stopped briefly on the snow surface. I imagined it was very much a case of 'who was more surprised to see whom?'

The bird soon tired of us and continued on its own journey and we did the same towards the northwest. That evening, George was busy writing his diary and began to complain of chest pains. I imagined it had something to do with indigestion and the unnatural proportion of time that was spent lying down whilst eating. It became clear that it was not a passing discomfort and within an hour George was lying face down on the tent floor barely able to speak with the pain. I gave him some water and tried to get him to breath deeply but gently and with time the pain lessened. Neither of us could explain the reason behind the sudden attack; not even heartburn can result in agony like I saw on his face. I gave George the night off any jobs to let him rest and hoped that the problem would not resurface. Aside from an underlying chest problem which may have gone undetected or extreme heartburn, we were at a loss as to the cause. Thankfully, there would be no re-occurrence.

We experienced a variety of weather conditions over the days that followed, as if a reminder as to the unpredictability of our adopted 'home'. On two days, my journal described that the 'wind speed kept increasing to more than thirty-five miles per hour and so we camped as a precaution. Frost-nipped private parts,' and 'Not a day to remember. Hand unbelievably cold to start and ability to do jobs impaired. Clear skies are retaining no heat.' The next, I wrote, 'A great day. Able to do jobs without excruciating pain.'

Whenever we were forced to temporarily erect the tent in very high winds, we were determined to get out skiing again that day. Winds always seem worse from inside the tent anyhow. It was a form of damage limitation to our mileage but also we needed to relieve the frustration and boredom of lying in the tent. Even a few miles gained on a bad day was a welcome mental boost and proof that we were still making progress. On one particular occasion, George and I did not even lay out our sleeping mats or unpack our rucksacks, such was our determination not to let the wind beat us. We nibbled on a single bar of chocolate and then went back out into the clouds of drift flying past at head-height, not the usual ankle-height.

Comfort on the expedition was often correlated to the state of cloud cover. Although cloud and the associated loss of contrast can affect navigation, the relative warmth can make life a great deal more productive. This is due to the blanket of cloud not allowing the sun's warmth to escape so easily and so keeping the surface layer of air warmer. This can make the difference between a clear day at minus thirty-five Celsius and a cloudy day at minus twenty-five. I cannot convey enough how large a difference this makes to general life. Only when temperatures rise to the mid-summer heights of minus five or above does wet snow affect ski and sledge movement. There

143

is a perfect window of operation for the smooth surfaces of the sledge runners and ski undersides. This is due to their interaction with the snow and ice surface which varies a great deal due to temperature. Too cold, around minus forty, and the snow forms crystals which cannot be melted by the pressure of the runner sliding over them. This creates a feeling of hauling through thick sand. Too warm, as temperatures approach zero, and the snow is saturated and wet, making it sticky. This would cause havoc with the unwaxed skis and skins. Between minus fifteen and minus twenty-five, we found the best skiing conditions and the sledges slid well, provided the snow was not deep.

Despite popular assumption, temperatures in the High Arctic and Antarctic are not constantly caught in the depths of dismal temperatures. As previously mentioned, quoted figures are usually exaggerated, a worst case scenario or only at the coldest point of the journey. This is especially true since most shorter expeditions of between one and two months are timed to experience the very best of the conditions. Few know that many expeditions, when starting out from the coast of Antarctica, ski in temperatures of only minus ten, suitable for wearing only a single layer. Likewise, temperatures on the second leg of Weber and Malakhov's North Pole return expedition reached highs causing the pair to overheat. Unfortunately for George and me, we would experience the full force of the spring weather and not enjoy the 'warmth' of August. Mercifully, we escaped the dark months of January and February. Such was the compromise we were forced to make in order to have reasonable sledging conditions.

For those with experience of navigation, especially in places with precious few points of reference, it may not come as a surprise that we had problems with this aspect of our journey. Besides the challenges of white-out already discussed, the innate workings of the human being seem to be the major flaw. We are just not very good at walking in a straight line. Or at least George and I are not. I was most certainly worse than

George. This occurred even on sunny days when we were able to use our own shadow as a sundial and tried to stay on track. Just a few moments of concentration lapse and we would veer off away from our intended path.

The reasons for this irritation are numerous. Firstly, people are not used to having to judge their direction on stimuli other than sight. As you walk down a street at home, you walk in a straight line because your mind is subconsciously and constantly watching the edges of the pavement and making corrections to your direction. Closing your eyes and attempting the same simple task becomes nigh on impossible. This was the challenge we faced. Even if we managed to identify something we considered a good landmark, perhaps a prominent sastruga to use as reference, soon a similar one appeared and we would then be unable to tell the difference. Day after day, week after week we went through this sequence of hope, contentment and then frustration at our own inability. Poor contrast and visibility simply exacerbated the problem and we became more reliant on our compasses. These were themselves unstable and jumpy due to our proximity to the Magnetic North Pole.

A second reason for our deviations came from the sledges. Our rope traces, via a bungee shock-cord, attached to loops on either side of our harnesses. Due to the enormous weight of the sledges, even though with our food and fuel consumption this slowly lessened, they affected our movement greatly. If one trace was slightly shorter than the other, it tugged at our backs momentarily before the other. This had the effect of gradually tugging us in one or the other direction. Until we had perfected the traces, I would still always curve to the right.

I vented into my journal, 'Irritated at how inept I am at walking in a straight line. Ten paces and I'm 45 degrees to the right. George still makes stats and talks of the end – good spirits.' George's statistics were a constant stream of numbers, similar to mine, and a vehicle to keeping him occupied mentally. I was not sure whether constant talk of the end of the journey was healthy, particularly at that early stage.

Chapter IX

'At times, during the long hours of steady tramping across the trackless snow-fields, one's thoughts flow in a clear and limpid stream.'
Sir Douglas Mawson

The boredom whilst in harness was a price to pay for our huge ambition and it would fast become the greatest torment either of us would have to bear. The sheer amount of time that George and I spent out in the featureless, white vastness of Greenland was beyond easy comprehension. I tried to rationalise it by comparing it to college-term periods back at home but these thoughts always seemed to fall somewhat short of the mark. The scales we had to consider were simply appalling. After all, our quest was mostly about mental stamina once the physical aspect has been rationalised.

There are an infinite number of ways to mentally prepare for a period of sensory deprivation and physical hardship and an equal number of ways to handle it once out there. There are overriding principles that have always run through my mind, on polar expeditions or not, which have been a foundation of strength. I do not believe in the tactic of blinkering oneself to the realities of the predicament in order not to become overwhelmed. This is an 'out of sight, out of mind' process, which is, in a way, a cheat and destined to reinforce failure once the otherwise unprepared soul is exposed to the raw facts.

One principle is that 'if you let the little things slip, the big things follow.' This is a question of standards and the art of keeping them high throughout, regardless of fatigue. It is so tempting to start letting small parts of your life slip, such as waking time and length of sledging sessions. They may seem

147

like the easiest course of action at the time and seem to have no real effect on the big picture. Quite the opposite is true as these are cumulative and will ultimately send those involved into a spiral of laziness and failure. I have found that this can be as relevant in any walk of life, not just in an extreme situation like the one George and I found ourselves in. Secondly, and more importantly to me, is the fact that 'no-one is in charge of your mind but you.' This is so often forgotten and can give way to excuses, blame and resignation to the 'inevitable'. The human mind is the most complex thing, especially when under major stress. The smallest things can fundamentally affect mood. Music for instance, which George and I utilised, can have the effect of transporting a person from a state of ecstatic excitement to despondency. People tend to reinforce their current temperament with more similar stimuli and end up in a spiral.

The difference, as far as I can tell, between those who appear outwardly stable and those who fluctuate from high to low is the ability to control their sensitivity to this. The very ability to realise and fully appreciate that you are in control of your own frame of mind is at once a form of mental strength. It is one thing to tell yourself this but another to actually believe it and let it manifest itself in the real world. Negativity and despair come from nowhere other than inside your own head and so it is only from the same place that these thoughts can be overcome. The temporary mental creation of an external source from which these thoughts come, can be a way that they become more powerful than they should. It seems that if 'someone else' is telling you something, it can support your own uncertainty. These are the mind processes natural to a human and have to be nipped in the bud if they are to be overcome. There is a fundamental difference between a macho blindness to the facts with the constant reinforcement of 'winning thoughts', and a genuine mental strength. The former will likely result in the accumulation of doubts and worries and the person will not have real control over their mind, only appearing to do so. This can explode when stresses go on for too long or become too intense. What I endeavoured to achieve, all considered, was the latter. As such, the epic journey across the icecap was slowly being achieved and I did not feel an anger or despair bubbling inside me. I found myself capable, and willing, to go on and I felt lucky and privileged that I had found a strategy of approaching the task sustainably.

Admittedly, the thoughts that swirled through my head were far-reaching and at times strange. They varied throughout the day. In the mornings I had a torrent of thoughts and these became a mere trickle by the end of the hard, last sessions of the day. In order not to be overcome by thoughts and not to waste their precious time-passing attributes, I queued them. Different topics of thought became designated to various sessions daily. Another bonus was that, due to my accumulating fatigue, I often found myself able to cover the same subjects on consecutive days and not notice the repetition. That way, thoughts and discussions with myself lasted a long time. The types of thoughts were usually related to the sort of mental stimulation I was lacking. On rare occasions, when the surface was hard enough not to require us to ski line astern and the wind was low, George and I would talk. This would be invaluable to both of us – conversation is an experience you do not miss so sorely until you are without it.

Other mental journeys were of one of two types. First were the long, rambling day dreams with many tangents. They were my personal favourite as you got literally lost in your thoughts and hours could pass blissfully before being shocked back to reality. The other sort were equally important but tended to account for less time and led to more clock-watching: a depressing pastime. These were structured thoughts where I methodically worked through a problem or a design. During my time sledging, I had arbitrarily invented a helicopter-mounted camera, written a cookbook and even designed my dream house. The extreme nature of our mental pressure is demonstrated by how I, bizarrely, mentally positioned where I wanted power sockets in this hypothetical house. Many of these thoughts have long since faded, thankfully, and most seem amusing now. A psychologist will probably tell you that this says all manner of things about my personality. However, at the time these thoughts served a purpose and got my mind through the long days.

Liquid water is a vitally important resource for any polar traveller. As any athlete will tell you, water and hydration is central to performance. Without this, nothing will make you perform adequately, especially when the task is great. There is, of course, one great benefit to polar expeditions when compared to those in the jungles, deserts and even at sea. There is fresh water everywhere around you; the only problem is that it is frozen, often thirty or more degrees below zero. The need to collect, store and carry large quantities is therefore not present and this is a great relief when considering the weight of a fully-laden sledge. Besides being heavy, it is also not advisable to melt lots of water and then store it in bottles, as the ambient temperatures will soon cause it to freeze. George and I had soon become familiar with the annoyance of water freezing into an ice block in the neck of a bottle, denying access to the liquid water beyond. A few violent stabs with a metal spoon usually solved the problem. A sensible system was to melt sufficient water for the one day. Since we had only one stove operating at a time and boiling a pan of ice took quite some time, this process could take hours just for a few litres of water. As such, we did not want to have to do this in the mornings. Instead, we boiled the water for the next day the night before. This had the added advantage of allowing us to use the plastic Nalgene water-bottles as hot water bottles throughout the night in our sleeping bags. I used to nestle one by my feet to thaw my toes and one alongside my torso. The effort taken to make water from ice meant that any spillages were taken to be a major disaster. We both managed to spill entire pans full of hot water onto the snow surface at one time or another. This was referred to as being a 'tent rhino', a term I first heard from Rich when he knocked over his mug of tea the previous year. This error was followed by desperate apologies and a promise to boil another at breakneck speed. Only once did one of our 'hot water bottles' leak into a vapour barrier in our sleeping bags during the night and this bottle was quickly relegated to backup use only.

By the arrival of May, we had been travelling for well over a month. The monotony of the expedition had started to fully set in and both George and I were coming to terms with the fact it would not be over soon. To make matters worse, snow conditions were poor and I noted that, 'sledges felt 180kgs again'. This was compounded by the return of sastrugi, again always at ninety degrees to our direction of travel. We also began to encounter large collections of barchans. These are dunes of powder snow, similar to those created from sand in the deserts. These new obstacles saw to it that we could not forge a straight path across the icecap as they could not be met head on with any success.

As an expected effect of our accumulated time on the ice, medical issues slowly began to appear, although none required treatment with the various pills and potions we had to cover most eventualities. Most required simple running repairs and included chafing on the inner thighs. This discomfort was easily alleviated by repositioning the merino wool base layers and trouser cords. More concerning was the onset of excruciatingly painful peeling of the skin on two of my fingers. This was the fallout from the frost injury I had sustained a few weeks previously. The middle and ring finger of my left hand began to peel back like a banana, revealing raw, red flesh beneath. I knew that the flesh was alive and healthy due to the good blood supply right to the tip of each finger but it was a definite case of frost nip. It was therefore not a threat to either my fingers or the expedition but a condition which must be treated with care to avoid re-injury. I ensured

151

that priority was given to hand-warmth over the cold days to come. The icecap itself was, by all accounts, devoid of life and so the only source of a potential infection would come from the bacteria we ourselves carried with us. This would need careful attention since an infection could spell an end to our hopes.

Day 38   2nd May
305 miles covered 'No longer dreaming about losing unsupported status which is nice!'

My sleep was a never-ending battle between the noise of the wind and the fatigue draining my mind and body. I began to realise that I was waking in the morning to the same recurring dream or nightmare, as I might consider it. I dreamt about taking a break from the expedition, flying home, having a home-cooked meal before flying back out to resume the journey. All of this took place amid blissful happiness and without thinking that something was wrong. Only towards the conclusion of the dream, as I resumed the expedition, did the realisation dawn on me that my convenient pit stop in England spelt the end of our unsupported status, quite obviously. Once awake in the tent, back in reality, it took a minute or so to realise that I had not, in fact, taken a short sojourn home and still held the precious unsupported status. This status, in reality, can be compromised by a variety of means, such as an emergency resupply, use of power support or an emergency evacuation of a team member. I was thankful to write the journal entry that marked the abrupt and unexplained end of such bizarre dreams.

On later reflection, I think these episodes illustrated a number of things about my state of mind at the time. Firstly I was, without being conscious of it, troubled about the security of the main purpose of the trip, travelling without aid. At that stage our mileage achievements were strong but still behind a strict schedule, defined by dwindling food supplies. We had since off-loaded around twenty kilograms of supplies into depots at fifty mile intervals. I simply did not know whether we would make it to the coast and back in time; I believed it but could not guarantee it. I suspect that it was mainly a result of being in the second month of the expedition, with many unknowns yet to come, and having it all to play for. Also, it shows how much weight and emphasis I put onto this man-made enigma, the unsupported status. It makes me again consider the complex support debate but ultimately reassures me that the simple way is, for me, the right way. To some outside the polar community it may seem pointless but to others it means a great deal. A parallel situation could be the satisfaction a pilot feels when landing an aircraft themself, manually, rather than with electronic aids doing the work for them. The pilot landed that plane, no-one else, and that is something to be valued.

The wind began to grow as George and I approached the four hundred mile point, past half-way across our first icecap crossing, and slowly began to lose altitude towards the west coast. Little did we know at the time, Day 39 of the expedition, but we would contend with this one stubborn wind for the next month and beyond. This constant tormentor came from the high ground above us on the icecap and introduced new headaches for our isolated double-act on the ice. In the evenings, as I prepared the tent for the night, shovelling snow onto the valance 'skirt', I began to realise that I had left small gaps in the 'snow seal' around the base of our home. The process of weighing down the valances was simply to keep the tent on the surface and stop air flowing underneath it and, as such, airtightness was not necessary. Under most conditions, even with a fair wind, this was not an issue. Unfortunately, as the days of sustained high winds continued, we developed a build-up of snow powder in the outer partitions of the tent, outside the main sleeping area. This blocked the ventilation panels at the head of the tent and covered our boots and other pieces of equipment banned from entering our inner

153

tent sanctuary. Needless to say, the experience of boots full of cold snow, which soon became cold water, was not to be recommended. As a result, I had to become far more diligent with my shovelling duties. This was easier said than done at a time in the day when I was physically exhausted and the evening temperatures were starting to plummet. The only thing on my mind was the warmth of my sleeping bag and rest. The result of plugging the gaps was that drift no longer entered the outer partition and our quality of life improved significantly as a result. Drift is to the Polar Regions what waves are to the sea: ever present except when conditions are dead still. As the building block which eventually creates the dreaded sastrugi, drift is a seemingly weightless cloud of snow powder propelled along by the wind a foot or so above the ground. Only when the full fury of the katabatic wind is unleashed does the drift become so tall it engulfs a skier. It is undeniably beautiful as it flows over the ice endlessly and has become the focus of so many filmmakers trying to capture the essence of an icecap.

Shovelling snow and ice onto the valances was only part of the story in our daily evening routine. The fact that I always began the first sledging session of the day as leader meant that, since we usually skied eight sessions, George concluded the day ahead. George, who had excellent discipline for finishing a session not one second too early, would ski to a halt when our travel for the day was over. Feelings were invariably those of relief and excitement for the warmth and food ahead. Indeed, I found that I would be thinking only of food for that last seventy minute session. Since the surface was, without fail, a patchwork of crusty areas, sastrugi and dunes, there were good and bad areas to pitch the tent. Some were very soft and powdery with dunes and despite the ease with which skis could be driven in as corner anchors, they were not suitable. This was because powerful winds could quickly come from nowhere in our unpredictable environment and rock-solid anchors were therefore vital. In addition, a soft covering in combination with our weight and heat during the night would dent the surface and lead to an uncomfortable night. The last thing we needed as we awoke for another day's toil was a stiff neck.

Other patches on the icecap were rock hard just a few inches under the surface and could not even be breached by an ice axe, rendering them useless for a good pitch. Nine times out of ten George, who was fifteen feet ahead of me as we concluded the day, would already have spotted a likely spot for us. Only rarely did I veto the location and decide to travel on for a minute or so and find somewhere better.

From this point on, as with most aspects of our life on the ice, we shifted into automatic pilot for the evening routine. Two items needed to be laid on top of the sledges during the day, one was the rolled up tent and the other was the solar panel performing its trickle-charging duties. It varied who carried what and so the first job was to position the tent-bearing sledge at the head of the pitch site. This was defined by the direction or likely future direction of the wind. As previously described, our tunnel design tent was sensitive to the direction of the wind and had to be placed aerodynamically. As a critical safety policy, we attached a loop of the tent onto a karabiner connected to the sledge to avoid a freak gust ripping our home from our grasp.

Next the windward corners were anchored with a pair of skis and the remainder of the tent 'sausage' allowed to unroll onto the snow. This was usually amply aided by the force of the wind. Since the bendy poles were already threaded through the skin of the tent and ready to tension, we quickly took our places on either side. Dependent on whose fingers were warmer and therefore most dexterous, one of us held a pole end in an eyelet whilst the other forced the pole into its tensioned state and clicked it into its relevant eyelet. This was repeated down the length of the tunnel and then, once erected into shape, we placed the final ski anchors at the leeward end.

As time went on, this routine became so well practised that we were able to complete it in a couple of minutes, vital in adverse conditions. We were now, much relieved, able to get under cover, although George usually do so first. His job was to clear out the inevitable ice and hoarfrost debris which had ended up in our living quarters from the previous night, despite our strict 'no snow in the tent' rule. For this, George used a vital piece of polar expedition equipment, the tent brush. This was, in truth, a washing up brush which cost fifty pence in England. Slightly short of company, alone on the ice, the pair of us gradually gave most inanimate objects a name. This is nothing new and particularly common amongst those who travel solo. We even borrowed the name for the brush, 'Mavis', from fellow Englishman Pen Hadow − it just seemed a good name. Beyond that, the tent was christened 'Terrance', and the sledges had various names that varied depending on how well they were behaving. There was a more serious purpose to cleaning ice out of the tent, rather than just to make it look neat and tidy. Whilst lashed to the top of a sledge, the tent was exposed to temperatures far below freezing, which kept the contents frozen. Once the tent had occupants, however, the sun warmed the air inside and our body warmth would melt the layer of frost and ice. This had the result of soaking our clothing and sleeping equipment, most of which was not waterproof.

Whilst George was doing the cleaning, I remained outside, dragging the second sledge into place outside the door and then passing in the items which were not already in our tent rucksacks. The absolute key, especially with lots of blowing drift, was to open the zip on the sledge canvas only as much as necessary, to avoid snow getting in. On the couple of occasions we failed to do so, we were greeted in the morning by a substantial weight of snow inside the sledge. This was not welcome given the fact the sledges already weighed a great deal. Also, we ran the risk of getting vital equipment, such as gloves, wet if the snow melted.

Once I had placed the only guy-line we used, the windward line attached to an ice axe, I was able to pile into the tent entrance. Embarrassingly, I often forgot I still had my hauling harness attached and so had to make an unwelcome extra trip outside. Meanwhile, George had been laying out our sleeping equipment. I proceeded to dig a two foot by two foot hole in the snow just inside the front door of the tent, before zipping up and keeping the external world outside, if only for a few precious hours. This hole served both as a cold and gas sink and also as a location to place one's feet in a makeshift seat.

The sink was a great success as the coldest air from the tent interior naturally flowed into the sink, away from us, especially after the stove was fired up. More importantly, since the sink hole was placed next to the cooking area, any undetected gas leak from the fuel bottle and apparatus would be likely to flow into the sink and decrease the chance of a disastrous tent fire. We did survive a potentially fatal error as a cigarette lighter, used in conjunction with 'flint and steels' to light the stove, was left near to the base. As both George and I were busy with other tasks in the tent, we both jumped with a start as we heard a crack with the volume of a gunshot. Frantically checking the stove and shotgun to ensure that a fire was not about to take hold, I saw the lighter some three feet from the stove. It had heated up by the windshield until the plastic canister punctured and exploded with a violence that belied its small size. On closer inspection, we could see a small hole in the side of the lighter through which the burning lighter fuel had shot. It was a major wake-up-call and reminder to further improve our 'drills' regarding flammables.

In the same way that George would do in the morning, I assembled the stove, pumped the fuel bottle and began to prepare our dinner. This would be substantial and consist of a main meal, which varied from chicken curry to shepherd's pie. The only unpopular option we found was chilli con carne. Although it tasted good and did not have major digestive

157

implications, eating it was an ordeal. We took great care in the protection of our lips from the cold, wind and sun but they were still permanently chapped and sore. The spice in the meal ensured that our lips stung badly for quite some while. The finale was my personal highlight of the day, hot chocolate drink. This was a Dutch blend chosen by Kees from Be-Well and tasted fantastic, as well as warming us and providing calories. We soon found that one half of a sachet was sufficient for a good mug and so enjoyed two mugs each per night.

Whilst eating, I had concurrently been melting snow for the next day, writing my diary and doing any odd jobs that were outstanding. I would also send the satellite update if it were my turn. This would include the technical details of our day's travel as well as a short message to the wider world. Sending this usually stimulated the download of any incoming messages. These were incredibly valuable and the few days when there were none caused a cloud to descend over our little world. By this point, George and I were so keen to sleep that our kit was tidied, our teeth brushed and then the inner door was zipped up. This sealed us into the sleeping capsule and allowed us to hang the alarm above my head and settle down. I cannot overstate how wonderful the feeling of reaching this state each day was. The pleasure never diminished and we truly appreciated every moment of getting ready for bed. After placing our socks and hot bottles in our 'slugs' (sleeping bags), we shuffled around and filled our slug compression sacks with our down jackets, which made ideal pillows. Then, with a quick, 'Goodnight!' we closed the head drawstrings to complete our cocoons.

Day 41   5th May
333 miles covered 'Usual saga of cold fingers in the morning. Managed to burn myself tonight on the bloody pan.'

Evening routine on the expedition did not, however, always go to plan. Aside from the sleeping mat stabbing incident, on one occasion I grabbed the red-hot pan lid with a bare hand and branded my finger with the shape of the handle. My expletives are still vivid in my mind to this day. It was made worse by the fact my hands were numb and so I did not let go of the burning metal until I heard a sizzling sound. Then, sure enough, the pain came.

Looking back now on the expedition in May, it seems like a no man's land of memories. Unlike other parts of the journey, which were consistent in their challenges and from which I derive very clear mental landmarks, May is a grey area. We were still moving slowly and approaching a cumulative five hundred miles, some days behind schedule. I can only suppose that the physical efforts and subsequent exhaustion made the days merge into a mix of woolly half-memories. My journal was equally confused as one day would declare a triumph and the next have a distinctly sombre tone. Consecutive days of my entries spoke of being 'horribly ill in the morning – too much ghee,' 'fewer bitter nights,' 'Fixed camera – catch up time!' and 'No movement. Really annoying.' Although George and I never discussed it in such terms, May was a time to get through. It was not a time to build up time ahead of schedule but rather a period to scramble through in any way we could. There was no glimmer of the end, or even the halfway point. In truth, the success or failure of the expedition would ultimately be forged in those cold and windy days of May.

A dramatic change occurred on one day when George and I, maddened by the unrelenting wind, chose to travel regardless. The icecap took on a bizarre appearance I never saw again for the remainder of our journey. Despite a total lack of cloud cover and good contrast, we could barely see the blue sky above as we exited the tent to begin our day. Such was the extreme nature of the drift and snow powder which flew around us from all directions. All the things which were usually clear, such as the sastrugi and even each other, were hazy and soft. There was a kind of ethereal feel to the place, if you could for a moment ignore the maelstrom going on all around you. Never before had I felt that I was in a more alien place.

One major hitch, which came from high winds and flying snow, was when George and I took a brief break on the front of our sledges between sessions. We naturally faced our backs into the wind to shield our faces. Since the wind was travelling at around forty-five miles per hour, this resulted in an area of low air pressure right in front of our faces and upper torsos. Clouds of snow then flew into this void and made it nigh on impossible to eat or drink in these vital rest stops. Regardless of whether we faced the wind or turned our backs on it, we ended up with a face full. Such inconveniences are a part of living in the Arctic, where nothing ever happens quite as you expect. The only strategy to overcome them was to either try out lots of variations to find a solution, or simply ignore them, which was easier said than done.

I wrote that night, we 'headed out into the heavy and bizarrely cold wind. Worsening fingers and George got a numb bum. Nearly forty below zero plus wind-chill in May. Why?' Wind-chill calculations that day put us well below minus sixty and into the extreme risk category for frost injury and hypothermia. In these conditions, exposed flesh will freeze in less than five minutes according to US government weather experts.

As we skied towards our target compass bearing, I heard a strange buzzing sound above my head. It must have been very loud since I could make it out over the howling of the wind. I turned round to ask George if he could hear it and saw that he was pointing to the sky, obviously having heard the same noise. It was the unmistakable sound of an aircraft engine. I knew that there were no trans-icecap flight-paths at low altitude this far north. Most of the flights occur across the thinner width of Greenland in the extreme south. It must

160

have been a charter aircraft – the Twin Otter operated by Air Greenland. The only reasonable explanation was that another expedition must have requested an emergency evacuation. It was May and as such, a few short, three-week guided trips were taking place. Later, Matt would confirm our suspicions, as he said that almost all other expeditions had aborted due to the conditions and illness. George and I had been in the environment for nearly two months by that point. We had, therefore, become well-conditioned to the brutal weather and our definition of 'bad' was consequentially different from most. I wondered how I would have felt to have been dropped straight from civilisation into that chaos.

Day 47   10th May
380 miles covered 'Morale starting to waiver – even culinary creations can't last forever. Low rations not good – had to share last night. Legs feel weak and got itches.'

Having undertaken a detailed set of calculations in the tent regarding our status with food and miles achieved, the picture was not good. We could not afford to eat full rations whilst not skiing full days as this would cause an accumulating supply deficit. Half-rations were the unavoidable solution. Due to lost hours skiing, we could not afford to eat food meant for later stages of the journey and rely on making up the time later. There were an infinite number of unknowns between then and the end of the trip. We could not rely on good luck. We might be delayed on the West Coast or have a delay before the polar high pressure of summer arrived to improve conditions.

The next day, however, brought us back onto full rations and a set plan in our heads of how we would get to the West Coast. I had broken this down into chunks so that we could concentrate on making targets in the short-term. Obviously, there was no point in getting to the West Coast and Baffin Bay if we then had insufficient supplies to return home. We had

161

some of our supplies safely laid in depots but these were far from being an insurance policy. We could be unable to access them for a number of reasons. To counter this I decided on a policy, which was that we must always be carrying enough supplies to keep us fed on half rations should two consecutive depots fail. This translated to approximately a week's rations. As a rather frightening statistic, our return journey planning necessitated that at times, in the middle sector of the expedition, we would have less than six days supplies in our sledges with up to fifty days yet to ski. There would be little room for error. Being stranded in the middle of the icecap without food or fuel would make for either a catastrophic or humiliating end to our plans.

The full rations, combined with the ever lightening sledges and slowly declining slopes, meant that we were finally skiing at full potential. We achieved and maintained speeds of around two miles per hour with sledges a little over 110kg. It became a competition between George and myself who could break the speed record for a session whilst leading out front. One day it was 1.9 miles per hour, then 2.0, then 2.1. We decided that despite our welcome new-found pace, we should rein each other in, as we found that we were becoming very fatigued. Our bodies had already been through a great deal and were not as resilient as we might have liked. Meanwhile, food continued to make its way into our every thought. 'My thoughts are increasingly of food. I get hungry in the day and crave to dig into my saved rations. Will Not. Drift continued. Keen to catch up on lost sleep.' Much sleep had been lost to the roar of the high winds.

Besides the desire for foods that were fresh, colourful and flavoursome, other pressures began to emerge now that we had been travelling for seven weeks or so. There is the undeniable fact that despite the low temperatures which can help considerably, hygiene is a problem. I had begun to develop maddeningly uncomfortable itches on my back in the first ski hauling session of many days. George and I had one change of underwear long-johns, made from merino wool, which were to be our reward for reaching the West Coast. This was over twenty days away and the one change was all our weight restrictions could allow. Unsurprisingly, as with any other basic job, washing was far more complex and uncomfortable than it is in most other environments. We regularly used wet wipes to undergo a basic clean but we both badly needed a deep cleanse. We had, as we both commented to the other with some dismay, begun to smell vaguely of digestive biscuits. After we had established that neither had secretly stashed any biscuits into sledges, our own clothes were the obvious culprits. On the evening of Day 51, George and I embarked on a rapid but welcome wet wipe extravaganza which improved our spirits no end.

I had also enjoyed a good half-hour session of cleaning my red woolly hat. It had remained on my head for the vast majority of the past two months, night and day, and so tended to collect enormous amounts of my hair which became interwoven into the fabric. By repeatedly tugging at the hat, I was able to free huge tufts of hair and ended up with a hat which felt, if not genuinely, refreshed and cleaned. My only other worry was the way that my socks were wearing. George and I had chosen different brands of sock and it seemed that his were wearing slightly better than mine, even if their insulation properties were not quite as good. I had accumulated a number of holes in the heels and so rotated the tube sock to designate a 'new heel'. There was, of course, a finite number of times I could do this and so the life of my first pair of socks was nearing the end. I had become strangely fond of my socks and vowed they would last me to the West Coast, whereupon the second set would be dug out of a dry-bag.

Chapter X

'We were the only pulsating creatures in a dead world of ice.'
Frederick Cook

A small revolution came to the expedition when I broached the topic of skiing side by side as opposed to one behind the other. In crevassed areas or where the snow was deep, line astern was the only option due to safety. However, we soon realised that we had been skiing on a good surface for some days and it was no longer necessary. We had been lost in our own thoughts for countless hauling sessions. Now there was a prospect of breaking the monotony by skiing side by side – allowing conversation. Of course, this was only viable in low winds and if it did not affect our pace on the ice, which was critically important at that point. Topics varied from our families to photography and from future travels to tetrathlon, a sport which George excelled at.

The evenings were often dominated by our jobs and practical conversation and so general discussion was a welcome change. It even allowed us to touch on something which we had barely talked about and fascinated me. George strongly advocated the use of health products made by a Japanese company that operated by a network of distributors. Following some research on the web before we left, it turned out that there was a lot of speculation about scams and pressure selling surrounding the company. Most of the claims about vitamin products and sleeping systems apparently had no scientific basis and the cost of the items was suspiciously high. I am generally a sceptic regarding anything I consider 'hocus-pocus' and this brand rang alarm bells. It turned out that despite my reasoning and protestations, the answer was just that those who had 'not tried it just would not understand.' I realised that I was banging my head against a brick wall and moved to another topic. In any case, our extended debate allowed us to pass a substantial amount of time and allowed me to learn a little more about what really made George who he was. Perhaps I was just being too methodical but I most certainly did not believe the middle of an icecap was the place to pursue something potentially divisive. We had thus far worked as a team almost without hitch and had a long time still to go as companions.

Beyond my concerns about the bizarre products as a principle, I had major misgivings about one particular aspect. One part of the 'system' was a magnetic insole with a high metal content. When I enquired as to their purpose, what followed was a stream of pseudoscience and I changed my angle of attack. I was seriously unhappy about George having metal inside his boots, next to his socks whilst in extreme low temperatures. Feet and toes, in particular, are susceptible to cold injury and placing a strong conductor of heat next to his foot seemed unwise beyond words. My protests were, however, to no avail and George continued with their use. Besides George's choice of footwear, we had bigger issues to deal with which put an end to our much appreciated period of being able to ski side by side. The wind had returned. Not only had it returned but it shifted to blow into our faces as we travelled, and the forecast for the next week was poor.

Day 55   19th May
483 miles covered 'Pinned under a blizzard. Only 3.6 miles [covered]. Two foot of powder flies through the air. The Arctic isn't giving an inch. Fingers are like wood and burn like hell on our sledging sessions.'

The Arctic again made a point of reminding us that we would not be permitted to crawl across its surface without being tested. It is no coincidence that the most violent and unpleasant conditions we experienced were also the ones that provided the most stunning vistas and phenomena. Sundogs were the first light shows of the day. They were the first we had seen since the aurora weeks back, when the sun dipped below the horizon and plunged the ice into darkness. Sundogs are a common name for parhelia, which are 'false suns' and appear to the sides of the sun to form a halo. They are caused by ice crystals in the air and appear in extremely low temperatures. George noticed the sundogs first and we attempted in vain to enjoy the unique experience. Most of our concentration was required to keep moving forward in a straight line and to avoid the large snow dunes that had suddenly appeared in our path.

The process of erecting the tent that night became a saga as we both struggled with dexterity in our fingers. It took both of our efforts to force a single tent pole into its eyelet and it was a great relief when we were finally able to collapse into the tent and take stock of our day. George turned to me and summed up the torrent of thoughts which must have been flying through both our minds with "At least we're not dead."

The next day saw yet more sundogs and I made a concerted effort to enjoy them. When I was researching polar expeditions by reading various accounts and speaking to veterans in person, a common piece of advice was to enjoy those special polar moments. There are so many sights and sounds that are entirely unique to the Arctic and Antarctic. It is so easy to become numb to your surroundings, especially when under pressure, and not fully appreciate those things which should define the experience. My efforts were rewarded as that morning, over the perfect parhelia which had formed, there was a complete double rainbow. I realised that it represented the widest variety of colour I had seen in months. These spectacles continued through most of the day's sledging until the wind lessened and the temperatures nose-dived as the evening drew near. We noticed that overnight, as Dagmar had forecasted, the wind became increasingly gentle and

167

turned to the northeast. This was welcome respite from the headwind which sapped our energy as we forged westward towards our halfway point. When the wind buffets your face-mask for prolonged periods, the risk from frostnip and frostbite increases substantially. We had made a point of increasing the frequency with which we checked each other's cheeks, ears and noses for good blood-flow. Luckily all was well, although I noted in my journal that I had chilly feet.

We had pushed past five hundred miles and the surface had become difficult yet again. I noted that it had become 'very uneven and bumpy. Jolts the back.' We also managed to cause the first bit of damage to our long-suffering tent. Whilst attempting to put up the tent in quicktime, a pole became snagged on part of the outer skin of the tent. Further pressure succeeded only in bending one of the sections of the pole and fracturing the end of another section. Since the damage was fairly minor and the pole still worked, I protected the end of the pole quickly with gaffer tape and fed it back into the tent. We only had one spare pole of each length and did not want to commit a precious replacement unless vital.

It was George who first suggested the idea of moving to night skiing. It is an undeniable fact that, as the weeks roll on in the Arctic into the summer, average temperatures slowly increase. Before long, daytime levels are up into the poor sledging window previously described. Although there was, for the central portion of the expedition, no real concept of night and day as the sun never set, the sun still dipped in the sky. This led to a drop in temperature during which we were usually having our tent time.

We were particularly conscious of our sub-optimal pace and the accumulated lag compared to our target schedule. Any increase in pace would be greatly appreciated to claw back some time. A colder surface and the increased glide it afforded could be just the boost we needed. This could be combined with the added glide we had from gradually shortening ski-skins. The sledge weights had slowly lessened as we had been laying depots at fifty-mile intervals. As the sledges began to slide more freely, this needed to be matched on the skis. By cutting strips off the high-friction adhesive skins, more smooth ski surface was exposed and the faster we could travel.

However, there was a limit to how far we could afford to trim the skins. Although, at that point descending slowly to the coast, we would have to climb back up as we began the return leg. This uphill hauling would again require grip. We did not want to entirely remove the skins, which were fixed in with screws, and so found a solution. Past a certain point we added smooth gaffer tape to the remaining skin in order to attain glide whilst not cutting off too much. This could be removed more easily later on if more grip was needed.

George believed that the night temperatures were more suitable than our current day temperatures and it was time to make the shift. He may well have been right and there was no proven solution to the problem. Since this would involve a twelve hour time-shift, we could either ski two days back-to-back or have an extended night's rest. Despite the desire to keep pushing I knew we could not choose the former.

I reasoned that the descent and climb back from the coast, and the technical ice we would encounter, would take its toll on us. We could ill-afford to start that phase of the expedition, now known randomly as 'Hector', more drained than necessary. The decision was thereby made to take an extended rest in order to begin skiing with a twelve hour shift. We would make good use of the time by undertaking a check of the inventory, making running repairs and melting plenty of ice. If the night change failed for any reason, we could easily make the change back and wait for a later date; it was worth trying.

Hector, the push to the coast, was something we had both been looking forward to for weeks. It represented the halfway point and, as such, was a concrete sign that the expedition was within our grasp. If we had sufficient supplies to get there, we knew we had enough food and fuel for the return buried in depots along the route. The only unknown was the fate of these depots. They were experimental to say the least. We would be hopping from resupply to resupply with precious little contingency in our possession. Regardless, it would be a mental victory, a break from the daily trudging step after step and then a move towards home.

George and I woke from a deep sleep as the sun was starting to ride low in the sky and knew it was time to get on the road. Within an hour of being on the move, it was clear we had changed too early. The surface was no better and the sun's different orientation made it difficult to navigate. I explained these thoughts to George and we immediately made the switch back. In all, we had, in fact, only 'lost' a couple of hours travel and a few bites of food in the transitionary periods. I promised that I would keep assessing the situation as I sensed George was eager to make the change.

It was around this time I became aware of the physical degradation that my body was enduring. Suddenly, I found myself able to wrap my fingers around my upper arms, something which would have been impossible in past weeks. Even my legs, which were being worked daily, were losing size and condition. The deficit of calories and especially protein was starting to have its insidious effect. My thoughts rolled into my journal as I wrote my concerns: 'Bitterly cold evening. Fingers too cold to write (effect of starvation?) Stunning sun and drift. Awful last two sessions.' It was my opinion that the slow onset of starvation was beginning to reduce our resistance to the cold. Although not as extreme as in March, the temperatures were still low as summer had not yet reached the cold North.

I also noted the need to lance a hard blister on my heel. A hard layer of skin had formed over a sore and swollen blister and so I needed to release the pressure. I passed a needle through the stove flame to sterilise it and plunged it deep into my heel with a squirm. Satisfyingly, the contents came flowing out and I proceeded to dress the wound before getting ready for sleep. I wrote increasingly about the coast and my excitement for it. The desire to see mountains and the sea was overwhelming.

The katabatic wind returned as we passed five hundred and seventy miles. This beckoned the descent to the coast in earnest, as the majority of the altitude to be lost would be in the final miles. The relatively sharp drop-off of the icecap on the coast was the main cause of the wind as it flowed off the plateau. Day 62 was particularly windy as I exclaimed on a new page, 'The wind still blows!' I also believed that a slow moving weather front was a contributor to our woes. To make matters worse, our weather forecasts were now not getting through at all and Matt explained that night that the satellite system providers and Iridium were working hard to find a fix, which they did a few days later.

Ever conscious of the need not to become complacent about our routines, we acknowledged that as the journey progressed, things would have to change. One example was the calorie balance throughout the day. We began to notice that we found the middle couple of sessions of the day particularly challenging and felt that more calories, as well as some more warmth, would help. By taking only a few spoonfuls of porridge and little ghee butter from our breakfasts, we made hot flasks of calorific porridge with a soup-like consistency. This would give us a much needed boost and re-warming drink as the day began to feel longer and more fatiguing. We found that the flasks served to keep warmth in the soups until the fourth session, after which we drank them. Eating our flapjacks, chocolate and nuts between sessions in the brief breaks, which we looked forward to immensely, was always a challenge. The gorilla mask, which would usually ice up, had to be peeled back to expose my mouth, whilst keeping my nose protected from the cold and wind. Using large, ungainly gloves, the aim was to then shovel in as much food as possible without dropping any; a mistake was heartbreaking. Large icicles that were caused by our breath and snot instantly

171

freezing and accumulating would always form from the bridge of our goggles and from our facemasks. These were very satisfying to snap.

We took some time one evening to rest in our sleeping bags and discuss the routes. First of all, we assessed our route out and the positions of the depots we had laid. Of course, they dictated the route we must take back. The path taken thus far had not been a straight line as might be imagined. Due to imperfect navigation in the early days, the shape of the plateau dome and our keenness to avoid proximity to the West Coast until necessary, we had travelled a soft S-shaped curve.

In order to make sure that important information and mapping was safe even if something happened to one of our sledges, we both had duplicate copies of everything from maps to permits and emergency telephone numbers. It never ceased to amuse us that instead of referring to the detailed satellite images of the icecap we had produced and waterproofed for the journey, we looked at a ripped-out page from an in-flight magazine. George had taken it from a waiting room in Iceland and it showed a tourist's overview of Greenland, including rudimentary contour lines. Bizarrely, we found it ideal for visualising progress and so used it throughout despite its increasingly dog-eared appearance.

Our attentions turned to the detailed satellite images of the West Coast, the glaciers and the overlaid lines of longitude and latitude. We had always nominated a target area to ski to, from which we would assess the route visually and using gut instinct. There was a huge zone of glacial tongues, crevasses and rocky moraine that we would need to negotiate. We planned to leave our sledges on the icecap and make the final ten-mile approach to the coast on skis and with only rucksacks on. We had small boot crampons for any particularly difficult ground. The biggest problem was keeping the weight of the rucksacks down as they had to contain all our essentials, including the huge tent, our food and fuel and sleeping kit. There was a reason sledges had been invented – to travel with heavy loads over snow and ice. Our attempts to increase speed and flexibility by leaving them behind would only work if the rucksack weights were very low.

Ultimately we loaded up the rucksacks, ready for a coastal push on three consecutive mornings, but these attempts proved to be premature. Having stood outside the tent, loaded the packs onto our backs and tried to move, the weight made us sink deep into the surface, even on skis. We persevered hauling our sledges in the meantime and travelled at an excellent pace despite them, setting our record of nineteen miles in a day.

Day 65   28th May

624 miles covered 'Wind speed >52mph. A day to remember for all the wrong reasons. Skis were snowed up and have to be de-iced with a knife. After only 90 minutes of slipping and sliding with storm force tail wind I called an end. Only just managed to erect tent. George spilt hot chocolate. Shared some.'

Day 65 was a truly awful day and encapsulated the most serious drama we had endured so far. I chose to use the complete story of our struggles with the tent as the preface of the book for this very reason. It was, however, the culmination of a day of struggle and very genuine fear. The morning conditions ensured that we had no visibility and the landscape resembled a sort of freezing hell. It was as if the entire surface had been picked up and was being thrown through the air. There was no point of reference to ski from and so we resorted to our white-out techniques from the weeks past. I knew from the outset that all was not well with the skis. It was the beginning of our long saga to optimise their glide and friction on the ice.

It soon became apparent that snow had become attached to the skins of the skis, had partially melted in the day and then refrozen rock hard overnight. This resulted in a hard layer of ice which rendered the skins useless. To make matters worse, the same thaw and refreeze cycle had begun to afflict the runners of our sledges. They felt like they weighed a ton, at a time when they should be near their lightest of the expedition. The pair of us forged onwards but I think we both knew that the day was about damage limitation rather than good mileage.

"This is getting crazy. We can stay out but it's the tent I'm worried about," I yelled at the top of my voice to George who was skiing only a foot or two away.

"Yeah you're right. My hands are feeling cold too and I can't warm them too easily," he replied. My own hands felt like they were entering a downward spiral of warmth. My wind speed reading as we left the tent was 48 miles per hour without gusts and it soon read 52.

"George, we're banging our heads against a wall out here," I said. "Let's push on a bit further and we'll make a call on the state of our hands. Then we'll call it a day. If the wind's still increasing we'll have dramas with the tent."

He nodded his agreement and we continued skiing in what we thought was roughly the right direction. We were only partially in control as the slippery surface and wind left us unstable on our feet. The deafening noise of the wind, combined with the knowledge that we were far from safe, sent my mind into a heightened sense of awareness. Those minutes are by far the most vivid from the expedition and I can still relive the moments months after with total clarity. The horrific thought then returned to me. What if we were unable to put the tent up? The wind seemed stronger than ever.

I poked George with the end of my ski pole, the only way to get his attention over the mayhem. He glanced over and I made a 'cut' hand gesture to signal it was time to get under cover. It was from that moment we endured the desperate struggle to get the tent up and stable. The fact that we did so probably relied a great deal on luck but also on an innate resolve to survive. We were undertaking awkward tasks with fingers that had long since lost feeling and any meaningful dexterity.

Regardless of the circumstances and testament to the design of modern polar tents, the tent stood firm once we had secured each corner and weighed down the snow valances. Still on an extreme adrenaline high and grateful to be out the wind, we set to our evening tasks with a real energy. We were in remarkably good moods considering the seriousness of the trial we had undergone. The only thing to dampen our spirits, however, was when George spilled his hot chocolate. It was our well-earned reward for a day of unusually hard work and his face changed from anticipation to anguish in a split-second. We shared the remaining mug, which did a magnificent job of warming us before it was time to sleep.

Even the next day, our experiences in the high winds dominated my thoughts. The tail-end of the katabatic storm that had rolled off the icecap was still with us. We both commented on strangely strong and cold gusts which 'made us shudder'. I sensed that all was not well with George as the day progressed. He skied very fast and was not keen on discussing anything in much detail. I am not sure whether there was something which had got to him particularly but I think the previous day must have had an effect. Despite being an extrovert character, he also had periods of introspective reflection during which I felt he used to dwell on difficulties. The storm had been a close call, we both knew it, and we had to learn lessons from it and then move on. Luckily, by the second half of the day, he was back to his old self. This late resurgence may have had something to do with our first sighting of a seabird.

Greenland has only the narrowest halo of inhabitable land around its coast and even this is largely devoid of life except for in the height of the summer. If we did not believe the coast was within our reach before, this bird confirmed it. The halfway point was seven hundred miles from Nagtivit, the furthest distance from our base-camp we would ever be.

It was therefore the most critical in terms of supplies and the long-term sustainability of the journey. Reaching the West Coast meant it was possible; we had everything to play for.

Just an hour before we were due to stop hauling, we both had our eyes fixed on the horizon. The sky was blue, the wind had dropped to a fresh breeze and we were playing a game. The first person to see the coast would win an extra serving of hot chocolate. George's eyesight was clearly sharper than mine as, all of a sudden, he let out a yelp of unbridled excitement.

"A mountain! It's a mountain. It's the coast!" he yelled at me. I looked over to see the tiniest speck of black over the icecap horizon. Indeed it was, the tip of a coastal mountain and the reward we needed most. Without another word we placed our ski poles into the snow, skied over to each other and hugged. We had made it to the West Coast, the real test of the viability of the expedition. For those few minutes we forgot that we still had to ski all the way to the edge of the icecap, which was still many miles away, and then start the long journey home. Distances of that sort no longer held the same dread they once did as our pace with sledges just below 90kg was approaching twenty miles per day. We had not travelled on unstable glacial ice since March and we knew that since it was now June, the advent of summer, there would be less snow cover.

Day 69   2nd June
691 miles covered 'Camped on top of glacier and a crevasse! Proceed to skis and rucksacks tomorrow. Quite nervous as it'll be the first technical section for ages. Want to get on with return.'

As we continued to approach the sea, the coast presented itself rapidly and we crested a large ice dome near the glacier system. For the first time we had a good view of the potential routes and locations of the crevasse fields, which were numerous. This had been impossible to do in detail

176

from satellite imagery, which was usually out of date or from the wrong time of year, when the ice was entirely different. There was a ribbon of mountains that was still shrouded in heavy snow and glacier tongues flowing through the gaps to the sea. We could just make out the sea and the huge icebergs floating in Baffin Bay. As we were beginning our journey all those months back, the sea would have been locked shut with pack-ice.

I called a halt to our approach with the sledges and said that we would launch our attempt on the coast the next day. We had plenty of jobs, such as preparing our rucksacks, pondering the best route and taking some photographs for sponsors. The visibility had closed in slightly which inhibited my attempts to see the dangerous ice ahead. On that account, we put up the tent on the dome crest and enjoyed our first 'room with a view' for months. George retired into the tent in order to organise it for our important planning evening as I retrieved our climbing gear and rope. Our harnesses, ropes, crampons and prusik loops had been stowed deep down in the sledges as they were not used on the icecap. It was remarkable how much space was now vacated in the sledge shells, having eaten or cached most of the food and fuel.

As I was returning to the tent on one of the final trips, my foot dropped straight through the surface of snow. I managed to catch my fall by twisting onto my side. Having yelled for George to come outside as quickly as he could, whilst watching his footing, I investigated the hole. It turned out that we had inadvertently set up camp on a crevasse.

We had tested the area with probes prior to putting up the tent but had clearly missed it. Using an ice axe and a probe, I excavated the area to ascertain the width and direction that the crevasse was travelling. It ran perpendicular to the flow of the ice and was only just over a foot wide. I hacked away at the two walls to make sure that I had found its full extent. Since we had found the crevasse and checked the surrounding area, we chose to stay put for the night as the surface seemed otherwise reliable. There was no guarantee that moving on would find us anywhere easier. It was, however, undeniably perturbing to find the floor of your tent could give way into a chasm of unknown size. Despite the fact we were no longer on the high slopes of the icecap at nearly nine thousand feet, there were still over a thousand feet of ice below our feet. Most of that altitude would need to be descended in those final few miles.

Having packed our rucksacks to an acceptable weight with all the necessary safety equipment, including the Personal Locator Beacon, we settled down to sleep knowing that we could expect an undisturbed sleep. My earlier concerns over the crevasse were due to the fact that I knew the heat from the tent would begin to warm and soften the ice surface underneath and possibly destabilise it. However, I was confident, after my investigations, that this would not happen. A last minute check of the satellite phone gave me an unexpected and pleasant surprise. A friend from university had become engaged to her boyfriend. I dutifully reported from the ice that the wedding date was saved! I closed my journal entry with: 'Great day but just want tomorrow to be over.'

On the morning of Day 70, we packed up our equipment and readied ourselves for a long ski. We aimed to reach the edge of the icecap and return to the sledges in one day and so we had to start early. Our camp was left in situ for us to return to for a well earned rest later that day. It was an odd feeling, for the very first time in over two months, to leave our sledges and the tent in place as we skied off downhill. The skis were our main safety item over the crevasses but we also moved throughout connected by a rope. The crevasses were plentiful and in multiple planes that made route selection difficult. They ranged from innocuous slots to medium size crevasses, easily capable of swallowing an unwary skier.

One great advantage was the speed at which we could ski. Without the sledges and with the descent towards the sea, we could pick up real speed. The icecap undulated in steep slopes and rises in these final miles. On the slopes, we approached real downhill skiing but had to keep an eye on our speed. Our skis were not designed for control on downhill sections and if we approached a crevasse, having spotted it too late, we might not be able to stop in time.

We dropped down over another crest to look back and see the ice that immediately adjoined our camp. Just a few metres over the top of an ice dome, out of sight of the tent, was a truly enormous crevasse field. It stretched hundreds of feet across and was one of the many sources of the main glacier systems. The crevasses were so active and disturbed that they were far more than cracks in the surface. These resembled the chaotic jumble of ice you are likely to see in the pressure zones and ridges of the Arctic Ocean.

George looked at me in amazement as if he could not believe that our tent was right next to the zone but we could not see it from our camp. The crevasse under our tent was no longer a mystery. There must have been hundreds of them snaking their way across, silently hidden from view by the snow layer. The only problem with the undulating surface was that after enjoying a quick descent of a slope, we then needed to ski up the opposite side. Navigation was not too easy either as the landmark references we were skiing from were obscured as we climbed up a slope.

Matt had mentioned before we left, backed up by our prior research, that areas near the coast as we approached June might begin to melt. The air temperatures were still decidedly arctic and we were at the highest latitude of the expedition. However, the intensity of the twenty-four hour sun accumulated and dips in the surface allowed small melt-pools to develop. These could be up to fifty feet across but would usually refreeze each night as the sun lowered in the sky and temperatures dropped. I was intrigued about these, irrespective of the climate change debate for which they unsurprisingly serve as evidence.

179

We spotted a melt-pool ahead and diverted to intercept it. It was evidently very shallow and the sun's reflection shone brightly out of the azure blue pool. On reaching it, we found it was entirely frozen and we were able to ski, or slide, over it. There were coloured spots and blemishes in the solid pool that we imagined were algae. The final undulation in the approach to the coast completed, George and I were then faced with the real test, the technical ice. The main glacier was totally impassable unless tackled siege-like over a number of days in full mountaineering style. I intended instead to aim for a large outcrop of rocky moraine that had a tail. This in turn extended down to the rocky headland and the sea.

Given George's apparent uneasiness and wide-eyed looks he gave each passing crevasse, I decided to route-find and have George on the rope fifteen feet or so behind. He was certainly not so much scared of them as he was intrigued. I often felt a tug on the rope as George had stopped to get his camera out and take a photograph down a chasm. It was yet another example of the bizarre human attraction to danger. I likened it to the overwhelming desire to walk right up to and look over the edge of sea-cliffs.

The surface became increasingly unstable, crevassed and rough. The ground consisted of sharp, crystal-like ice that tore at the skis and made us travel a hopelessly indirect route towards our goal, the moraine. We reached the moraine outcrop and looked down the glacier to assess the way forward. It was at that moment that I realised we had reached our furthest point. The ice deteriorated significantly thereafter and I could see row upon row of crevassed ice and melt zones which looked incredibly unstable. Our path was blocked.

Should we have had the luxury of time, we could have spent days slowly working our way down the final few hundred yards to sea level and the bay itself. Time was not on our side as we had taken a few more days than ideal to reach the West Coast. This was largely due to accumulating lost hours in storms and the slow pace in the sastrugi fields early on. Apart from the small contingency of food we had in the sledges for emergencies, we did not have a single flapjack to spare. Besides, it would have taken days to backtrack and move up the coast to find a better access point. We simply did not have that opportunity and there may not have been any chance of finding a better route.

We had crossed the icecap, descended from it onto the huge glacier but did not reach sea level. It was an undeniable disappointment. The sea was tantalisingly close but yet just out of reach. George and I had, due to weight constraints, only the bare essentials for glacier travel and I was not willing to let us end up at the bottom of a crevasse for the sake of pride. I thought of the great Norwegian polar pioneer, Fridtjof Nansen's words, 'I demolish my bridges behind me – then there is no choice but forward'. We had indeed demolished our own bridges and made our commitment to that glacier. We had also committed to the return journey by unloading our sledges into caches along the route. So be it. I knew the return was physically possible and turned my mind to it.

We had arrived at our halfway point and this was a signal that the remainder of the journey was only ours to throw away through weakness or complacency. We were healthy, if thin and tired, and we had laid our depots as planned. It was now up to us to work our way between them at pace and to get home. Nothing seemed more poignant on this occasion than to film a brief video diary for our collection and eat half a banana flapjack each. With floods of thoughts coursing through our minds, we turned for home. The route back up to the sledges and tent was long and would take more time, as we would have to travel uphill on quite a steep gradient. To makes life trickier for us, the surface was hard and icy, meaning that our tracks from the way down were scratchy and sporadic.

A few hours later, it was a great relief to find ourselves on relatively flat ice again, despite having a few minor moments with a crevasse or two. They were only small slots but nothing comes close to that heart-stopping moment when your foot breaks through the surface and you experience that falling feeling. Before long, George and I spotted the familiar shapes of the tent and our sledges. For us, they represented sanctuary and survival.

Chapter XI

'Never stop because you are afraid – you are never so likely to be wrong.
Never keep a line of retreat: it is a wretched invention.'
Fridtjof Nansen

George and I skied with real vigour towards our tents, enjoying our first steps in a homeward direction. For the first time I started to feel the long-term effects of our toil. I felt drained and weak in my body and weary in my mind, yet my spirit and resolve was as strong as ever. I smiled to myself as I believed that as long as the desire remained, my body would be able to hold on for as long as necessary. However, I knew also that the greatest tests were perhaps yet to come.

We had been skiing for seventy days, longer than many large scale past expeditions to the Poles. I wondered what it would be like for them to have achieved their goal and call in their aircraft for pick up. The elation and relief must be indescribable. We had elected to make the return, indeed it was fundamental to the purpose of the expedition. We had set out to ski further without any support than anyone previously. We both knew that we too would experience completion but the great prize was forty or so days in the future. The West Coast, despite the mental stimulation it provided, was something of a 'false summit' for us. We had promised ourselves an undergarment change once at the coast, our only one of the trip, but we decided to delay. Our trip down the glacier had been very hard work, especially given that we were not used to anything apart from putting one ski in front of the other, day after day. It was enormously tempting to just collapse into the tent, wash and then get underway the next day. We had made reasonably good time back to the tent and still had two or three hours of skiing before the official end of our sledging day. In a possibly unpopular decision, I said we should collapse the tent and make headway onto the icecap. I did not want to linger on the coast and felt we should regain our sense of icecap routine as soon as possible. The wind was still blowing in the same katabatic manner as before. The welcome tailwind from the descent had therefore become a headwind and this managed to chill us through our clothing despite the air temperature being a great deal better than in March or April.

Day 71   4th June
716 miles covered 'Lovely summer's day apart from the 30mph headwind and drift! The ice hills are very steep – lots of stress on legs. George being a little careless. Kicked over a Nalgene into the stove and loses concentration whilst navigating. Sure he will sharpen up once back on full ghee!'

In order to take advantage of the lie of the ice on our approach to the coast, George and I had decided on a curved route from our final depot instead of a straight line. We mulled over this decision in the tent whilst finally enjoying our wet wipe bath and base layer change. The feeling of fresh fabric on my skin was wonderful and I was happy to be rid of their skin and muck-encrusted predecessors. We looked at each other dolefully as we changed. We could both see the true scale of each other's weight loss, especially from the upper body. Also, our bodies had not seen real daylight in over two months and they looked it – pale and unhealthy. My thinning waist had left my trousers struggling to stay up. Since I only had the single pair of outer trousers, I made do with a do-it-yourself solution. Using a reel of thread brought for miscellaneous repairs and using one of the staple skills of the polar traveller, I set to sewing the waistband into a bite. This resulted in making the waist a couple of inches slimmer although the neatness of my handiwork was not stellar.

184

Combined with a belt made from a rucksack utility strap, it was a great improvement.

We were enthused by the idea of not retracing our route back to that final depot. We had limited supplies and we felt that the benefit of flatter ice would not be so beneficial on the inevitable climb. The straighter route could save us a number of miles. The main question, however, was the major unknown – had our depot survived? The final one was clearly the most likely to be intact, given it had only been laid a week or so previously. If that had been destroyed, we would be in real trouble.

Whilst enjoying a short break during our day in the harness, I made a brief call home to report the good news of reaching the coast. My frustrations at George's phone usage soon returned as I wrote 'George makes more than six phone calls – he can see I'm not impressed. Totally unnecessary'. This time, I was sorely tempted to kick up a fuss but held back at the last moment. We were about to enter a critical phase of the journey. We had got on well thus far and bad blood between us would achieve nothing.

The next day did not bring much respite from the rising tension in the tent as a small supplies crisis brewed. We had meticulously planned every last item of food throughout the trip. Every depot had contained the correct number of daily food packages: three days for fifty mile depots and six days for hundred mile depots. We had set out with exactly one hundred and ten days of food and fuel each. The first sign that all was not well was as George was sorting through his sledge to make certain items more accessible. He had done a makeshift 'stock check' just to ease his mind and found what appeared to be a shortfall. He called to me inside the tent and I casually replied, "Are you sure?" He was, and I was soon summoned outside to check my own sledge. Sure enough, I found exactly the same. The difference between reality and what we expected was not dramatic but any miscalculation in our complex plans could be very serious indeed.

We recounted and recounted in disbelief and I even asked George to check the bottom of his sledge for holes. What a nightmare it would be to be slowly trudging our way home, dropping food parcels out of the bottom of our sledges as we went. Having resigned ourselves to the idea of having less food than expected, we retired to the tent to recalculate our required future mileage averages and our new plan to get to the first depot. Once there, we would be feeding off the depot system and everything would return to the original plan.

I found that we needed to cover an average of seventeen miles per day to reach the depot without having to ration, but this would eat into our contingency. My journal noted that this would be enough to 'survive okay'. Over and above the confusion and potential ill-effects the shortage had on our expedition, I was unable to explain how I had made such a stupid error. Struggling to comprehend and unwilling to go straight to sleep after we had eaten, I recalculated our projections from the very start. To my surprise and partial relief, we did in fact have exactly what we should have on Day 72 of the expedition, except for one sachet of hot chocolate which had curiously gone missing. The miscalculation had been made when planning the coastal approach and had simply been a little over-optimistic.

I was not surprised that our ability to make mathematical assessments and think methodically had suffered. We were suffering by this point from an extreme and prolonged mental exhaustion combined with inadequate food to work to our full ability. The effect of cold on the human ability to think has also been well documented. I had made the error in my plans and George had to return to his sledges twice that evening to retrieve forgotten items. We were both showing the effects. Our progress was encouragingly strong as the gradient relaxed and we completed the initial climb. The surface was crusty despite being a little soft and there were few sastrugi. Mercifully, the wind had also dropped and we proceeded to achieve a number of consecutive days in excess of seventeen miles, our target. The blues skies and big distances were, as ever, not to last as winds rose again above thirty-five miles per hour.

Day 75   8th June
727 miles covered 'Horrendous day. Windy with no visibility. Little conversation whilst hauling. Little sleep due to howling. Breaks can't be enjoyed due to the wind and drift. Mentally empty by the end. NEED improvement.'

On reflection, it was astounding how often the tone of my journal entries changed as the conditions varied. A single good day could make up for a week of torture. Such was the fickle nature of the icecap and our moods that closely matched it. Conspicuously absent was any mention of giving up or finding a way out. I do not remember ever thinking that way. You often read of polar explorers dreaming up elaborate ways of escaping their ordeal whilst saving face, by injuring either themselves or others. Even the worst days and the correspondingly bad journal entries still looked to the future and improvement. Unlike the early days, even on days with heavy drift and wind, we were still now able to complete a reasonable distance by the end of our day. This accumulation was instrumental to the continued viability of the big dream.

I began to think of our time on the icecap in an odd way as we fast approached the second half of the third month. Instead of things being a day or week ago and the expedition seeming like a brief separation from reality, it became reality. It was as if there had never before been anything or anywhere else. I thought in terms of the different 'ages and seasons' of the expedition. We were, as I joked to George, living on the icecap and not just visiting. I just hoped we would keep our concentration, avoid mistakes and not become permanent occupants of the desolate landscape.

The much anticipated first depot was fast approaching, only a week away, as we were routinely posting daily progress in excess of fifteen miles. However, in order to maintain a narrow margin of contingency in terms of supplies, I made the difficult decision to introduce minor rationing again. This was always an unpleasant concept for both of us but the resulting peace of mind, that there was something being held in reserve, was invaluable. Although we were travelling mostly without weather updates from Matt's office back in Switzerland, they would be of little value anyhow. The conditions changed so regularly, from low winds and clear skies to blizzards and no visibility, that we simply expected the worst and hoped for the best. Our spirits were high as a pair, largely due to the excitement of making progress towards the thousand mile point and, ultimately, home.

One unknown about the route home would be the state of the surface. The icecap varies from week to week and even day to day based on the recent weather, especially the sun and wind. At present, the surface we were enjoying was what I described at the time as 'crusty underfoot and with only isolated sastrugi'. This was a major encouragement, as was the anticipation of going back onto full hot chocolate rations again! One concern was that, since we were now at seven thousand feet, only a thousand or so beneath our expedition maximum, we were experiencing the best expected surface. We knew nothing about the final five hundred miles that had caused us such torment all those months ago on the route out.

By the eightieth day, we had skied firmly into June and the advent of summer was upon us. Temperatures were undeniably improved from weeks past and, although we had fewer challenges from the intense cold, the summer meant that the surface would start to deteriorate. Given our previous attempt to change to night-time skiing and the subsequent back-track, I was cautious about doing so again. It would not be too long until, as we were travelling southeast, the sun would start to set again in the evenings. This would give us the opportunity to switch to a better surface as the sun's warmth left the icecap for a few hours. Our final day's hauling before we hoped to find the food cache dealt us a blow we could not have predicted. In a bizarre change of weather, the clouds closed in and whiteout returned. The wind grew and it then began snowing heavily. This combination resulted in a day of freak high temperatures, comfortably above freezing. Although water resistant, our smocks and trousers were not waterproof 'hard-shells'. As I hauled my sledge sombrely through the blizzard, I noticed white snowflakes landing en masse on my black sleeve. Unlike before, they did not fall off or stay in place frozen. I watched as they melted into the fabric. Before long our clothing was sodden and, with the wind, we began to chill even as we skied.

I knew that I had to make a quick decision on how we would deal with such an unlikely problem. By skiing on, we would just become more and more wet and would need to dry off eventually. I decided to call an end to our day, never a pleasant decision, to get ourselves ready for when the conditions cooled and improved. George needed no coercion whatsoever as he was clearly just as fed up as I was. We were so committed to reaching the cache in good time that any delay was thoroughly objectionable.

One piece of good news was that we had been particularly efficient with our use of stove fuel over the past weeks and therefore carried a strong contingency. Since we had been able to use only a quarter of a litre of fuel per person per day, we had around two litres over and above our safety backup. I resolved that we burn a proportion of this to run the stove for the remainder of the day. Each wet item of clothing, from our sodden gloves to our smocks, could be held over the stove on a carefully positioned ski pole. This would be the only way to make our clothing fit to wear again. In order to avoid a condensation build-up and making the tent into a sauna, we opened the ventilation flaps. These had been important

189

throughout the expedition in allowing air flow through the tent without letting in drift snow. Carbon monoxide build-up can be a silent killer in a sealed tent and the tell-tale sign had always been a suddenly weak roar from the stove as it struggled for oxygen. The process of drying was laborious but it allowed me time to speak to my brother for only the second time during the expedition. Each part of every garment had to be held above the stove separately, in order for us to see the tell-tale clouds of vapour rise from the fabrics. Our battery power stores for the satellite phones, GPS handsets and our iPods had become a little lower than I liked and so we set up the solar panel on the tent roof and recharged the flat batteries.

Day 81   14th June
858 miles covered 'Depot ahoy! Colder tonight and snow getting into everything!'

Although we had clothing that still felt damp to the touch, we simply had to get moving as the eighty-first day dawned. Our food supply was almost exhausted and the depot was only a few miles away. Our spirits were raised by a let up in the snowfall, although visibility was very poor. We agreed that it would be a great test of our recorded GPS coordinates as we would be unlikely to see the cairn until we skied into it, if it was still there at all! In the final mile leading up to the known location of our food and fuel cache, I took out the GPS and led the way, following the small digital compass needle towards our goal. That last half hour was most probably the most nervous I was at any point on the journey. The feasibility of our entire homeward leg back to safety depended on the survival of our ice marker cairns.

I thought back to the pioneering days of polar exploration when the option of an aircraft pick up from an expedition's goal was impossible. The return was then an unavoidable and integral part of the endeavour; and so it was with us. The difference was that if we felt our survival was at risk, we could request an emergency evacuation, although this was heavily weather-dependent. I wondered whether the same feeling of excitement and anxiety gripped them as they approached the location where they expected to find a resupply. It was in those moments of high tension that I realised how important it was to me to travel in such a traditional and pure form, albeit not undertaking a repeat of a past journey.

As the mist closed in, we saw a white speck half a mile away. On closer inspection and to our delight, this eventually revealed itself to be a fully intact cairn. There was a tail of drift which had built up on the leeward side of the ice structure but it was there. The relief was indescribable. As a pair, George and I now knew that, in principle, our gamble of using depots to lighten our sledges had paid off. There was, however, a long way to go. We were on the depot 'train' now and needed to keep intercepting the caches every three days in order not to run out of food.

One of my mental tools to stave off the boredom of our increasingly long hauling days, which now regularly included a ninth session, came to an abrupt end before reaching the next depot. My music player had fallen into the snow, become wet, and refused to operate. Although battery limitations meant the music was a treat rather than a constant form of entertainment, it had become a great strength. Perhaps this was because it was a reminder of a world outside the expedition. After all that time, it was important to remind myself that the real world did indeed still exist.

In a generous gesture, George lent me his spare iPod with a whole new range of music and 'Blackadder' talking books. As the conditions began to settle and we regained our full rations, my mind, full of optimism, began to drift to the thought of the next big milestone. Only a handful of people had previously travelled over one thousand miles in the Polar Regions and only a tiny number had done so without power or resupply support. As our strong daily hauls accumulated, we were fast approaching that totally arbitrary but nonetheless significant barrier.

The slow and delightful realisation dawned that the weather, now in mid-June, had settled into a period of polar high pressure. This tends to be dominated by more reasonable temperatures, blue skies and calmer winds – typical in the summer seasons of both Arctic and Antarctic. We had fought through and survived the horrendously challenging spring and now needed to avoid complacency, keep our bodies healthy and complete those last few hundred miles.

I had to keep reminding myself of the sheer scale of what we were attempting. The concept of talking about 'only a few hundred miles' was only in comparison to the total distance and those miles could bring much difficulty and even failure at this late stage. We had been a few days behind my 'ideal world' schedule since week five and had more or less maintained the correct pace ever since. As such, our situation with supplies was not comfortable and so, with encouragement from George, we said that our days should increase in length to try and buy back some time.

One evening, during a perhaps prematurely nostalgic final ski session, George and I realised that we had not recorded our journey sufficiently in terms of photographs. We reasoned that the final days would likely be long and hard and so we should take advantage of the blue skies. In half an hour, we took a whole range of photographs, some for ourselves and some for our sponsors and supporters. A major regret remains the relative lack of photographs taken during March and April. A number of factors contributed – unreliable battery packs and sheer exhaustion. The enormous sastrugi and extreme low temperatures would have provided a pictorial story in themselves. Satisfied, we returned to the serious business of finding a suitable pitching site for our evening camp. Before finishing my evening tasks of securing the sledges and the aerodynamics of the tent, I took a moment for myself in the unusually peaceful evening sun.

192

The evenings were becoming deeper as the sun came closer each day to touching the ice horizon. The colours in the sky became increasingly varied and the ominous chill returned to the air. We had been enjoying minimum temperatures from minus five to minus ten Celsius over the past few days and I knew these would come to an end as the sun set once again. A light snow drift made the entire surface look fluid, but it lacked the menace of earlier times. I felt thoroughly happy and privileged to be standing where I was, looking at the sights that few will ever see. I was tired, sore and concerned for the future but for those few moments it did not matter one bit.

Day 86   19th June
924 miles covered 'Skies cleared in the morning with a rare gentle tailwind. Shin hurts a lot and sledge felt heavy – tough day despite nice weather. Dagmar worried about forecasts not getting through.'

The feeling of a particularly heavy sledge had returned, despite their weights being just over half their horrendous starting load. This was due to the return of the tiresome thaw-freeze cycle that caused our ski skins and sledge runners to ice up. Due to the intensity of the twenty-four hour sun and the friction of ski on snow, the ice melted into a film over its surface. The accompanying cold temperatures then froze this into a tough ice layer which destroyed the glide of both ski and runner. The only certain cure to this problem was to attack the surfaces with a metal tent peg manually and hack off the offending ice. This usually brought relief for most of the day and allowed us to travel again at our potential speed of a sprightly two miles per hour. As well as the hard ice layer, the warmer snow was becoming sticky on our ski skins and made movement feel like wading through treacle. Our skins, although by that stage shortened, were the culprits. We found that with a little experimentation, more gaffer tape over the skins worked well.

I received a number of satellite messages on the evening of the eighty-eighth day that prompted a long tent discussion regarding our strategy for our homecoming. Both our sponsor's public relations team and Matt Spenceley were interested in when we projected we would reach the East Coast, the glacier and complete the journey. Our only way of making such a calculation was by extrapolating our current pace and hoping that nothing would hold us up along the way. What we knew was that we were both degrading physically due to slow starvation and the fatigue of our muscles and joints. Mentally, we were in remarkable shape and I foresaw no issues in this respect. We also knew the technical glacier system at the coast which, in its new snow-less summer guise, would slow our pace considerably. Beyond that, there were only the unknown unknowns: those we could not predict.

I gave an estimate and target of 14th July, 111 days after we had set off from the same location all those months ago. If we were able to make that date and meet our pick up then we would complete our journey only a day late, after nearly four months. This would be remarkable, less than one percent error in our timekeeping. The prospect of success and returning home excited us so much that we enjoyed a single jelly baby each as a treat and ate our favourite freeze-dried meal that night, 'lamb pilaf' curry.

To make life even better, we had enjoyed respite from our ski glide woes due to a period of cold weather caused by our being above eight thousand feet and having clear blue skies. The only dilemmas caused by altitude were that the stove seemed to burn less efficiently, and our faces became swollen, a common complaint on high icecaps. Most badly affected tended to be the areas around our eyes, which puffed out awfully. At times I found that it even began to affect my peripheral vision, but it was entirely reversible once at lower altitude.

It seemed, in a way, even more cruel, given our optimism and good recent progress, that day eighty-nine dealt such a blow to our prospects of reaching the coast safe and intact. 'My left ski had snapped – which is a potentially major problem,' I understated in my journal. This was, in reality, a major disaster as our reaching the Nagtivit Glacier in time before our food ran out depended on maintaining a fast pace. My left ski, which was quickly and rather unfairly christened 'Rodney', had cracked just behind my heel, causing my boot to fall backwards as I placed pressure on it. Astoundingly, it had cracked through the entire thickness of the wooden core and also the metal ski edges. Rodney was a write-off in his present state. As a short-term solution to get us to the end of the day, I created a splint using spare tent stakes but this only partially supported my weight.

That evening, an eye-watering decision was made and I brought Rodney inside for surgery. It felt like I was betraying an old friend but I resolved to finish the job of snapping him fully in half and then repairing him. Using the serrated part of my 'ankle' knife, kept in a pocket on my right boot for crevasse emergencies, I severed the remaining wood splinters and the two halves parted company. The splint used for the final hours of that day was clearly inadequate and a long-term solution was needed. After all, my makeshift repair would have to last around four hundred miles to the end of the expedition, including potentially rough ice on the East Coast. Having cleaned up both ends of splinters and sharp metal, George and I both set to work lashing the broken rear section underneath the longer front section which had the binding attached. One would hold the two halves together as the other used a spare tent guy line to tightly hold them together. George's extraordinary knowledge of knots was a great help and the resulting fix was very neat. The final touch involved reattaching the skin over the join and inevitable half-inch step caused by the overlap.

Rodney, once ready again for use, was around a foot shorter than his other half, by now known naturally as Delboy. This asymmetry in length and the step made the ski

195

behave differently to normal but it was a vast improvement on the splint, or not using the rear section at all. I did not wish to endure the miles of sledging without skis, as Scott's indomitable companion Henry Bowers did on the ill-fated 1911-12 *Terra Nova* expedition. In any case, we had made our best effort and would have to hope it held together long enough to get us home. I do not believe that Rodney's failure was down to flawed ski design. Their manufacturers later assessed the breakage and showed me the particular model's excellent reliability record. I am convinced that no ski could be guaranteed to perform for huge distances and, in particular, through all the stresses caused by rock-solid sastrugi.

Our second encounter with a depot came on Day 90 and we were no less nervous about locating it than with the first. The visibility was good and as we approached our predesignated GPS coordinate, it became clear that the job would not be as simple as before. The additional time the depot had needed to endure had led to much more erosion from the wind. The GPS's accuracy was critical as we certainly would have missed the bump had we not been taken to within twenty feet of it. A long digging session with the shovel later, we were reunited with our food, fuel and rubbish, and ready to push on to the next depot with stomachs satisfied for at least the following few days.

Day 91   24th June
1003 miles covered 'One thousand miles! What a wonderful milestone − and it passed so quietly! A colder day but still with the high pressure system which we pray will hold.'

There are few great goals in polar expeditions, ones that have an enduring appeal and are free from accusations of contrivance. For me and for others, the thousand-mile barrier is one. No matter how it is achieved, supported or unsupported, with or without resupply, it is a reward for dedication. Despite our thousandth mile in unbroken steps passing by appearing to look very much like any other, it represented a great achievement for George and myself as a team. For me in particular, it was a poignant moment. My earliest polar dreams and indeed my first project, the doomed 'Journey South 2007', was set to cover almost exactly one thousand miles and break that distance unsupported for the first time in the Antarctic. Due to our previous funding woes, the project never came to fruition but this achievement on what was essentially a reincarnation of the Antarctic journey meant a lot to me. My satellite update to our online 'blog' that night enthused about joining the 'handful who had done so'. Our short-term reward was a handful of fruit pastilles – a taste of fruit which had been absent for so long.

Despite the gradual build-up of cloud that evening and into the next day, we dismissed it as 'nothing too sinister' and were fairly confident that the weather was beginning to settle. As we skied yet another strong sixteen-mile day, my attention turned again to my troublesome ski. The fact that it comprised of two half skis lashed together with a large bump halfway down had a significant effect on its ability to glide. Consequently, with one ski-step I moved forward as I expected and then with the other I experienced far more resistance. This asymmetry to the repetitive action of hauling began to cause me additional aches and pains in my hips and lower back. The best solution I could think of was to alternate my skis fairly regularly, despite the fact the left binding was different to its right-hand equivalent.

The broken ski was a serious setback but I had to keep it in perspective. I still had the ski, more or less, and could ski reasonably on it. I had not lost it down a crevasse, injured myself or broken something critical like the stove or the tent. We could move onwards and for that I was glad. Rodney the ski did not seem to hold a grudge over George's and my heavy-handed surgical skills.

Amidst the considerable implications of the broken ski, we were, nonetheless, approaching 1070 miles. This was the

197

previous unsupported distance record in the Polar Regions and had always remained the primary focus of the journey. Just as for any other polar symbol of achievement, such as the various South Poles or North Poles, there is nothing different about that particular patch of snow or ice to any other. The 'barriers' of reaching a Pole or surpassing a distance record are not physical and are some of the classic arbitrary measures of exploratory success. I was having a challenging day getting used to my 'new' ski which behaved very differently to its intact counterpart and let the biggest moment of the journey almost slip past. We rewarded ourselves with a little extra hot chocolate and some more fruit pastilles. It was not a time to get ahead of ourselves, however. We still had over three hundred miles to ski and we did not know if we would have any further equipment breakages. Every step we took beyond this point extended the record further.

Another day saw yet another depot in our sights. Our excitement about how well our depots had survived was evident and we skied at some of the best speeds of the expedition, despite our increasing fatigue. Our GPS led us into the final mile to the depot and in the bright sunlight on a smooth snow surface, George exclaimed that he could see a white dot. It must have been hundreds of yards away but he was totally convinced and stopped to point it out. Surely enough, I then also saw the small blemish against the icecap and confirmed it was exactly on the bearing directed by the GPS. We skied like crazy towards our target and finally completed the last few steps. Our GPS had been correct to less than three feet. Incredibly, what George had first spied from nearly a mile away was only a foot-high bump on the ground. The glare of the sun had reflected onto the sloped surface and made it shine like a beacon. Our luck was truly on the up and the prospect of another three days of supplies safely in our sledges was great.

The stark facts regarding our depots were not encouraging for the future. As we entered the final fortnight of the expedition, our bodies would be at their most degraded and in need of nutrition. Those final weeks also contained those depots which had been out at the mercy of the icecap and its winds for the longest. The depot laid only fifty miles into the expedition would have been left alone for over three months. A great deal could happen in that time, including the periods of extremely high winds that we knew had occurred for certain. The contents of that Depot 'A' would have to fuel us for the tricky final descent to the coast, across the numerous crevasse zones. I put such thoughts to the back of my mind for the time being; little could be done about them anyhow. Instead, I wrote in my journal that 'my mind was well occupied' and hopefully, 'Not long to go.' The next day, I would be too tired to make an entry to the journal.

Other signs of the south and the coast began to make themselves known, even if we had not yet reached our altitude summit of nearly nine thousand feet. There were hills beginning to appear on the icecap and the sun was riding very low in the sky during the night. Another depot and our favourite meal, shepherd's pie, made up for the hard hauling over the changeable surface.

Day 100   3rd July
1154 miles covered 'Windy to start – looked fairly ominous, but not as bad as dramatic clouds looked. First drift for ages.'

As the culmination of the expedition came into view and we began our slow descent from 8,600 feet, our public relations representative from Tiso sent a message requesting a phone call to discuss arrangements for coverage on our return. We knew this was about the time when we would have to start dealing with the inconvenient 'real world' problems of press and business, but there was a problem. We had agreed a time local to the Edinburgh office but did not know exactly what time it was. We did not know our time-zone and had long since adopted our own timing system for our wristwatches.

199

We really were in our own little world, without a care for the conventions of the Western World.

Our time in the tent coincided with what we decided was the middle of the night in England and so our only option was to phone Greenland Home Rule in Nuuk on the West Coast. In what must have been the most surreal phone call the switchboard operator had ever received, I asked seriously down the line, "Good day. I was wondering if you could tell me what the time is? We're on the icecap and have somewhat lost track." Clearly amused and entertained by the change from his normal job, the friendly voice informed me of the local time and from that we worked out the British Summer Time equivalent.

On reading through my journal in depth for the first time since the expedition began, some things became apparent from the entries of Day 104 onwards. Whilst the daily mileages approached nineteen miles, a quick pace, the length of the entries became much shorter and the handwriting almost illegible. The recurring theme remained 'a long day' and my language became far more basic, less enthusiastic and less verbose. Both George and I were beginning to suffer and the onslaught came from every angle: physical fatigue and mental exhaustion. This inescapably brings us back to the topic of why? Why design an expedition which you know will result in pushing you to the very limits? I believe it reflects largely on my not wishing to sit amongst a crowd of other expeditions and also involves a curiosity about true physical extremes.

Although we found the next depot accurately using the cairn and GPS readings, I noted that I had major concerns regarding the last two depots. Their cairns were not as large as those which followed and probing the area with a pole for the supplies would take aeons given the radius accuracy of the GPS. Despite the partial cloud cover, the gloominess of the landscape led us to believe that the sun had set for the first time in months. Sadly, it was not to be the spectacular light-show we had hoped for. That would have to wait. Correspondingly, the temperatures had begun to dip once more to around minus twenty Celsius. These anxious thoughts and string of disappointments began to affect George obviously; it was the first time I had seen a chink in his characteristically irrepressible positivity. He seemed to have overcome his worries by the end of the day but it was something I had to watch carefully, in terms of my own mood as well as his. Loss of determination and focus at this pivotal stage would be catastrophic.

Chapter XII

'The only thing that overcomes hard luck is hard work.'
Harry Golden

Disaster struck on Day 107. Our worst fears had been realised. Having finally made our change to nights, we had skied eighteen hours out of twenty-four and covered over twenty-seven miles. The sun was, by this point, setting each day, usually to our rear. For a few brief moments, as the temperatures noticeably dropped, we paused to look behind and marvel at the beauty of the colours in the sky and the deep blue the ice assumed. We had our final two depots to go – corresponding to one hundred miles to our predesignated coastal pick up point. We had both wondered to ourselves, would we be able to locate these final and most important caches? They had been laid many months before and had been required to withstand the longest time exposed to the ravages of the polar spring. In my gut I had expected the worst for these two final lifelines.

As we had both done so many times before when approaching a depot location, we had our final break sitting on the front of our sledges, side by side. Looking at each other sombrely, George and I exchanged our hopes for which meals we would find inside and, on this occasion, excitement at a fruit pastille treat buried with the depot. There was always a little tension at these moments, not between us as a pair, but between us and the depot itself. It was not only the apprehension of an unknown but an apprehension of something we knew we could not afford to go awry. As we closed in on the position marked on my high-precision GPS handset, we were not greeted with a raised cairn on the

203

surface. Instead, the ground was featureless with a patchwork of sastrugi, flat zones and dunes. I remember a sick feeling in the depths of my stomach.

"It's finally happened – we knew the last two would be most difficult to locate," I said to an equally distraught-looking George. "We're just going to have to probe some likely looking spots." He nodded his agreement.

More in hope rather than expectation, George retrieved the seven foot telescopic tent pole we used as a probe and began testing the raised areas of ice in a ten foot radius of the GPS best-guess. Since the depots were only dug a foot under the surface, it should be relatively easy to strike the hard ghee butter tin or fuel container. We had no luck and after a quarter of an hour or so, we began to get cold. At that point, it became a matter of priorities. We could either spend the few hours poking holes in increasingly large tracts of the Arctic and have a chance of finding our much-needed food or push on. After we had tried the area directly around where the GPS pointed us, it was clear we had another problem. Due to a number of factors, mostly due to the wind and general weather over past weeks, there was a rock hard ice layer a foot or so beneath the snow surface. This meant that any meaningful excavation would involve the laborious and energy-sapping use of the ice axes to break through it. This made my decision much more simple. We could end up wasting time and energy searching the area for our cache and still end up with nothing. Using the final scraps of our food contingency, I drew up a punishing ski schedule to reach the final depot and an equally eye-watering food rationing system. We would have to cover the longest distances of the journey on skeleton rations if we wanted any chance of making it to the coast and succeeding in our quest.

Looking back at where our depot should have been with a desolate mix of feelings, we turned to the next target and skied off towards the horizon. By now the weather had clouded over and we sensed that we were in for a rough ride.

Yet again, the Arctic was not giving even an inch and we were being punished for the smallest mistakes. There was no doubt the depots should have been larger and better marked, despite the accurate and well backed up GPS locations. There was no value in dwelling on the facts and we had to march on. Besides, we barely had the energy to commit to anything as frivolous as feeling sorry for ourselves. The only option apart from forging on was barely worth thinking about, especially with our goal within sight and with all those months behind us. We were out of range of the coastal helicopter and so the sole Twin Otter would have to be scrambled should we be unable to continue. What a pathetic way to end such a journey and, as a final blow, it would not be covered by our extremely specific insurance policy. After confirming in my mind our proximity to the helicopter and Twin Otter with the map, I put such thoughts out of my mind.

The next day's journal makes for depressing reading, with yet further deteriorating handwriting. 'On three flapjacks per day and hypoglycaemic. Dizzy whilst even on good ground.' Only a single day into our desperate bid for the coast on minimal rations, the effects were surfacing. We were both beginning to show the symptoms of hypoglycaemia, low sugar levels in the blood, especially towards the end of sledging sessions. These included shaky and jerky movement, dizziness, headache and difficulty paying attention. The one morsel of good news was that we had an excess of stove fuel, meaning that we were able to melt plenty of snow for drinking.

It is enormously hard, even for those familiar with polar expeditions, to empathise with the most desperate moments of past journeys. For many in the past, there was no hope of rescue and so their peril was more terrifyingly imminent. Cherry-Garrard wrote on his quest for emperor penguin eggs that: 'such extremity of suffering can not be measured: madness or death may give relief. But this I know: on this journey we were already beginning to think of death as a friend. As we groped our way back that night, sleepless, icy and dog tired in the dark, a crevasse seemed an almost friendly gift.'

The vast majority of those living now will never experience such a stark threat on their life and, despite elegant literature, the feelings and fears remain alien. In those cold and desperately hungry final days on the icecap, I caught a glimpse of the mindset ensnaring them. Certainly, we were there of our own volition and had the possibility of a ski-plane. We were walking like ghosts across the landscape with empty, soulless eyes and with one aim: the safety of the East Coast.

In a satellite phone call to Matt Spenceley to explain the situation, we spoke about ways of using the small amounts of ghee butter we had to add energy to our flapjack. Eating the ghee raw would be a last resort and would, most likely, result in vomiting. Additionally, I broached the topic of our pick up plan, which had intentionally been left flexible until this point. The first and cheapest option was dependent on sea ice conditions, a boat piloted by Georg sent to the foot of a glacier. If this proved impossible then the helicopter could again be chartered and sent to the edge of the icecap to meet us. Both options opened a number of possibilities as to which glacier we should aim for and therefore the end point. Within the area directly surrounding Tasiilaq, there were a number of major glaciers flowing into the sea, one of which was the Nagtivit, our start point. Our task was therefore to make our way to that region and await a report about the sea ice conditions.

Waking on Day 109, I did not believe that things could have become worse for our prospects. George was complaining of the same things as me. My stomach was so empty and my over-worked body so deprived of energy that every movement hurt and I craved every nibble of food. To my horror, on opening the tent door to a dull and grey whiteout with low winds, there had been over a foot of soft snowfall during the day, our night time. Sledging that day slowed to a

206

snail's pace at the very time when we needed to be achieving daily averages of around twenty miles in order to be in with a chance of making it. Once we were on the move, the snow began to fall again. The snow was so thick that our skis and boots carved a deep canyon in the snowpack and our sledge had to displace yet more. The physical effort required was comparable to the early days and we were travelling at well below a mile per hour. Our total that day would be only eight miles, a third of what was required.

After our brief inter-session breaks for water, food being conspicuous by its absence, we realised that we were struggling to get back on our feet. George informed me that he felt incredibly ill and had no energy whatsoever. His speech was slurred and he found it hard to focus on my face when speaking to me. I was in no better shape and we used each other as supports as we rose to begin another attempt at skiing. The snow was piling up on the canvases of the sledges and so this had to be cleared regularly in order to avoid hauling more weight than necessary. The sledges complained noisily as they were forced through the sludge of snow, creaking as they went.

If the conditions remained as they were, we did not have a chance of making the coast, which was more than sixty miles to the southeast. We would continue to ski at our slow pace on the ever-dwindling scraps of food until they ran out. We would then fall where we stood, with luck communicating our position via satellite phone or Personal Locator Beacon, and await rescue. Having travelled over thirteen hundred miles, it would be heart-breaking to fail almost within sight of the end. We did, however, have a final life-line – our final 'fifty-mile' depot. It was not on a straight path between ourselves and our current target, the Hahn Glacier and so would require a slight detour to intercept it. It was another gamble worth considering. There was an outside chance that the cairn there would be intact and its contents retrievable. This would provide us with three days of full rations with which we could

207

most likely complete the journey to the coast. On the other hand, if we again failed to locate our food, we would have added distance to our route with no reward. I decided that we would make a push for the last depot, that the reward of a resupply was worth the risk.

Thoroughly exhausted and discouraged after a horrendous day of fighting our way for every step towards home, we collapsed into the tent and ate our meagre food allowance for the day which was, in this case, half a flapjack each. It was a far cry from the 5,600kcal intake we had enjoyed for the majority of the hauling journey and only served to make us feel hungrier. The concept of more days like that one was beyond comprehension yet our resolve remained. We had come so far and worked too hard to fall at the final furlong.

Day 110   13th July
1334 miles covered 'What a turnaround! The deep snow hardened and we get visibility, a tailwind and a gradient. George concerned about glacier.'

As if by a miracle and most certainly the first occasion on the expedition when we had anything approaching good luck, the snow hardened. It could not have come at a better time and we simply could not believe our luck. As we stood on the edge, staring failure in the face, we were handed a critical lifeline. The weather, aided by the increasing time the sun spent below the horizon, had chilled considerably and this had caused the thick snow layer to crust over. Instead of our skis and sledges sinking hopelessly into the soup of soft snow, we were able to skim over the top without our weight causing the crust to collapse. This had a revolutionary effect on our progress, especially with the slight decline gained as we descended the icecap once more. Regardless of this, the misery of almost zero rations continued and we grew still weaker. At the pace we were travelling at that point, we hoped to reach the depot location early the next day but held out little hope for success. Again, if there was no cairn then we could not afford the time taken to excavate the area methodically.

Apart from my thinly detailed journal entries, those days beyond the 107th are but a mess of rough recollections in my mind. Each day seemed to flow seamlessly into the next and I have few lucid memories of individual events or the order in which they occurred. On that day with the improved surface, our pace was fast and we were travelling with 'empty fuel tanks'. We had to go that speed; we had little option. On one occasion, I was skiing second to George, a few feet behind, when I felt the power give way from one side of my body and I slowly slumped to the ground. I tried to let out a yell to alert George but all that appeared was a weak yelp. By pure chance, he looked over his shoulder and skied back to help me back to my feet.

Having regained my balance and having assured George that I was okay to continue we got back on the trail, myself in the lead. Only half an hour or so later, I sensed that all was not well behind me. I stopped and slowly and deliberately turned to look behind. Surely enough, George had stopped and was slumped over, staring blankly at the ground. I called out his name and got a vague response so I unhooked my rope traces and went back to see what could be done. George's body began to sway and so I helped him rest on the nose of his sledge for a moment and handed him some water, also drinking some myself. I could not offer him or myself food, so water was the only option for some sort of boost. There was little to be gained from staying still and so we fitted our harness traces again and lent forward to take the weight of the sledges. Incredibly, the effects of reasonable weather and the good surface, which was the flattest of the expedition to date, allowed us to travel nineteen miles in a single day despite periods of semi-consciousness.

There was no doubt that we were both suffering from the advanced effects of hypoglycaemia and exhaustion caused by sledging for upwards of fifteen hours daily on fewer calories

209

than a single chocolate bar. The remaining scraps of ghee butter could be nibbled occasionally but it resulted in instant nausea due to its unpalatable high fat content. The greatest risk was when skiing one behind the other. If one of us were to pass out again and the other not notice, then we could become separated with unthinkable consequences. Even worse, if we were both overcome at the same time then neither would be able to help the other back to his feet, erect the tent or activate the emergency beacon. The situation was becoming undeniably desperate yet we skied on. In hindsight, sitting in a comfortable chair in the warmth of England, this could be construed as unwise in the extreme, even irresponsible. However, decisions of this nature are made 'on location' and are therefore subject to the pressures and sentiments of the moment. The consequences of decision-making at the critical moment are well documented. On one hand was the decision of Ernest Shackleton to abandon his South Pole attempt ninety-three miles from the Pole and, in doing so, certainly saving his own life and those of his companions. On the other, there are tragic stories of inexperienced clients and under-pressure guides on Mount Everest pushing to the summit despite the best advice and never returning home. I felt that the situation George and I were in fell somewhere in the middle – a calculated risk to finish the job combined with a desire to come home alive.

We had already skied over thirteen hundred miles unsupported, had secured the record and had nothing more to prove to ourselves or anyone else. However, it was not completion. We had to reach the edge of the icecap in order to have reached our goal. The East Coast was not yet in sight; it was something I expectantly checked the horizon for regularly. Every mile took us closer to the 'drop-off' to the coast where we could expect to find steeper gradients and therefore reduce our energy output, of which we had precious little in reserve. The epic sastrugi fields were, thankfully, no more; the long months of wind, snow and sun had made sure of that.

Having covered 1,354 miles in total as the crow flies, my final journal entry was on the 111th day, some twenty to thirty miles from our destination. I simply did not have the energy nor inclination to write any longer. My singular focus was to get to the coast and the safety it represented – nothing else mattered in the slightest. The last words of my journal noted that Rodney, the ski, had precious little glide on the surface and so it was painful to ski. We spotted the mountains only a day later; at first, we saw small, dark dots where the sky met the icecap which was bathed orange in the setting sun. Although I had not set foot in that particular range, which extends north from Tasiilaq and Kulusuk up to Mount Forel, the second highest peak in Greenland, it had become very familiar. For the 'Trans Greenland', it represented a symbol of homecoming and success as well as something other than ice to fix our eyes on. On the nearer side of the Sermilik Fjord, I had made first ascents of peaks with Adam, Rich and Wilki in the 'Journey South 2007' days. At that time, we had climbed in spectacular weather with the same long sunsets and dramatic clouds. From the summit of one mountain, we had looked out over the fjord, the coastal range beyond and the icecap to the west. The stunning silhouettes against a blood-red sky had transported us into Tolkein's land of Mordor. And so it was again. Amid the preoccupations my mind was dealing with, I did make a conscious effort to appreciate the landscape we were presented with. The mountains, now fully in view, were only partially covered in snow as July had taken hold. The shapes they cast against the sky were impressive – much more so than the more gentle shapes on the West Coast range. Some were jagged fingers pointing high into the sky and they represented many of the most technical peaks yet to be climbed in the world.

Soon we had reached the locality of the final depot that held the key to the manner in which we would cover the final

211

miles of the expedition. If we could find the treasures stored underground, which included another 'treat' packet of fruit pastilles, then we could refuel our bodies and make our way to the coast in reasonable shape. If not, which I feared more likely, then we would have to continue travelling without food to the end, which could still be either helicopter or boat pick up. We were convinced that the cairn would not have survived and we would go through the frustrating process of walking directly over the depot just a foot or so beneath the surface without knowing it. In hindsight, the application of a kevlar cane or similar item to fix to the depot and reach above the surface would have solved the problem.

As we reached the position the GPS designated, our suspicions were confirmed as we were presented with flat icecap with gentle, uniform ripples in its surface. It was another beautiful evening with cold temperatures, low winds and an orange glow from the sun. Our long shadows were cast hundreds of feet across the ice. In all honesty, I did not want to ponder the loss of the supplies any longer and wanted to spend hours digging for them even less. We took turns probing a circle around the GPS coordinate for an hour or so and were arrested by the same hard under-layer of ice beneath the snow as before. With relief at knowing our fate, at least in this respect, we could focus our minds on what must be done. Failure and evacuation was not an avenue we considered and so we hatched our plan to make those final miles to the glaciers. Now that I knew we had no more supplies available to dig up, I made a decision to ski to the Hahn Glacier, the direct neighbour of the Nagtivit. This was reinforced by Matt saying that a pick up from the foot of the Nagtivit by boat would be unlikely due to sea ice. This would get us to the edge of the icecap, close enough to keep the helicopter in range whilst not unnecessarily adding miles to our journey.

George and I spoke at length through the exhausting final sessions of the day about how we wanted to undertake the final push to the coast and completion. We settled on another long day of fifteen hours skiing, followed by a through-the-night push to the very end, without tent-time. This would limit the additional number of days we would have to suffer for and the last 'day' would give us a mental crutch of 'we will be finished at the end of these sessions.' Meanwhile, through the continued haze of our hypoglycaemic state, our pace was excellent. We were now descending the edge of the icecap dome at quite a rate with light sledges of around 80kg. For some rare moments, we had real glide on our skis and the sledges followed happily after us. The surface was smooth, with low friction and it even felt icy in places. The inevitable side-effect of this was that the sledges picked up too much speed. It is very difficult to control the movement of a sledge hell-bent on overtaking its hauler. Sometimes, it is best to let the petulant dead-weight have its own way and let it go down first, having reversed the rope traces. This had drawbacks, as this meant the skier would have limited control over direction, especially important in the crevassed region we were entering. Being the beginning of summer, the glaciers would become 'dry glaciers' and the icecap itself had less snow cover. This leads to crevasses being more exposed and snow bridges far more precarious than before. The other option to control the sledges was to apply some of the trimmed skins from our skis to the runners. This increased their dragging friction and slowed them down, a bizarre state of affairs considering the past months. In March, the concept of wanting to slow our sledges down would have resulted in mutiny.

The idea of covering the final miles of the expedition with well behaved sledges and simply skiing in a straight line to the pick up was not to be – we knew that all along. However, given our state of mind, a simple conclusion was what we needed more than anything. Every few sessions, we were able to nibble at small blocks of hardened ghee butter with flakes of flapjack inset for 'flavour'. This was all we had to keep us fuelled for that last week. With our sledges more in control than their owners, we ate up the miles towards the

213

contours, glaciers and mountains of the Hahn Glacier region. Despite being barely capable of performing the most basic tasks, such as erecting the tent and zipping up the canvas on our sledges, we made a point of reminding each other of the risks. Most people know that the descent of a mountain is the most deadly time. People become tired, complacent and just desperate to get away from the thing with them still in its jaws. For us it was the same; the final few miles would be the most dangerous in terms of crevasse fall, hypoglycaemic fainting and there was still the risk of a freak katabatic storm flowing off the icecap. I wondered how we would fare putting up the tent in fifty mile per hour winds in our compromised state. Following what we hoped would be our final night on the icecap, we set off for the last, long day.

The time in the tent had been torture. We desperately needed the rest but there was the irresistible urge to get going and finish, with the end perhaps less than a marathon away. Neither of us slept well as the feeling of hunger was not even slightly alleviated by the nibbles of fatty food – the resulting stomach pain was agony. It was an odd thought to consider that our morning routines and habits would only be run that one final time. Each action as we exited the tent, collapsed it and attached our sledges was a ritual. Very suddenly, the icecap changed as we entered the complex fjord and glacier systems of the coast. There were long, steep slopes that were difficult to navigate on skis and were covered, especially in the upper regions, with parallel lines that indicated narrow crevasses. As we negotiated one of these dramatic bowls, we could see down, between the rocky outcrops, to glimpse the sea and icebergs floating free from pack ice. The end was becoming very real, although I do not believe I was able to appreciate it fully. My mind was alternating between excitement, nonchalance and feeling half asleep. Beyond the final U-shaped bowl sat adjacent to a small sea inlet, we climbed slightly onto what appeared to be a ridge. Given the lack of landmarks and perspective we had to contend with on the icecap, it was hard

214

to see what was really a bowl, a ridge or a slope; the landscape was so abstract. Having narrowly avoided a zone of three foot wide crevasses we had not previously spied, we crested the 'ridge' to see what was actually a gradually rising slope. This eventually gave way to a steep 'valley' in the ice and another long climb onto a huge dome. We were now very close to the scene of the 'Journey South 2007' training expedition a year previous. This dome, that we could begin to assess fairly well, signalled the transition as the coastal glaciers met the icecap. Our final task was to descend into the dip, climb the dome and then descend off the other side, off the icecap and onto the Hahn Glacier. As ever, our perception of distance was far from accurate and the valley with its dome was, in fact, a monster. Our sledges felt light on the bare ice and it was mostly a case of controlling our movement amongst the crevasses. Often on the slopes, I let my sledge run freely alongside me, only giving it a tug with the traces when it began to forge its own path.

Having spoken directly to Hans, our pilot, via the satellite phone regarding our location, we began the final few miles of skiing. Despite the awful state our bodies were in and the semi-consciousness in which I had spent the previous few days, I remember those moments more vividly than the rest of the expedition. It was as if the true realisation the end was near had shifted my mind into another gear. I remembered each slope, each view and, it seems, each individual crevasse as we snaked our way round our indirect route to the pick up point. As is true for all coastal areas in Polar Regions, the ice was broken, twisted and malformed as it flowed its way irrepressibly towards the sea.

We may have hauled many more miles that day than we had achieved 'as the crow flies'. To avoid opening an impossible can of worms, polar expedition lengths are always measured from start to finish in a straight line. Otherwise, it would not be possible to truly calculate the real distance covered, around features such as mountains, crevasse fields

215

and open water. The only time when this convention is altered is when there is a return journey being attempted, in which case it is clearly two straight lines, and with a traverse, the mid-point being a Pole, either North or South. In this case, the distance is measured from the coast to the Pole and then from the Pole to the opposite coast, not always at the same continuous angle. Our own expedition had travelled many more miles than would be recorded on completion, largely due to the coastal disturbances and our curved route over the icecap to follow altitude contours.

In sight of the final dome that represented our final hours, we paused and ate our last individual blocks of chocolate, only a tiny mouthful but enough to push us on. It was about at this time when I looked over to my right and saw what I was certain was a tent a few hundred feet away. The shape, colour and position convinced me that we were not alone in these final stages of our journey. I called excitedly over to George and pointed out my discovery. He did not seem sure and so I skied slightly off line to investigate. Only when I crested a particular ridge of ice did it present itself as a mountain in the far distance, much to our disappointment.

I reflected later on what this meant in terms of my state of mind. My perilously low levels of energy were barely sufficient to drive my legs, let alone be mentally lucid. It was not surprising that this condition, which could be compared to being under the influence of alcohol, had skewed my ability to recognise objects. Also, I now believe that the sighting of the tent was more hope than belief. We had both been subconsciously crying out for the smallest signs and thoughts of civilisation, no matter what form they took. I wanted that mountain to be a tent. I wondered who lived in it, what they were doing and what their own story was. I needed people again. I had not allowed myself to ponder these thoughts too deeply in the final weeks. The end seemed near two weeks from the coast but only relative to the total length of the expedition. Two weeks was still an age in terms of skiing into nothingness. Now, so close to the end, despite the periods of wondering if we would ever make it, I finally gave in to the urges to think of anything I wanted. I was totally indulgent in my mind's wanderings in those last hours.

I could not, however, take my mind off the matters in hand. We had long since entered a region of the icecap that represented a significant danger in terms of crevasses. A complacent mistake at this stage could mean failure or even death just moments from success. Along with trying to 'read' the ice as much as possible in order to spy a good route towards our destination, I used the GPS extensively. George had entered the predesignated helicopter landing spot as 'HOME' in the unit's memory and this was what the arrow pointed to on the screen. The feeling of seeing this was indescribable, especially as it finally read '1.0 Miles'. These last miles seemed to alternate between taking an age and then shooting past almost without noticing. In order to give the pilot a good chance of finding a safe spot to touch down, we had chosen a smaller ice dome on the glacier-icecap transition as a meeting point and so had to ski slightly beyond it in order to descend and leave the icecap, thereby completing the double traverse.

The yards fell away on the GPS and it finally announced our arrival. We had done it. This tiny bit of technology, used infrequently on our spartan and relatively low tech expedition, had confirmed our success. I stopped, breathed deeply and looked over to George. We had skied the final yards side by side to avoid precedence and smiles grew across our faces. I placed my ski poles into the ice and clipped my traces onto them. I skied over to George, shook hands and we hugged each other. One thousand, three hundred and seventy four miles in one hundred and thirteen days, and four years of struggle. We had skied further without support than any person in history and had experienced the Arctic in exactly the manner that I had intended. It had been clean, simple, raw and, importantly, novel polar travel. Unable to stand for much longer, both of us sat down on our sledges to rest before starting to pull them up towards the landing spot. I decided that the gradient of the ice slope was too much to safely land the helicopter and so set about moving higher up to flatter ice and communicated these new coordinates back to the pilot.

Day 113   16th July
1374 miles covered Message transmitted to expedition website: 'EXPEDITION COMPLETE AT 0832! HAULED 1,374 MILES AS CROW FLIES IN 113 DAYS. THE TISO TRANS GREENLAND IS NOW THE LONGEST FULLY UNSUPPORTED POLAR JOURNEY IN HISTORY.'

We made some important satellite calls as we began to prepare our equipment for the flights, strapping our skis and poles to the sledge and marking a landing site with black bin liners filled with snow. I dug out our flares ready to deploy as the helicopter came closer. If the pilot missed our position then he would have to return to Tasiilaq, leaving us to pay for a second extraction flight. We were so drained that this procedure took a number of hours and we spent a lot of the time lying motionless on a roll mat and trying to take in the situation.

My thoughts were mixed, as could be expected. After one hundred and thirteen days, I wanted to experience home so badly. I wanted to leave the icecap – it had driven my body and mind to places I did not previously know existed but it was time to move on. I craved fresh food, people's faces and new conversation. Despite all of this, my final days on the icecap and the ordeal they represented, I loved that place. For some, one polar expedition is enough for them. I felt that for George this was the case. He had been to the Arctic, travelled in an extreme manner that few ever will, achieved his aim and seemed content that he would never try anything as huge again. Noting this in 2018 – how wrong I was! On my own part I felt an extraordinary pride in my expedition and its success in a season when the majority of expeditions were compromised one way or another. For me it was the start of something, not a culmination, and I vowed even at that stage to return to push other boundaries at both ends of the Earth.

As we sat on the dome, awaiting the designated time for our pick up, we were able to survey the scene fully. The final hours had been long and tortuous, especially given the increasingly desperate state our bodies were in. The relief was that we did not have to walk, or haul, a single step further. Looking down the glacier towards the sea, it was clear that the East Coast, at least in the area we were located, was more dramatic than our West Coast half-way point. The glaciers were steeper and the mountains more impressive. As a small concession by the icecap on our final day, we were treated to low winds and a cloudless sky. The sea itself was obscured by a spectacular inversion layer that resembled a blanket of low-lying cloud. These are common in the coastal Polar Regions and are due to the air counter-intuitively rising in temperature as the altitude increases. We were also able to see two of the peaks I had stood atop a year before. Most striking however, given the experiences of the past four months, was the stillness. The icecap and glacier seemed peaceful, a totally different beast to the place which had put up so many barriers to our presence. Throughout the entire expedition, for a bird looking down on us, we must have looked like a couple of ants slowly crawling their way across an endless white sheet. There was never any question of conquering the icecap; any such notion is impossible. The Arctic is always in charge and will either let you scamper across its surface or it will not.

In the back of my mind was the timing mistake of the last year with regard to the helicopter pick up. I anxiously scanned the mountainous horizon, looking for the glint of metal in the sun and listening for the tell-tale 'whoop-whoop' of the rotors. It was a shame we could not exit the icecap via the Nagtivit and using Georg's boat, but the sea ice was

219

thick and the glacier some miles away. It would have made for a more traditional, satisfying ending. This conclusion I only came to some days after, since at the time the one and only thing I could think of was getting back to civilisation, and food, as fast as physically possible. We had been almost entirely without food for over a week and had travelled over one hundred miles in that time.

Surely enough, exactly at the agreed time, George spotted a glint on the horizon between two mountains and then over the next few seconds, the reassuring sound become audible. It was our first glimpse of another person since setting off one hundred and thirteen days before. It took another five minutes or so for the helicopter to approach to within a mile of our dome and then it stopped and hovered. The pilot was searching the glacier edge for the black dots – George and me. Afraid that he would miss us and the black landing markers we had laid out, I released a single mini-flare. Moments later, the helicopter turned to face us and began its final approach. We knew that the pilots who flew the Greenlandic aircraft enjoy having a bit of fun and that Hans, our pilot, knew how exhausted we had become. His parting words on the satellite phone had been, "Hope you don't mind a close landing! Saves you moving your gear to the heli!" So as not to disappoint, Hans brought the red and white Bell 222 closer and closer to our waiting spot, ignored the carefully laid out landing markers and brought it to rest roughly five feet from where we were crouching.

Unable to control his excitement for one minute longer, George exclaimed at the top of his voice, "That is the best thing, ever. Wahoo!" The truth was that Hans could never fully appreciate how glad we were to see him. I think he was a little taken aback as he was greeted with embraces from two smelly men who resembled starved convicts. This exuberance served only to further exhaust us. The overwhelming delight was that we were being picked up having successfully completed our aim, man-hauling further without support than any person in history. We would have liked to travel from sea-level to sea-level, but this was made impossible on the West Coast and was only a second priority. In order to minimise the amount of fuss, we had prepared our sledges for flight, skis and poles strapped tightly to the outside of the sledge canvases. It took only a few minutes to lift them, with Hans' help, into the fuselage of the helicopter. The Bell 222 required only one pilot, so George went to the side door to take up position next to him. I used the rear sliding door and went in the back with the sledges, which gave me the best opportunities to photograph the coast out of the windows. In a final farewell to the icecap – my home for so long – I took a final glance back over my shoulder and then lifted my large polar boot slowly off the snow for the last time. We were on our way home.

With an enthusiastic burst of throttle, Hans started the engine up once more and the rotors slowly spun into motion. I did not know where to look first. I had had the opportunity to look at my surroundings for so long, without interruption, but now we were about to leave. I had the urge to commit everything around me to memory, perhaps for fear of forgetting the place. We slowly lifted off from the ice in a snowstorm caused by the rotor downdraft and spun around to face out towards the sea. As we began to gain altitude and speed, the whole area around where we had made our desperate last efforts to reach the edge of the icecap, our route and the surrounding fjords, mountains and crevasse zones were suddenly so obvious. What was extraordinary, although not unexpected, was the different appearance the entire region had to when we set off. This is not a reflection on climate change but simply on the seasons and the length of time we had been away. Although the flight to Tasiilaq would take only around twenty minutes, there was so much to see. The mountains had only a splattering of snow and the fjords were now filled with icebergs and growlers (smaller, low-lying bergs), rather than being locked shut with pack-ice as in March. The rock was a deep brown and looked crumbly, a very definite challenge for innovative climbers seeking new ascents. We could see out all the way to sea, which was now a rich blue colour with a smaller number of massive icebergs majestically making their way along the coast. In March, the sea was a jigsaw puzzle of ice pans as far as the eye could see; the sunlight glinted off it like a giant mirror.

Eventually, after one of the most enjoyable flights imaginable and with certainly amongst the best views, I fully relaxed. I thought previously that completing the expedition, climbing aboard the helicopter and flying to safety would be the most enormous transition from extreme stress to overwhelming relief. Although that flight was undeniably the biggest weight of responsibility lifted off my shoulders, I had not experienced the tension and stress in those last days that I had anticipated. I did not have the spare mental capacity to indulge in such unproductive thoughts. Every effort had been dedicated solely to getting George and myself to the finish-line – everything else paled into insignificance. Tasiilaq, now thawed from the icy shackles of winter, came into view. The village in summer is a hive of activity, being larger than Kulusuk and having a reasonably-sized dock where ships from the Royal Arctic Line could come alongside and offload imports.

Chapter XIII

*'Polar exploration is at once the cleanest and most isolated way of
having a bad time which has yet been devised.'*
Apsley Cherry-Garrard

We circled the small helipad that was placed outside the main village on a small spit of rock and then made our descent. The staff, a mix of Danish, Icelandic and Inuit, in the small office beside the helipad had come outside to watch us land. Once we came to rest on solid ground we again thanked Hans and then worked with the staff to haul the sledges onto trolleys out of the storage area. Having cleared the area for the pilot to continue his day's work, shuttling locals between the villages, we were able to relax for a moment. The staff had been, apart from the pilot, the last people we had bade farewell to in March and, fittingly, they were the first to greet us. Unfortunately for them, we did not smell as fresh as we did on the outward flight so they physically recoiled once within a few feet! No offence was taken; we had only washed properly and changed clothes once in four months.

Our immediate craving was of course for food and the staff were generous beyond the call of duty. They were also hospitable enough to let us briefly use their internet connection, a novelty then in the Arctic, providing they were allowed to speak to us from a distance. I was intrigued to see the comments on our daily dispatches on the website and to check my bulging email account, mostly with junk mail. It was the first part of our return to communication and we loved every minute. The messages of support, both public and private, were very touching and I felt that our attempt to communicate our story live, despite basic technology, had done its job.

Matt called the satellite phone to congratulate us soon after and to inform us of what he had arranged in terms of schedule. He commented that most of his guides had been out and back on shorter expeditions with clients three times during our double-crossing. Knowing how we must be feeling, he had devised a plan without any unnecessary rush and this included a night and a meal at one of the small guesthouses in Tasiilaq. It would give us an opportunity to visit the village shop and satisfy the craving for food for the first time. Our first challenge was to get our sledges which, despite not containing any food or fuel, still weighed nearly 150kg together, up the steep hill to the guesthouse. As was so typical of the kind nature of Inuit who call Tasiilaq home, a local with an old truck noticed our puzzled looks and offered to help. We were soon hurtling up the steep rocky face of the hill and were delivered to the front door of the guesthouse. Having introduced ourselves to the owner and asked directions, we stumbled our way across the village to the well-stocked shop, which provided for the whole community. The expedition had an unexpected side effect on us physically: our ability to walk. Every day on the icecap, we had made sliding and shuffling movements on our skis and had walked perhaps ten paces per day to and from our sledges during tent-time. We had forgotten how to walk, somewhat like the phenomenon reported by seafarers regaining their 'land-legs' after a long voyage. I found it hard to walk in a straight line without following the roadside or something similar. My legs, weak as they were due to starvation, seemed to try to recruit the wrong muscles for this usually most instinctive action.

More by luck than judgement, we made our way to the shop front and our eyes could have popped out of ours heads as we saw the food on offer. Any concern about our 'eyes being bigger than our stomachs' had long since been relegated to the backs of our minds as we ploughed our way from shelf to shelf. We bought bread, jam, fruit (an expensive luxury) and cake, and had only just got outside when we realised we could not last one moment longer. A mixture of smiles and bemused looks greeted us as passers-by wondered why two bearded Westerners were devouring half a ton of food like ravenous animals. It fast became clear that we had indeed bought far too much food and that our stomachs were a fraction of the size they were before we set out on the ice. With the prospect of dinner in the guesthouse, courtesy of Matt, we gave the rest of our food to the owners and other guests so it did not go to waste. I still found it hard to control the rate at which I ate and so much of our time was spent either eating or recovering from eating too much.

Now that the waters surrounding Tasiilaq and Kulusuk were largely free from sea ice, we were able to forgo the helicopter shuttle to Kulusuk and instead enlisted the services of Georg and his boat, *Mugu*, the same boat we had our hair-raising adventure in the previous year. He would collect us from the rocky landing spot near the helicopter pad the next morning, ready for our flight to Iceland some hours later. As ever in the Arctic, any water or air travel was totally at the mercy of the weather. Excited to be in Iceland and then back in London within forty-eight hours, we prayed the polar high-pressure would hold. Having had a brief half-hour nap on our beds in the guesthouse, a bizarre and thoroughly pleasant experience, I went outside to speak to George, who was slowly working his way through the battered contents of his sledge. We had decided to empty them, clean out the sledges and consolidate all our supplies into a single sledge. The empty sledge could also stack neatly into the other, making the freight back to the UK, by sea this time, much easier. We still did not have a clean change of clothes as these were stored in Matt's hut in Kulusuk, so we continued to wander around, still with fairly dreamy and vacant expressions, smelling of four months' physical toil.

The handful of adventurous tourists, who had made it as far as Tasiilaq and shared the guesthouse, were clearly unimpressed as we laid our equipment out for a stock-take on the wooden platform outside. I had always felt that since Kulusuk and Tasiilaq had always been a staging post for expeditions, never a destination in themselves, I had somewhat neglected them. I was determined not to do so this time around, despite our limited hours until the boat shuttle. We decided to eat dinner, then move the sledges down the steep hill to the sea and then instead of going to bed, go for a wander through the village in the midnight light. The food served that night was just what we needed: not too much bulk but lots of small dishes that showed off the traditional Inuit cooking. We enjoyed dried narwhal and all manner of small fish. The effort to move the sledges back down the hill became quite a saga. It was late at night and so we could not enlist the help of a local again. Instead, we each took a side strap in hand and began to lift them down, a few hundred feet at a time. We became exhausted very quickly and eventually fashioned two shoulder straps to take some of the weight. The slopes were far steeper than we envisaged and our progress was out of control more often than not. However, in one piece and having managed to avoid scraping the fragile runners on the ground, we reached the shoreline. Having placed the sledges out of the way behind a rock, George and I began the walk back into Tasiilaq. The contents of the sledges easily exceeded £10,000 in value but we were confident that they would be safe left there for a few hours.

In the glow of the summer night-time in Greenland, I began to feel genuinely at ease and able to enjoy the place for what it is, not a launching point for an expedition but a vibrant community. It certainly had its problems such as alcoholism, especially in the winter, and a very basic waste management system. Any non-organic waste, such as plastics and metal, was simply pushed over a cliff into an ever growing pile on the rocks below. This was a shame, a world away from the quaint

Western image of Inuit, but it was reality and a reflection of the fact that they were as keen as any to embrace the benefits of the modern world.

The small wooden houses, most of them painted in bright primary colours, were in varying states of repair and some had added signs of social status, such as a snowmobile shelter or veranda. Many had long lines of small fish hanging out to dry across their front porches. Once we had reached the steep inlet which provided cover from the elements for the shipping dock, I suggested we took a rest on a rock to take it all in. There was a small whale swimming close to the settlement in the fjord and I could see a group of locals quickly heading to their boats, clearly keen to catch the animal for meat and the multitude of other uses the Inuit have for their quarry. It was, at its very heart, despite the occasional foreign visitors and influences of the West, a traditional hunting village. The overwhelming atmosphere of the place was of contentment and friendliness; nothing was too much trouble. We could see the church beyond a row of houses, now free of the snow build up of March, the last time we had seen it. Although it was past midnight, most of the children were playing a game of football in a large dusty rectangle left clear in the centre. With not a cloud in the sky and a light breeze, it seemed like the idyllic place to live, although as anyone with Arctic experience knows, it can turn on you in the blink of an eye. In 1970, a *piteraq* had blown through all the way down the icecap and hit Tasiilaq with full force. It caused widespread destruction to the mostly wooden structures and showed that even the coast is not immune from the ravages of the icecap.

Whilst we were still in Greenland, concentrating on allowing our minds and bodies to begin recovering, we were blissfully unaware of any implications of the expedition back in the UK. Our title sponsors, Tiso, had begun a press coverage campaign and word of the success of the expedition had begun to circulate the expedition community. For a few days more, however, I did not even want to be part of that world just yet, or to consider the enormity of the sheer distance we had travelled. Having continued our slow walk around the settlement, meeting the various sled dogs chained to rocks outside each cabin, we made our way back to the guesthouse and arranged our own breakfast. Yet again, I overfed myself. We knew that a fast journey in a boat would not be the best way to settle our stomachs.

I had almost overlooked how well George and I still got on, even after we had been airlifted the day before. There is so much talk of expedition partnerships quickly fracturing upon completion but nothing seemed to have changed. We had both had our faults on the expedition; it would be impossible not to. As I noticed whilst reading through my journal entries, the times when George had irritated me had been few and far between and mostly very minor. I hoped that George's own account read similarly to mine! As he has since observed, we both filled different niches within our team; he was the 'impulsive energiser' and I was more 'calm and calculated'. There is no doubt that, at times, we both had to bite our tongues to keep the peace but the important thing is that we both did so. On stressful expeditions, it is so easy to allow a storm to brew in a teacup over very little and, after all, we had our own very real storms to deal with. The end result was that we were able to complement each other as a team and concentrate on the important thing – achieving consistent progress towards our goal.

The sun was again beginning to rise higher in the sky to beckon a new day but for us it was time to move on. Georg was due with his boat and so we made our way down to the shore. Regular as clockwork, his little boat flew around the edge of the headland and came to rest against the rocks. Georg's beaming smile was visible from behind the wheel and he leapt onto the shore energetically, wearing his trademark blue boiler-suit. He walked up to us, shook our hands without a word and gave my beard a tug. George's had, as had become a running joke between us, stopped growing after a few weeks into the expedition. After a fair amount of work, the sledges were aboard and we made the trip across the mostly ice-free water to Kulusuk. There had been far more ice in July the previous year. As Georg took the helm and ran the engine flat-out, we travelled in a series of violent bumps as the hull hit the water, giving our stomachs a lesson in moderation.

Kulusuk was unrecognisable from the last time we had seen it and we docked in the small harbour – a dog-sled route all those months ago. Since there was no jetty, the task was to haul the heavy sledges up over the rocks onto the dusty area beside the petrol storage tanks. The rocks were slippery and covered with the entrails and half-butchered carcasses of seals. The hunters of Kulusuk counted seal, narwhal, polar bear and fish as their most common quarry. Taking narwhal and bear is carefully controlled by quota in the Arctic although bears are often shot if they enter the boundaries of a settlement. The pelts, meat, claws and teeth are sought after amongst the locals and are used with little waste.

Before long, it became clear that George and I were simply not physically capable of being any use with heavy lifting. The smallest tasks fatigued us and we needed to keep sitting down to take rests. Georg had clearly appreciated the ordeal our bodies had been through and, in a gesture so typical of the man, signalled that we should go up to his house and make a cup of tea for us all. As we walked slowly and deliberately like a pair of zombies up the hill to his blue cabin, Georg recruited a few villagers who helped to carry the sledges onto the back of his all-terrain vehicle. We heard the engine stop just outside the front window and saw Georg man-handle the sledges onto the ground, where they would stay for some weeks until the Royal Arctic Line next sent a ship to carry freight away from Greenland. Only items which had no immediate use were therefore left in place.

Halfway through enjoying our cup of tea with Georg and his son, and after being endlessly offered all sorts of confectionary, an elderly Inuit man came into the front room and made himself a drink. I was struck by the community spirit that existed in Kulusuk, where anyone can walk into a neighbour's kitchen and make themselves at home. The man sat down opposite us and smiled with a wide, toothless grin. The state of people's teeth in Kulusuk always saddened me, as sweet foods had become more popular but dental care lagged far behind.

Although we would have to wait until Reykjavik for our first shower, a change of clothes was next on the menu. As we brought back the weapon, ammunition and flares to Matt's hut, we changed into non-expedition clothes. The feeling of fresh, clean fabric and normal shoes was exceptional although it was also the point when I noticed quite how ill I was feeling. I was having to sit down every five minutes or so and George likewise. It is entirely predictable that after a diet brutally high in fats and low in volume, our stomachs had made major adjustments over the course of the expedition. Culminating with a week-long period of total starvation and then an influx of rich foods, our poor insides must have been wondering what had hit them. We had expected to take time to readjust to normal food, just as we had taken time months before to wean onto a high-fat diet. This was now catching up with us with a vengeance.

All that was left to do was bid farewell to Georg and his family, before making our way along the dusty path back to the airstrip. There were small glacial areas all around the village on the slopes, slowly dripping onto the thawed ground. The habitable halo around Greenland is, in the height of summer, remarkably fertile and wild plants grow all around. We had been offered a ride from a local on his quad-bike from Kulusuk to the terminal but we were in no rush, had only light rucksacks and wanted to spend our final hours in Greenland at a slower pace. Before our flight from the airstrip, now devoid of the huge snow drifts of March, we had a fascinating conversation with a group of Americans taking advantage of the brief summer window of amenable weather. They were totally stunned at how long we had been travelling and asked a string of questions which lasted until we were called to board the aircraft. It was at once very flattering to have a group of people so interested in what we had been through, whilst also allowing reality to sink in.

Our triumphant arrival into Iceland and the night-long celebrations we had planned for weeks on the icecap did not transpire. This was despite our very best intentions and efforts. The large bowls of nachos, fruit and pints of Viking beer placed on our restaurant table were what we had dreamed of in the darkest moments of the expedition. After half a pint of beer and half a dozen nachos, George looked at me and said, "Shall we just go back?" mirroring my own thoughts exactly. The big night out in Reykjavik was not to be. That evening, I spent some hours making my way through my email backlog as George tried to sleep. He had been affected far worse, initially at least, than I had from the diet change. His first, much anticipated, evening back in civilisation was tainted by frequent visits to the bathroom.

Testament to the efficiency of Matt Spenceley's operation, despite not knowing our expedition finish date until the last moment, our flights were organised with precious little delay and we were due to fly to London the very next morning. Having cleaned the guesthouse out of the vast majority of their breakfast stocks for the next five years, we made the taxi journey to the airport. It became apparent, as we sat in the terminal eating pizza, that despite our hour long showers and clean clothes, we still smelt horrendous. I was later cheerily informed by my family that we both smelled of digestive biscuits, an aroma George and I had noticed in the early days of the expedition. The major plus-side from the situation was that on our final flight from Iceland, no-one was willing to sit within a row of us. I have never experienced so much space in economy class! It was on that flight that my own illness caught up with me and I went through the same period of extreme tiredness and nausea that George had since recovered from. I was so incapable that I had to sit on a seat and spot my rucksack on the baggage carousel from a distance. It was late on a Friday night and we were standing only a few hundred feet from where we had said our goodbyes to family and friends in March. Walking through customs, I caught a glimpse of our families and so George and I made our slow approach. Completely subconsciously, we had adopted our side-by-side skiing formation from the expedition: George on the left and me on the right. There was no particular reason for this but it had become a habit. Our minds were clearly still not free from the shackles of day-to-day expedition life and we laughed it off. My mother was the first from my family to brave the overpowering smell and welcome me back home. I gather that after farewells to the Bullards, it was not possible to stop me talking from the start to the end of the two hour journey back to the south coast. They did humour my stories with the windows firmly wound down.

The expedition was over and I was home. The sledges and their contents took a further three months to find their way by sea freight from Tasiilaq to Hampshire via Denmark. The following days involved a number of press and television appearances before I was able to shed the now very itchy beard, which had been a necessity for any publicity opportunities. The most important job was to thank the huge team of individuals who had put their time, effort and money into making the expedition a success. This success was, a week after returning home, starting to sink in. We had skied further, without assistance or support, than any other human-beings in history. This was not exciting or satisfying in a smug, self-important way; rather it was very humbling. I had briefly seen what it was like to achieve something truly, and without caveat or justification, on the edge of human physical ability. The much over-used terms of 'pushing the envelope' and 'breaking barriers' now took on some real meaning to me. I also appreciated how close we had come on a number of occasions to things going very wrong. Rather than making me

232

want to rest and bask in the sun, it inspired me to want to go even further in the future, in terms of trying new ideas in the remote areas of the world.

My catalogue of projects including those which did not, due to funding losses, reach the ice had raised nigh on £40,000 for cancer charities. This was something that motivated me to return to the Polar Regions and use the inevitable publicity from the journeys for something positive. On our return to England, George and I were invited up to the London head office of Breast Cancer Haven for a tour and a coffee to say thank you. The facility was impressive with a large, serene reception area. The building itself was divided into various zones; some were for one-to-one consultations with the charity volunteers and some for group activities. Having spoken at length with a number of the staff, with whom George was already familiar, I was even more convinced that we had chosen an excellent cause to support.

Our luck continued into the press and media world without negative commentaries coming to my attention about our journey. All were complimentary and recognised, I hoped, that we did what we did for the right reasons and tried to be as transparent as possible. I never made any secret of the fact that the deep, driving force behind my determination to complete the expedition was one of ambition and the competitive spirit that accompanies it. This competition is increasingly rare to find as an overt public motivation when speaking to those who travel in the Polar Regions or climb mountains. It is more fashionable and strategic, particularly where sponsors are involved, to follow an ethics or environment-first line, leaving the traditional ambition and rivalry between expeditions to be almost censored. Competition is healthy and nothing to be ashamed about – it is to be found at the core of modern expedition books published before the millennium. Consistent through the pages of Shackleton's *South*, Mike Stroud's *Shadows On The Wasteland*, Weber and Malakhov's *Polar Attack* and Ran Fiennes' *Mind Over Matter*, is an honest acceptance of wishing to be the best. At least, there is an acceptance or awareness of the expeditions going on elsewhere or in the past. Much of the later shift towards a 'softly-softly' approach is perhaps due to a culture with a growing fear of judgement, the scramble for limited sponsors and the increased number of people developing their own plans. I advocate a return to a more open and honest arena for polar expeditions where classic competition is encouraged, and an end to world record claims of 'first to compose music at the North Pole'. It is about the basics of what you do well, not about finding yet more obscure ways of doing so.

There had been, without doubt, a great strength in George's and my teamwork on the ice. In the fallout of the expedition I considered where the basis of this success lay. Two similar personalities, whether they are both passive or dominant, can be seen as a recipe for problems as the tempo of an expedition rises. Evidence for this is strewn through history.

On Robert Scott's first foray into the interior of the Antarctic he and his junior companion, Ernest Shackleton, had a tempestuous relationship. Shackleton's personality and attributes as a leader of men was to become famously evident over the following decade and this can largely be seen to be a battle of wills of two polar titans. Ultimately, only one would reach the South Pole whilst in command of an expedition, Scott perishing on his return in 1912. Shackleton, although leading the dramatic and epic rescue of his stranded men in 1914, would also meet his end in the Antarctic. He died of natural causes in 1922 and was laid to rest on South Georgia Island in the sub-Antarctic. Scott and Shackleton were both strong personalities with their own strategies and were unlikely to accept being downtrodden. This was most likely the cause of the friction. There were later misgivings regarding Shackleton's use of McMurdo Sound as a launching point for the South Pole as Scott considered it 'his' territory, following an agreement between the men.

It was the complementary nature of George and my characters that I believe ensured our eventual success. We both shared the same core attributes of being mentally steady with the imagination to occupy our minds for long periods. As has unravelled through the book, George's impulsiveness and energy was just as important as my keenness to maintain efficiency and sustainability. The two intertwined excellently to produce a machine able to persist under extreme stress and still able to persist as friends in the aftermath.

Epilogue

The question that usually follows directly after 'Why?' is 'What next?' Just five weeks after our arrival back in England from the Arctic, I entered Young Officer training for the Royal Marines Commandos. This world famous sixty-week course is considered one of the most demanding in the world. Physically, my body was a wreck, largely I believe due to the final couple of weeks on the ice. I was proud of our sustainability for the expedition as a whole, giving me confidence for future expeditions. However, the loss of the depots and resulting starvation took an enormous toll on our health.

I was not able to rest fully and recover from the expedition because of the looming fitness requirements of the Marines, the UK's most selective and physically demanding regular unit. Within a week of returning, I was running long distances and training hard in the gym. The thought of turning up at Commando Training Centre in poor shape was alien to me and I was determined to give myself a good platform on which to train. I remained in the regulars for about a year and, after a badly timed series of injuries, withdrew. I left behind a reliable pay-packet and a stable career path but I realised that I had regained the flexibility I had inwardly craved. One friend commented that an energy was back in my eye after being absent for a time.

Aside from pursuing my ambitions as a wildlife and expedition photographer and on the speaking circuit, the polar world remains a priority. Far from the expedition being the culmination of a dream, it was the springboard from which other travels will develop. It proved, prior to the period of starvation, that an expedition of such a tough physical nature can be largely sustainable on 5500kcal per day.

Our weight loss for the opening one hundred days was gradual and controllable. We experienced no sudden weight loss, muscle weakness or major illness. This was on a refined but fairly traditional diet of high fat levels combined with top quality protein and complex carbohydrates. Importantly, we achieved this under the 'holy grail' of a kilogram of food per day. In addition, despite the brutal weight constraints, the food was palatable and even enjoyable. No food became a chore. This told me that, without the sudden loss of supplies, we could have continued on our journey further, both physically and mentally.

It is no secret in the expedition world that few major polar expeditions are left to be achieved. The North Pole has been achieved overland, unsupported and also in the horrific polar night of winter, albeit with air drops. The Arctic has also been crossed unsupported via the North Pole and a return unsupported trek from the North Pole was achieved in 1995. In the Antarctic, similar is true. The South Pole has been reached overland and unsupported. However, the Antarctic, in completeness, has not been crossed without support, only with the aid of kites. Also, the Pole has not been reached in the polar winter, where winds and temperatures are a hyperbole without exaggeration. Finally, not since 1911 has a return expedition to the South Pole taken place successfully and without resupply.

Those who claim that 'everything has been done; everything discovered', are plainly mistaken and the outlook is not bleak in the slightest. The expeditions listed above are not modern, contrived publicity stunts but raw and elemental expeditions consistent with the oldest traditions of the pioneers, yet perfectly at home in the modern day. There is, therefore, no need to make up records about reaching a Pole, backwards on a pogo stick, in order to secure backing. All that is required is the dedication, vision and raw ability to take on the remaining great polar 'firsts'. After all, a speed record or 'youngest' record can be broken tomorrow.

Indeed, our own 'longest unsupported polar journey' did fall to Aleksander Gamme, although only by a small margin. I hope I will get the chance to exceed that distance again myself. Ben Saunders did eventually ski further than George and me in the Antarctic, although he lost his unsupported status. His honesty regarding expeditions and unpretentious belief in doing things 'properly' was, and is, admirable. However, a true first lasts forever. There is a reason the likes of Amundsen, Nansen, Herbert and Ousland stand shoulders above a crowd, albeit a crowd of limited size.

The other side of the coin is less inspiring and saddens me greatly. On browsing the travel section of a bookstore, I read on the inside cover of a book, *Race to the Pole*, 'with national pride at stake, can they re-write history and beat the Norwegians?' Aghast, I left the book firmly on the bookshop shelf. The facts of the expedition were veiled with embellishment and cannot even be compared roughly with the exploits of those Norwegians one hundred years ago. Quite how they felt that racing two modern-day Norwegians, who ultimately beat them comfortably, could overshadow the victory of Amundsen in 1911-12 confuses me, let alone 'rewrites history'. The race to the Pole between Scott and Amundsen has become legend for a good reason. Their efforts were genuinely courageous, pioneering and honourable. This modern team, by their own admission, descended into argument, severe frost injury and melodrama after barely a week. The undeniable facts are that polar expedition teams do not have to argue; George Bullard and I and many others are an example of that.

Due to celebrity and a major documentary, the heavily controlled three-week 'Polar Race' of which the book told the story, received worldwide adulation for skiing a relatively short distance, with close medical support and an enforced rest stop. There is nothing at all wrong with the event, only the way in which it is exaggerated to the public. Few know that in the preceding Arctic season, Russia's Matvey Shparo and Boris Smolin reached the Geographic North Pole in the depths of winter. They endured total darkness for eighty-four days and genuine air temperatures approaching minus sixty. The shame is that only a small group of people were able to follow their progress on an incomprehensibly tough expedition due to a low publicity budget – at least on the basis that the Russian venture had little traction amongst Western audiences.

These are the key points resulting from the reflective threads running through this book. No polar journey is more worthy than any other. Anyone who argues otherwise serves only to allow the community to descend into snobbishness. If you wish to see the South Pole, you can avoid pretensions of grandeur and fly there direct by chartered Twin Otter. Due to the complexities of publicity, ambitions and egos, commercial journeys are too often represented in ways that do not reflect their difficulty or novelty. Only those who invest time in appreciating the full spectrum will be able to separate the real specimen from the fake. The encouraging fact is that once you sift through the television celebrity expeditions, there is a foundation of ground-breaking polar travellers quietly going about their business.

These words, therefore, give a clue to my future intentions and expeditions. I can confirm beyond all doubt that the nature and scale of what I will attempt to attain will not be compromised by publicity stunt or headline grabbing. Instead they will attempt to continue pushing boundaries both in terms of endurance but also mental stamina within a team. There is no need for man-haul journeys to be seen as antiquated and quaint reminders of a golden past-era, rather as a pure and classic form of polar travel. It is no accident that, for surface travel, human-powered expeditions have also been proven to be the most efficient in terms of distances achieved without resupply. Man-hauling has never been more relevant or effective. Whether you consider it, as Robert Scott did, the most 'noble' form of polar expedition, is a personal decision. I believe it to be the most rewarding.

240

Also, an area I feel should be more deeply explored from my own point of view is communication to a global audience. Our plans for the 'Journey South' to the South Pole involved high budget photo and video updates transmitted via satellite to our website for a large audience to follow. This approach is vital to maximising the social value of an expedition, which in its fundamental form is selfish. The documentary would also have allowed a huge number of people to experience a large scale independent expedition.

The 'Long Haul' expedition had severe budget restraints despite the generous input from sponsors, Tiso, Doxa Watches, AST-UK and BeWell. We simply did not have the funding to afford elaborate technology; it was, instead, invested in quality safety equipment that would aid the journey's success. Our contact with the outside world was limited to SMS style updates to a blog on the website and private voice calls to the logistics team and our families. My future journeys will be designed to spread the word more broadly without compromising the purity and seriousness of the expedition.

The 'Long Haul' was far more than walking in a straight line for four months. If asked to sum up the purpose of the project beyond the obvious benefits to charity and satisfied ambition, then the real prize is perspective. Perspective is a privilege that comes to a person only having experienced something massive, be it a glimpse at your own mortality as in the case of Rich Smith or having survived an impossibly large ice sheet for four months with a single companion. I call it a privilege because that is what it really is. You cannot buy or be given perspective. Rather, you have to find it yourself through experiences and then use its enormous worth in a positive manner. I am indebted to those who, through support or sponsorship, gave me the opportunity to grasp that privilege.

The expedition was a very literal manifestation of endeavour, teamwork and stamina. Beyond that, however, it paves the way for the beginning of other great journeys, some

241

of which will be undertaken in the cold lands of the North and South but also at home, a place succinctly summed up by actor and writer Stephen Fry: 'Just landed. England's still here I am delighted to note.'

The Tiso Trans Greenland Expedition 2008

The Team	Alex Hibbert
	George Bullard
Base Leader (Kulusuk)	Matt Spenceley
Liaison (Kulusuk)	Georg Utuaq
Meteorological (Switzerland)	Dagmar Ineichen
Polar Advisors	Steve Bull
	Pen Hadow
Charity	Breast Cancer Haven
	The Rowans Hospice
Partners and Sponsors	Tiso Outdoor Specialists (Title)
	BeWell Nutritional Products
	Doxa Watches
	131 Design
	Applied Satellite Technology
	Hiscox Specialist Insurance
	ISO Active

It took four months for George and I to complete the double traverse of the icecap. This provided ample opportunity to consider the dedication, energy and innovation of our friends, family and supporters. Our journey would have never set out on the ice if they had not pushed us through the hardest and darkest moments, both in England and the Arctic. Hauling a sledge in a straight line is one of the most elegantly simple undertakings possible but the efforts required by so many to allow us to do so were mammoth. The smallest action, such as fast-tracking a visa application, can have such a profound effect on the long-term survival of a project. This springboard from which I launch my path in life is something for which I will never be able thank you enough. With certainty, I would not have stood a chance without your support. This list of titans reflects the thousands of hours dedicated to the dream:

George Bullard *with whom I shared some of the most horrific and most rewarding moments of my life so far.*

My family *particularly my long suffering mother, father and brother. Without their unconditional support and hours of hard work, I would never have left the starting blocks. 'The Long Haul' is also testament to their time and input.*

Matt Spenceley, Georg Utuaq and Dagmar Ineichen *of Pirhuk*
Louise Ramsay, Scott Shaw and team *of Tiso Outdoor Specialists*
James Henderson *of Doxa Watches*
Kees de Nijs and Brian Welsby *of BeWell Nutritional Products*
Gail Baird and Dan Bernard *of 131 Design*
The Honourable Alexandra Foley
Pen Hadow
Steve Bull
Captain Chris and Maureen Page RN
Dr. Mike Stroud Kirsten Eriksen *of the Danish Polar Centre*
Craig Mathieson
Hannah McKeand
Eric Philips *of Icetrek*
Jim Krawiecki *of the British Mountaineering Council*
Tom and Tina Sjogren *of ExplorersWeb*
Lisa Parker *of Hiscox Specialist Insurance*
Brian Taylor *of Taylors Cuisine*
Anna Staszewska *of The Bodleian Library, Oxford*
Captain Sean Chapple RM
Marianne Elmelund *of the Danish Embassy, London*
Shane Winser and Nick Leevers *of the Royal Geographical Society*
Shirley Greenall
Ben Saunders
Andy Ward
Will Steger

Geoff Somers
Roz Savage

In preparation for the 'Journey South 2007' and 'North08' Expeditions (postponed):

Adam Griffiths, Richard Smith and Andrew Wilkinson
It was the cruelest of blows that we were not able to undertake our journey together. The three years spent planning and training together were a privilege and an education.

Admiral Sir Nigel Essenhigh GCB DL, Patron
Frank Prendergast, Charlie Gauvain and team *of Eye Film and Television*
Tina Fotherby and team *of Yes Consultancy*
Simon Harris Ward and Chip Cunliffe *of the Catlin Arctic Survey*
Peter Lyberth *of Air Greenland Charters*
Victor Boyarsky *of VICAAR*
Patrick Woodhead *of White Desert*
Victor Serov *of TAC*
Mike Sharp *of Antarctic Logistics and Expeditions*
Steve Penikett and Steven Testart *of Kenn Borek Air*
Admiral Sir Jonathon Band GCB DL ADC, First Sea Lord Royal Navy
Dr. Mike Grocott and Dr. Dan Martin *of University College London*
Doniert Macfarlane *of Remote Medical Support*
Alex Gough *of the British Antarctic Survey*
Trevor Green *of Radarvision*
Charlie Newington-Bridges *of ABN AMRO*
Stephen Ross *of the Foreign and Commonwealth Office*
Tanya Frost *of Microsoft*
Bear Grylls
Clark Carter
Lewis McNaught
Phil Coates

A Brief History of Polar Exploration

Antarctic

1773 James Cook made the first forays within the Antarctic Circle but did not make conclusive sightings of Terra Australis Incognita, the 'Unknown Southern Land'.

1821 Captain John Davis, an American sealer, was the most likely to have set foot on the continent for the first time. The region is now known as the Davis Coast.

1823 British explorer James Weddell sailed into the region now known as the Weddell Sea.

1897-99 Multi-national expedition onboard *Belgica* unintentionally overwintered in Antarctic coastal ice. Crew members included Norwegian, Roald Amundsen and Frederick Cook.

1901-04 Discovery expedition, led by Englishman, Robert Falcon Scott, came within 463 nautical miles of the Geographic South Pole.

1907-09 Nimrod expedition, led by former member of Discovery expedition, Ernest Shackleton, reached a furthest south 97 nautical miles short of the Pole.

1911 Roald Amundsen (*Fram*) reached the Geographic South Pole for the first time, beating Englishman, Robert Falcon Scott (*Terra Nova*), whose team perished on the return trip.

1911-14 Australian, Douglas Mawson led an under-reported expedition around Commonwealth Bay from his ship, *Aurora*. His sledging journey ended in disaster with team members, Ninnis and Mertz, perishing. Ninnis fell through a crevasse bridge along with six dogs and significant supplies. Mertz would later die from vitamin A overdose after eating dog liver. After Mawson returned the 100 miles to his base alone, the first man to see him exclaimed, 'My God, which one are you?'

1914 Shackleton's attempt to cross the continent via the South Pole ended with the loss of his ship, *Endurance*. Shackleton entered polar legend after leading his crew to safety on Elephant Island and then South Georgia aboard open lifeboats.

1955-58 The Antarctic continent was crossed overland for the first time by Dr Vivian Fuch's Commonwealth Trans-Antarctic Expedition. Along with Sir Edmund Hillary, they used converted farm tractors to cover 2,158 statute miles in 99 days.

1959 The Antarctic Treaty was internationally signed to protect the continent and islands south of 60 degrees. It outlaws, amongst others, any military activity or establishment of territorial claims.

1980-81 Englishman Ranulph Fiennes' Trans-Globe expedition crossed the Arctic and Antarctic along with Oliver Shepard and Charlie Burton.

1985 Foundation of Adventure Network International, offering the first commercial and private access to the Antarctic interior.

1985-86 Robert Swan, Roger Mear and Gareth Wood reached the South Pole along Scott's original route in 70 days. The route covered around 900 miles although their unsupported claim is disputed due to meals received from a US camp. Their ship due to extract them, *Southern Quest*, was crushed and sank. Scientific teams then had to fly the team to New Zealand. The expense and commitment of this rescue has caused a long running friction between the expedition and scientific communities.

1989-90 American Will Steger led the first and only dogsled traverse of the Antarctic continent, covering 3,741 statute miles with resupplies.

1992-93 Norwegian Erling Kagge reached the South Pole from Berkner Island fully unsupported and solo. He travelled 810 miles on the one-way journey to the Pole. In the same season, British Ranulph Fiennes and Dr. Mike Stroud attempted a crossing of the Antarctic without resupply. They reached some miles onto the Ross Ice Shelf after 97 days before requesting aircraft pickup, both having suffered major physical degradation.

1996-97 Børge Ousland of Norway completed a crossing of the continent from Berkner Island to McMurdo Base with the aid of parasails but no resupplies.

2000/01 Norweigans Rolf Bae and Eirik Sonneland crossed the continent via a long 2,400 mile route from Troll Base to the Scott Base using kites. They spent a total of 14 months on the ice, including overwintering.

2006 Rune Gjeldnes, a Norwegian Arctic veteran, completed the longest solo polar journey para-sailing across the icecap. He travelled 2,980 miles from Novo Base to Terra Nova Base.

2011 Aleksander Gamme of Norway skis 1,404 miles in a return journey to the South Pole from the non-coastal Hercules Inlet. This breaks our record for the Longest Unsupported Polar Journey in history, and still stands.

2011 Christian Eide skis the established Hercules Inlet partial route in a record 24 days, 1 hour and 13 minutes. This sets a bar unlikely to be matched in the short term.

2014 Ben Saunders and Tarka L'Herpiniere ski 1,795 miles over 105 days from the Ross Sea coast to the South Pole and back. They received an emergency air drop on the return leg.

Arctic

Pre-expeditions Inuit, Greek and Viking voyages reached far into the lands and oceans of the North.

1596-97 Willem Barentsz discovered Spitsbergen on a Dutch voyage.

1845 Sir John Franklin led an ill-fated expedition through a new portion of the Northwest Passage. The entire crew would perish from starvation, the cold and illness after the ships were abandoned in hope of escape.

1875-76 The British Arctic Expedition of Sir George Nares attempted the North Pole via the Smith Sounds but instead succeeded in charting Greenlandic and Canadian coastlines.

1878-79 The Northeast Passage was first navigated by the Finnish *Vega* expedition of Adolf Erik Nordenskiöld.

1888 A Norwegian expedition led by Fridtjof Nansen made the first crossing of Greenland in 41 days. He famously declared 'Death or the West Coast'.

1893-96 Nansen returned to the Arctic to attempt the North Pole from his icebound ship, *Fram*. He and Johansen set out on skis from the ship and reached beyond the 86th degree.

1908 Dr Frederick Cook claimed to have successfully reached the Geographic North Pole from Cape Stallworthy with two Inuit and dog teams. His claim is widely disputed due to incorrect sextant calculations and little concrete evidence.

1909 American, Robert Peary, Matthew Henson and four Inuit claimed to have reached the Pole in only 37 days from Cape Columbia, again using dogs. This claim is also disputed due to navigational inconsistencies but not proven either way. Peary was described by author Fergus Fleming as 'undoubtedly the most driven, possibly the most successful and probably the most unpleasant man in the annals of polar exploration.'

1968-69 Ralph Plaisted of the USA and his team reached the North Pole without question from Ward Hunt Island, Canada. They received resupplies and used skidoo transport. The next year, the large-scale British expedition led by Wally Herbert made a 15-month crossing of the Arctic Ocean, the first to do so. They travelled from Point Barrow in Alaska to Spitsbergen.

1988 The Soviet-Canadian Polar Bridge Expedition, comprising a number of major polar names, crossed the Arctic Ocean from Russia to Canada. Involved were Dmitri Shparo, Misha Malakhov and Richard Weber.

1994 Norwegian Børge Ousland became the first person to ski unsupported and the first to ski solo to the North Pole. He reached the Pole in 52 days from the Russian side at Cape Arktichevskiy.

1995 The first and, to date, only return expedition to the North Pole without support, was completed by Richard Weber and Misha Malakhov. They travelled for 108 days with ice in a perilous state by the time they reached the Canadian coast.

2000 The 1,070 statute mile expedition by Tory Larsen and Rune Gjeldnes of Norway crossed the Arctic Ocean without any support for the first time in 109 days. They were assessed in Canada on completion to be 48 hours from death.

2003 Englishman, Pen Hadow became the first person to ski solo and unsupported to the North Pole from Canada.

2006 Børge Ousland and South African, Mike Horn reached the North Pole, narrowly failing to do so in the polar winter. The sun rose shortly before completion of their 61 day expedition.

2008 Russians, Matvey Shparo and Boris Smolin reached the North Pole with resupplies after 84 days in the polar winter. They had to operate in 24 hour darkness, crossing open water with only head torches and in temperatures approaching minus sixty.

2008 The British 'Tiso Trans Greenland Expedition' completed a return traverse of the Greenlandic icecap in 113 days. Alex Hibbert and George Bullard travelled 1,374 statute miles and achieved the longest polar journey fully without support.

2014 Ryan Waters and Eric Larsen complete the last unsupported North Pole expedition since 2010. There have been at the time of press (autumn 2018) none since.

Notes on Equipment and Rations

The business of team equipment and food for the expedition has been discussed throughout the book, although it was not the place for enormous amounts of detail. For those of a more technical inclination or those also planning an expedition, here are more in-depth thoughts. Every polar traveller will have their own opinions and experiences and mine is simply one. I am, on the one hand, an unsupported expedition leader and so value practicality and efficiency. On the other hand, I do not subscribe to obsessive weight-saving at any cost, something I believe involves diminishing returns on investment.

Clothing

Clothing is the aspect of polar travel that has transformed most, with the possible exception of communications, over the past century. The furs, skins and other natural materials used to create the garments of yesteryear had a great number of attributes, many still used to this day. They did, however, usually entail significant drawbacks that led to polar expeditions seeking new solutions. These included the insidious build up of ice inside sleeping bags and smocks, plus significant bulk and weight. Since modern expeditions commenced in the late 1980s, in terms of outer layers there have been a limited number of textiles that have proven useful on polar expeditions. This is due to the requirement for light weight, insulation, breathability and the limited need for waterproofness. Ventile cotton was the preferred material on many expeditions throughout the later part of the twentieth century and has a lot to recommend itself. It was a favourite of Ran Fiennes, for example. It is soft, windproof and breathable. Once wet, a very rare occurrence in the Polar Regions due to the lack of rain, it takes a long time to dry out. Ventile was largely superseded by Gore-tex in the 1990s, despite its expense and reduced breathability. This was largely due to its properties as a good waterproofer. For polar applications, it was therefore not an obvious improvement. Pertex was the next innovation which combined excellent ventilation and wind-proofing. Although Pertex materials are water-resistant, most cannot withstand heavy saturation with rain. After extensive research and testing, Pertex (a nylon weave) with a warm pile lining (together termed 'softshell') was the material George and I used for our outer protection throughout the expedition. Only on one occasion, during wet snow, did the system let us down. In terms of underwear, the best option for us was merino wool. This smart wool has a special weave and consistency which makes it hardwearing, comfortable and able to withstand being worn for weeks on end. Cotton or loose-weave wools are a distant second and third for this application as the wearer can suffer from reduced insulation over time and chafing. Recent wisdom has considered fashionable weaves with bamboo, a reversion back to synthetics, or open mesh weaves. The debate rumbles on. Our heads were protected from the cold, wind and sun by thick balaclavas and woolly hats. These were specially designed to allow our breath to escape and allow us to eat whilst keeping our exposed noses and cheeks warm.

Our sleeping bags were goose-down filled with cold ratings around the minus twenty to minus thirty Celsius range. On most occasions, this allowed us to sleep in relative comfort, although the inclusion of a waterproof vapour barrier was necessary to keep the down dry and lofty. Synthetic bags are larger and heavier for a given cold rating and for icecap travel were not deemed optimum, although are now the mainstay of my winter travel sleeping system. Double bags, with a thinner outer bag, can also aid moisture control.

Tents

In the Polar Regions, there are two main designs of tent that can be used, domes (geodesic) and tunnels. Domes are very stable in high winds from changing directions but can be cramped and are slower to pitch. On the other hand, tunnel tents must be pitched aerodynamically along the direction which the wind is blowing. A cross-wind will cause them to be thrown around very violently and can lead to breakages. The living space in a tunnel tent is perfect for polar applications with a long sleeping area and separate partition that can be used for storage and cooking. Having tested both types in Greenland in 2007, the decision to use a tunnel tent was an easy one. Dome tents remain the shelter of choice for serious mountaineering applications, or on icecaps with unpredictable wind direction.

Also available are traditional pyramid or tipi-style nordic tents. These have a number of advantages including all round tensioning against wind and a low surface area above waist-height, despite being tall enough to stand up inside. Often, you can also benefit from breathable tent fabrics. However, space inside can be difficult to make best use of, and optimising good fabric tension is a challenge. Plus, there tends to be a weight penalty.

Skis and boots

The main contenders in back-country skis specialised for polar icecap travel are Åsnes, Fischer and Atomic. Much of the decision surrounding ski choice is down to personal preference and experience. In reality, they all produce excellent, reliable skis. I used Fischer E109 skis and one did, admittedly, snap after one thousand miles of hard use over rock-solid sastrugi. I am not convinced that any other ski would fare any better and that particular ski design has never suffered a failure of that nature before. One thousand miles is

259

simply a very long distance. I do now however use narrower models to help glide and efficiency, unless I know floatation in deep snow is needed. Also, very short skis, as stubby as 130cm, can be useful amongst broken sea ice where constant direction change is needed.

For use on icecaps where, unlike sea ice rubble, there is little need to constantly change direction, a boot and binding combination should be chosen for sustainability and comfort. There are a number of rigid boot and binding systems such as Alfa Mørdre boots and Salomon and Rottefella bindings. These are strongly preferred by Europeans and particularly by skiers from the Nordics. However, we required a softer, more flexible solution that did not lead to the horrendous bone infections and raw flesh seen on the Fiennes-Stroud 1992-93 expedition. Sorel boots are excellent polar 'mukluks' but were unavailable when we sourced our equipment and so we used two pairs of similar Baffin boots. These proved excellent and avoided excess blisters or discomfort although I do question their cold rating of minus one hundred degrees. We suffered cold toes at only thirty below zero. In the years that have followed, I've found that lighter boots two 'levels' down in the range are adequate in the coldest temperatures, provided a vapour barrier and sock system keeps insulation bone dry.

Medication

Due to both a desire to stay medication-free and also good personal care throughout the expedition, only a single pill was used in the entire four months. In order to prepare for other eventualities, our medical kit contained a wide variety of items. These ranged from ibuprofen and codeine for pain relief to powerful broad-spectrum antibiotics for infection control.

Food

The age-old wisdom for polar travel was to use high fat diets to keep energy high and weight low. There has, in recent years, been a great deal of research and experimentation in this field. Some polar expeditions have been strong advocates of a diet higher in more readily usable carbohydrates and reducing the fat content. In order to maintain a high calorie intake, this means that the weight of food must increase, since carbohydrates contain less energy per kilogram than fat. This solution makes a great deal of sense for shorter expeditions where sledges are lighter and speed is critical. One common misconception is that expeditions should eat seven or even eight thousand calories per day. The body is not typically capable of metabolising and efficiently using this quantity of fat-derived energy, let alone the extreme weight penalty it entails. Due to the need to keep sledge weights haul-able and because of the proven track record of modern high-fat diets, George and I opted for a five-and-a-half thousand calorie ration pack. This provided high levels of energy in a palatable form below a kilogram per day. We found it critical to have variety in our evening meals and so had a rotation of a number of meals, examples being lamb curry and beef stroganoff.

Since the Long Haul, I've used carefully designed rations totalling approaching nine thousand calories per day on long, 18+ hour ski days. Remarkably, over a fortnight I still lost significant weight. Also, the quality and taste of dried food has improved a great deal, and some even have begun to resemble the meal they profess to be. Encouraging.

Technology

Technology on polar expeditions is directly related to the level of funding the team has available. The days of highly limited and unreliable communications ended only a few years ago, when large, heavy radios were the only options. Modern expeditions can make use of satellite communications and the ability to send text, photographs and even video to the world in almost realtime. Expense and weight are most certainly a concern and it was my decision to commit the limited funds for the 'Tiso Trans Greenland' to 'mission-critical' equipment. As a consequence, our expedition was conspicuously low-tech, involving two satellite phones for safety support and for sending and receiving short messages. Many of our outgoing messages would automatically appear on the expedition website, which was followed by hundreds around the world. We did not send long lengths of prose or other media – something I had mixed feelings about. It is, undeniably, a fantastic thing to keep in touch with supporters and bring them into your expedition world. Conversely, I think that a part of the challenge of polar travel is a sense of isolation and self-reliance, which we most certainly achieved.

Tech is unsurprisingly the area where in the last decade most progress has been made. 'iPhone' had only just become a word when George and I stepped onto the ice.

We struggled with cameras, especially their battery systems, and the quality of video meant that our ambitions of even a short film of our expedition weren't realised. Our satellite phone worked, but resembled a relic of the 1990s.

My recent expeditions have seen perhaps their most dramatic changes in regard to how we have been able to record our experiences. We can shoot 4K video on the same camera as we take still images. Sound can be easily recorded to broadcast standards. Batteries, whilst still the flawed lithium system long due for replacement, are able to be charged more efficiently and have cleverer power management.

We can also upload data, not just the SMS messages or voice calls of the Long Haul. Currently this means, at the Poles, small images, but a next generation Iridium satellite network due imminently promises a bandwidth that could support on-location video upload without a ten-kilo transmitter.

I'm certain each year will offer us yet more. It's what we do with it that will be counted.

Glossary

ALCI	Antarctic Logistics Centre International
ALE	Antarctic Logistics and Expeditions
ANI	Adventure Network International
Antarctic	Region often defined by areas south of 60 degrees South, or Antarctic Circle
Arctic	Region often defined by areas north of 60 degrees North, or Arctic Circle
BAS	British Antarctic Survey
Bell 212/222	Small helicopters operated by Air Greenland
BSES	British Schools Exploration Society, now British Exploring
CASE	Centre for Altitude, Space and Extreme Environment Medicine
Crevasse	Fissure in snow or ice that can be hundreds of feet deep
DPC	Danish Polar Centre, now under Greenlandic government control
Growlers	Small and low-lying icebergs
Karabiner	Metal climbing loop with a sprung and often lockable gate
Katabatic	Cooling air flowing down off an icecap or glacier
Man-hauling	The manual hauling of supplies, usually in sledges or 'pulks'
Miles	Statute (common) or Nautical
Moraine	Glacially formed accumulation of debris, such as soil or rock

Mukluk	Traditional soft polar boot with indigenous Alaskan/Yukon origins
Novo	Novolazarevskaya Station, a former Soviet Antarctic coastal research station
Nunatak	Mountain peak which penetrates the surface of an icecap or glacier
OUEC	Oxford University Exploration Club
Patriot Hills	Commercial summer base camp on the Antarctic interior, now moved to Union Glacier
PLB	Personal Locator Beacon
POC	Potential Officers Course, Royal Marines
RGS	Royal Geographical Society
Sastrugi	Ridges and furrows, often up to five feet high, caused by wind and snow drift
Sledge	Otherwise known as a 'pulk' or 'pulka', allows transport of expedition supplies
Twin Otter	Versatile twin-engined aircraft able to be fitted with skis
UCL	University College London
Unsupported	Travelling without assistance from resupplies or external power
Valance	Skirt running around a tent which, when loaded with snow, helps stabilise the structure
White Gas	Otherwise known as Naphtha – used as a clean-burning stove fuel
Without resupply	Travelling without resupply from aircraft or depots laid by a third party

Useful Conversions

°F	°C
30	-1
15	-9
0	-18
-15	-26
-30	-34
-45	-43
-60	-51

Mile

Statute	Nautical
1.61km	1.85km
1,760yd	2,025yd
0.87 nm	1.15 st. mile

Bibliography

Amundsen, Roald, *The South Pole*, London, 1912

Avery, Tom, *Pole Dance*, London, 2004

Cherry-Garrard, Apsley, *The Worst Journey in the World*, London, 1922

Crane, David, *Scott of the Antarctic*, London, 2005

Eliot, T.S., *The Waste Land and other Poems*, London, 1940

Fiennes, Ranulph, *Mad, Bad and Dangerous to Know*, London, 2007

Fuchs, Vivian, *The Crossing of Antarctica*, Boston, 1958

Hadow, Pen, *Solo*, London, 2004

Huntford, Roland, *Shackleton*, London, 1985

Hurley, Frank, *Argonauts of the South*, New York and London, 1925

Krakauer, Jon, *Into Thin Air*, New York, 1997

Mawson, Douglas, *The Home of the Blizzard*, New York, 1998

Scott, Robert Falcon, *Journals*, Oxford, 2006 (first
   published 1914)
Shackleton, Ernest, *South*, London, 1919
Solomon, Susan, *The Coldest March*, New Haven, 2001
Stroud, Mike, *Shadows on the Wasteland*, London, 1993
Stroud, Mike, *Survival Of The Fittest*, London, 1999
Woodhead, Patrick, *Misadventures in a White Desert*,
London, 2003
   Weber, Richard and Malakhov, Mikhail, *Polar Attack*,
      Toronto, 1996